MW01052666

The Liability Century

The Liability Century

*Insurance and Tort Law from
the Progressive Era to 9/11*

Kenneth S. Abraham

Harvard University Press
Cambridge, Massachusetts
London, England
2008

Library of Congress Cataloging-in-Publication Data

Abraham, Kenneth S., 1946–
The liability century : insurance and tort law from the Progressive Era to 9/11 / Kenneth
S. Abraham.
p.   cm.
Includes bibliographical references and index.
ISBN-13: 978-0-674-02768-8 (alk. paper)
1. Liability (Law)—United States—History.   2. Insurance, Liability—United States—
History.   3. Torts—United States—History.   4. Damages—United States—History.
KF1250 .A7127 2008
346.7303—dc22
2007031806

For the Rheubans and the Thomsons

Contents

Acknowledgments

I cannot begin to thank everyone who has contributed to or supported the intellectual work that has gone into this book, because in a sense it is the product of nearly forty years of study. But the contributions of certain people stand out. Guido Calabresi first kindled my interest in tort law, and his work has inspired me ever since. My first dean, Michael J. Kelly, encouraged me to begin teaching and studying insurance, and has been a loyal and supportive friend in the ensuing decades. My colleague, Jeffrey O'Connell, has been a source of support and wisdom, as well as an invaluable intellectual resource, for many years. And in various ways Vincent Blasi, Oscar Gray, John Jeffries, Leslie Kendrick, Lance Liebman, Kyle Logue, Robert Rabin, Glen Robinson, David Rosenberg, Alan Schwartz, Kip Viscusi, Paul Weiler, and G. Edward White, with whom I have collaborated or who have given me extensive advice on a draft of the book, have influenced both my thinking and what the book eventually became.

I began writing the book while I was a Visiting Professor at Harvard Law School and I am grateful to the staff of the Harvard Law Library for its assistance during that period. But the lion's share of my work on the book occurred after I returned to the University of Virginia School of Law, where I have relied heavily on the reference staff of our library here. Their energy and expertise has been invaluable, and their enthusiasm in providing it has made working with them a pleasure.

Finally, a number of very capable research assistants facilitated my work in countless ways. These include James Burke, Margaret Cantrell, Nuala Droney, Sarah Hughes, Andrew Genz, Lara Loyd, Robert Ludwig, Logan Sawyer, Julia Schwartz, Emily Tabak, and Katherine Twomey.

The Liability Century

Introduction

Astronomers have discovered a solar formation they call a "binary star." This formation consists of two suns, each in orbit around the other. Their center of gravity lies at a point in between them, and they revolve around that center of gravity. Neither star could remain where it is, or as it is, without the other. They are two separate bodies, but each is dependent on the other for its place in the universe.

The tort liability and insurance systems are very much like the two suns in a binary star, dependent on each other for their position in our legal system. For more than a century these two systems have influenced each other's course of development. Neither would be anything like what it is today if the other had not existed and developed along with it. Today the two systems constantly interact, and almost no effort to understand or reform one of them can take place without understanding the role played by the other.

There is hardly any aspect of contemporary life in the United States that goes untouched by tort law or insurance. Virtually every activity that a business or professional contemplates must be scrutinized in advance for its possible liability and insurance implications.[1] Not only are both the tort and insurance systems enormously important from both an economic and social standpoint, but neither stands alone. They interact and influence each other's development, shape, and scope. The tort system, not only as it exists on paper but also how it works in practice, is a product of the insurance system, just as the insurance system is a product of the tort system.

The Two Systems and Their Interaction

We can begin with a simple understanding of what insurance is. As I shall use the term, "insurance" is a transaction that performs two functions: risk transfer and risk distribution, or spreading. Many transactions fit this description. But in insurance the transferee of risk, the insurer, accepts the transfer of risks as part of its business and not as the incident of another transaction. In accepting the transfer of a large number of risks, the insurer diversifies and thereby reduces its overall risk, by taking advantage of the law of averages. For the insurer, the whole risk is smaller than the sum of its parts. The insurer is thus a vehicle for distributing the risk of loss among its policyholders.

In the Unites States, insurance figures prominently in both tort liability and in nontort methods of compensating the victims of injury, illness, and death. We have vast systems of private insurance that provide health, disability, life, auto, workers' compensation, liability, and property insurance to businesses, individuals, and families. All told we spend approximately $900 billion annually on these different forms of private insurance—about 7 percent of the country's gross domestic product—plus an additional $600 billion dollars each year for publicly provided "social" insurance such as Medicare, Medicaid, and Social Security Disability insurance. The total compensation that insurance pays for injury, illness, and death in this county is thus in the neighborhood of $1.5 trillion per year.

These extensive sources of insurance developed as components of the unique and partial system of social welfare that emerged in the United States over a period of more than a century.[2] Tort liability expanded at the same time the social welfare system developed, in part because that system has never provided more than incomplete protection. More important, tort liability expanded because the movement toward greater social welfare reflected the increasing socialization and spreading of risk. The expansion of tort liability was part of this trend. More tort liability helped to socialize the risk of suffering accidental personal injury. But the particular ways tort liability expanded, the particular new forms of liability that developed, and the particular shape of the current tort system were influenced by the sources of insurance that were developing at the same time as tort law. Insurance was a principal mechanism by which tort law spread risk. And so new forms of insurance developed along with the expansion of tort liability, sometimes before and sometimes after a new form of tort liability was created.

But of course tort is not only a part of our system of social welfare; it is also a part of the extensive system of health and safety regulation that emerged in the United States at the same time as our social welfare system. As we will see below, the multiple functions that tort and liability insurance are now expected to perform make it almost inevitable that in practice the way they operate will fall short of the ideal.

The tort system and the liability insurance that commonly accompanies tort thus function alongside, and arguably as part of, our larger system of compensation for the consequences of injury, illness, and death. As significant as tort may be, however, it pales in comparison to the roughly $1.5 trillion per year system of compensation of which it is a part. I estimate that for the portion of tort that addresses personal injury, illness, and death, the direct cost of the tort system is approximately $200 billion—about 13 percent of the larger system.[3] A very substantial proportion of these direct tort costs—surely 75 percent, and probably more—are covered by liability insurance. Annual tort costs today reflect a more than one-hundred-fold cost increase since 1950, when tort costs were less than $2 billion. The increase in direct tort costs during this period has outstripped economic growth by a factor of 3. It is impossible, however, to estimate the additional indirect costs of the tort system that are in incurred in the form of forgone productivity, research, and development. But it would also be extremely difficult to estimate or place a value on the benefits of the tort system that accrue from the investment we make in it. These benefits include the health and life saved from damage or destruction by the additional safety the threat of liability generates, as well as reduction of the adverse effects of illness, injury, and death that tort achieves by providing monetary compensation for at least some of the consequences of the tortiously caused harm that does occur.

The interaction of tort, liability insurance, and these other sources of insurance-based compensation is continuous and complex. I will provide just two brief examples of this phenomenon, since in a sense this entire book is comprised of examples of how, often in unseen ways, tort law and insurance interact with each other at both the structural and operational levels. Perhaps the most politically visible tort law issue these days is whether to place monetary ceilings on the amount of damages for "pain and suffering" that are available in tort suits. But participants in this debate rarely recognize or acknowledge the role that liability insurance has played in making it possible for this issue to arise at all. Only because liability insurance is so readily available to individuals and small businesses can lawsuits claiming hundreds of thousands or even millions of dollars for pain and suffering from such defendants even be imagined.

Tort liability and liability insurance have an interactive impact on each other that has resulted in a decades-long arms race. Often the sequence has begun with tort law expanding the scope of liability or permitting ever-larger recoveries. Liability insurance then responds by providing insurance against the new liabilities and greater amounts of coverage. Escalation then proceeds another rung up the ladder, as tort law targets defendants covered by the new forms of insurance and imposes even larger amounts of liability, in order to ensure that there is sufficient deterrence of now-insured conduct, and because prior increases in awards have ratcheted up what are now considered appropriate levels of compensation. In other settings the sequence of interaction takes place in reverse. Here liability insurance comes into existence first, and tort law then seeks it out by creating new forms of liability, at least partly in response to the availability of this insurance as a source of compensation. Whether it is tort liability or liability insurance that has come first, however, they have had a reciprocal, one-way ratchet effect on each other that has resulted in both increasingly large tort recoveries and increasingly large amounts of liability insurance that covers these liabilities. Indeed, in certain domains this effect has been so great that bankruptcy and other liability-limiting devices are sometimes employed to create partial shelter from these liabilities.[4]

A second prominent subject of tort reform debate is whether to modify the "collateral source" rule that governs whether tort plaintiffs are allowed to recover damages for losses that their health and disability insurance have already paid, or whether these sums should instead be deducted from tort awards. This can be a significant issue, however, only because of the proliferation of health and disability insurance that has become available to the vast majority of the U.S. population in the last 50 years. If hundreds of billions of dollars of health and disability insurance benefits were not paid each year, the proper relationship between these different sources of compensation would have little practical importance.

In addition, the ready availability of health and disability insurance to tort victims actually may have been helping to inflate the amounts that are awarded in tort, in two ways. First, in virtually all routine cases involving comparatively small amounts of damages, and even in some cases involving substantial damages, a plaintiff's medical expenses are used as a baseline for computing settlement offers. This approach is taken because in practice the damages that juries award for pain and suffering tend to be roughly proportional to the amount of medical expenses the plaintiff has incurred on account of his or her injuries. As we will see in later chapters, the more health insurance that is available to tort victims, the higher their medical expenses will be, and consequently the larger tort settlements and awards are likely to be. Expanding health insurance may thus have a multiplier effect on tort payments. Second, health and disability insurance benefits that are paid soon after an injury occurs provide tort plaintiffs with access to what amounts to a capital market, thereby giving plaintiffs greater capacity to resist "low-ball" offers of settlement from defendants or their liability insurers. Because plaintiffs already have insurance against their out-of-pocket losses, they feel less pressure to settle their tort cases. As a result, these cases are either litigated or settled for more than they would have been in the days before health and disability insurance were as widespread as they are now. Paradoxically, then, instead of reducing the importance of tort, the spread of health and disability insurance probably has helped to fuel the expansion of tort liability.

The pain and suffering and collateral source examples reveal the way certain features of our system are so fundamental that they are almost invisible. Yet often it is precisely the hidden interactions between tort and insurance that make the tort system what it is, and that generate reform issues in the first place. Tort and insurance have become so inextricably and unavoidably intertwined that often one system is not even seen to influence features of the other that would not and could not have come into being, or would not continue to exist in their current form, without the other system. Unless these relationships are recognized and understood, proposals for tort reform may prescribe solutions that do not really address the concerns they are designed to solve.

Why This Project?

Over the years many legal scholars have thought that insurance influences tort law in important ways, but have rarely been able to say exactly how that influence operates. Insurance has been a bit like the skunk at a lawn party, present in everyone's mind but nonetheless ignored. Beginning as early as the enterprise liability scholarship of William O. Douglas, and continuing with the initial work of Fleming James, Jr., a decade or so later, legal scholars argued for the expansion of tort liability on the ground that potential defendants can more easily insure against liability than potential victims.[5] The enterprise liability theory was, among other things, an insurance rationale for expanding tort liability.

More subtly, a later generation of scholars, led most prominently by Guido Calabresi, employed economic analysis in their study of tort law.[6] They brought rigorous concern with the deterrent effect of tort liability into tort theory. Many also thought that distributional concerns, including access to insurance on the part of both potential injurers and potential victims, could appropriately figure in the determination of liability rules. They recognized, however, that these considerations did not always argue in favor of expanding liability. But neither James nor Calabresi, nor those who have for several decades been writing in the shadow of their work, had much to say about how insurance actually figures in these determinations. The insurance rationale for tort liability has been attacked by such scholars as Richard Epstein and George Priest, on the ground that the rationale has in fact been operating not only in tort scholarship but also in judicial decisions, and that the rationale has created problems for both tort liability and insurance.[7] And that rationale has been defended by such scholars as Jon Hanson, Kyle Logue, and Gregory Keating.[8] On the other hand, as prominent a figure as Dean William Prosser, author of the leading torts treatise of the twentieth century, argued that the availability of insurance actually has only rarely figured in the shaping of tort law doctrine.[9]

It is time to try to make sense of, and where possible to disentangle, these conflicting contentions, and to explore the relationship between tort and insurance. We need to get a handle on how insurance has influenced tort law, and how tort law has influenced insurance. It is one thing to assert in a general way that the availability of insurance influences the course of tort law development, or that when tort liability expands, insurance against the new form of liability is likely to be created. It is quite another thing to understand how this has and has not actually occurred in different fields of tort liability.

The main reason that this kind of examination has never been undertaken, I think, is that there is almost no one who is interested enough in both fields to have done it. Torts scholars have stayed away from insurance because it is in a sense a subspecialty of the field of contract law, and because it is highly technical. Learning about insurance and insurance law requires a substantial investment of intellectual capital. Torts is a required subject in all law schools, and many law professors teach the subject. But insurance law is an elective course, and for some people insurance has an ambulance-chasing air about it that tends to undermine its respectability. Securities law, in contrast, certainly has no greater economic or legal importance than insurance law but is generally held in higher regard as a subject of scholarship. At the very least it is a more prominent subject. For these reasons, there are far fewer insurance law scholars than there are tort scholars. Conversely, outside of the law schools there are insurance specialists in schools of business and departments of economics, but they tend not to know much, if anything, about tort law. The result is that there is very little overlap between those who write about torts and those who write about insurance and insurance law.

I began studying insurance and insurance law over 30 years ago when, as a new torts teacher, I encountered Justice Roger Traynor's concurrence in *Escola v. Coca Cola Bottling Co. of Fresno*.[10] As I indicate in more detail in Chapter 5, Traynor argued that the manufacturers of consumer products should be held strictly liable for injuries caused by defects in their products, on the ground, among others, that manufacturers are in a better position to insure against the risk of injury than are the purchasers of products. When I sought to determine whether this was true, I found little in the literature that was helpful. So I began to teach myself about insurance and insurance law, type of insurance after type of insurance, and doctrine after doctrine. I learned that general principles go only part of the way toward explaining how insurance works and how it affects, and is affected by, tort liability. There is no substitute for understanding the particulars that emerge from looking at issues from the ground up rather than from the top down.

I propose, therefore, to pursue the matters that are the subject of this book from the ground up as well, by examining the role insurance has played in tort, and (to a lesser extent) the role tort has played in insurance at particular periods and in particular fields of liability. Insurance can be a dauntingly technical field, but because often the devil is indeed in the details, there is no substitute for understanding them. Whenever necessary, therefore, along the way I will introduce the reader to the way insurance works and to the standard coverage provisions and exclusions that have been included in the insurance policies that figure in my analysis.

The story of the relationship between tort and insurance begins with a chapter on the period just prior to the introduction of liability insurance in this country late in the nineteenth century. I then trace the way the influence of insurance was felt as time went on, organizing my inquiry largely by focusing on a series of well-recognized fields of liability. Subsequent chapters address workers' compensation, auto, medical, and products liability, the decline of tort law's no-duty and limited-duty rules, and the special case of the 9/11 Victim's Compensation Fund. A number of the insights I develop about what happened in these different fields of liability are local; significant as I hope the insights sometimes are, they do not carry over to the other fields. But certain general themes do emerge and repeat themselves. I will have something to say about these themes in the concluding chapter.

The Normative Assumptions Underlying the Positive Project

There are many places in the pages that follow where a specific insight about how tort and insurance have interacted may be relevant or responsive to a standard criticism of, or defense against a criticism of, the way tort liability or the tort system operates.[11] In fact, however, a major part of my message is that much of the way tort functions is the result of structural features heavily involving its interaction with insurance. For this reason, certain standard doctrinal reforms, whether proposed or actually enacted, may not have much long-term impact on features of the system with which critics of tort are dissatisfied. While this point may of course have normative implications, I have no general reform or antireform agenda that I am attempting to advance in the pages that follow, other than encouraging more realistic recognition of the limits of both tort and insurance, in view of their relationship to each other.

My objective throughout the book is thus largely positive rather than normative. That is, I aim mainly to describe and analyze the interaction of tort and insurance, and not to argue that particular interactions have or have not been a good or a bad thing. Nor do I aim to lay the groundwork for tort reform, or to make a case that tort should not be reformed in any of the many ways that have been proposed over the years. Nevertheless, I do think that there is a sense in which the contemporary tort system poses a public policy predicament, as the tone and sometimes the substance of my analysis undoubtedly will reveal. It may be useful at the outset, therefore, to be explicit about what I mean.

The one thing almost everyone would agree on is that there is no contemporary consensus about what the goals of tort law are or should be. In the domain of personal injury the principal candidates are promoting optimal deterrence, ensuring compensation for the victims of injury, providing corrective justice or moral redress, or some combination of these.[12] In my view the most accurate description of the system as it actually operates, and as those who are involved in or observe the system understand it, is that tort is in practice a system of mixed goals. And probably most middle-of-the-road, pragmatic legal scholars and practitioners would argue that the system should pursue this mixture of goals, although there is no generally accepted theory about how much weight each goal should have. In a system of mixed goals, much turns on context.

In contrast, further away from the pragmatic center are those who think that the system now does pursue, or should pursue only one of these goals, largely to the exclusion of the others, recognizing that pursuing one goal will still be accompanied by a series of side effects. Thus, for example, deterrence might be seen as the goal of the system, and compensation of accident victims seen as a side effect, or means of achieving that goal. Or corrective justice might be seen as the goal of the system, with deterrence seen as a side effect of pursuing corrective justice.

There are several problems, however, that none of the above accounts address. First, the system probably is not terribly good at achieving any of its possible goals, though our data on the issue is itself very spotty. As a mechanism for deterring unsafe behavior, the efficacy of tort liability is uncertain, but it certainly falls far short of the ideal.[13] The threat of liability sends signals to potential defendants but among other things the signals are often vague; enforcement is inconsistent and sometimes inaccurate; potential defendants usually have liability insurance whose premiums may not be closely calibrated to their risk of loss; many potential defendants are in a position to receive only the most blunt of signals ("be reasonably careful"); and not all potential defendants have full control over the causes of accidents. As to just the latter, think of the massive number of auto accidents, for example, that are caused by the inevitable, sporadic inadvertence of drivers that the system labels negligent.[14]

Further, as a method of ensuring compensation to victims, tort liability is both unsystematic and inefficient. The percentage of their losses that victims are paid varies enormously, and is inversely proportional to the severity of injury. Seriously injured victims tend to recover less than their out-of-pocket costs; those with minor injuries are more likely to recover a sum exceeding these costs. Perhaps more important, the tort system spends more on the costs of administration and counsel fees than it pays to victims. One recent estimate is that only 46 percent of all tort expenditures is paid to victims.[15] A bit more than half of all money expended on automobile liability goes to victims.[16] Products liability and medical malpractice, however, pay a considerably smaller portion of their expenditures to victims—perhaps as little as one-third.[17] In contrast, nontort sources of compensation such as health, disability, and life insurance, and workers' compensation, pay a much higher percentage of their total expenditures—some upward of 90 percent—to victims.[18]

Finally, as a method of providing what has been variously called corrective justice, restorative justice, and civil redress, the system is also only partially successful. The corrective justice ideal envisions a wrongdoer acknowledging wrongdoing and providing compensation that rectifies the moral imbalance between injurer and victim. Yet most cases are settled with a partial payment that acknowledges no wrongdoing. In addition, often the defendant is a sizable corporation whose shareholders at the time of payment are not the same individuals and institutions who were shareholders at the time of the alleged wrongdoing. And of course, because much of the time the defendant is insured, it is a pool of policyholders who bear the direct cost of correction or rectification, not the individual defendant. For all these reasons, corrective justice in tort usually is attenuated at best.

All this pertains to the effectiveness of tort, viewed on its own. Another problem is that tort is not the only system we have for deterring unsafe conduct and compensating the victims of illness and injury. To promote safety we also rely on administrative regulation of risky activity at both the federal and state levels, and on consumer choice in markets for products and services that present an array of alternatives with different levels of safety, price, functionality, and other characteristics. Both regulation and the market play at least as significant a role as tort, and together probably a more significant role in many settings, in promoting safety. Similarly, as I indicated earlier, tort is only a small part of the universe of sources providing compensation for injury, illness, and death. Less than 10 percent of all such compensation comes from tort.

Yet just as tort is far from being as effective as would be ideal at achieving any of the goals we might wish to ascribe to it, these other systems of safety prevention and loss insurance also are highly imperfect. Defective products slip through our systems of safety regulation; a considerable amount of medical malpractice occurs; toxic material is carelessly or intentionally discharged into the environment; more than 40 million people in this country have no health insurance; most workers have insufficient or no long-term disability insurance; and the average family has a decidedly inadequate amount of life insurance to protect it in the event of the death of one or both of its breadwinners.

In short, in many ways tort is not very good at what it does or at what it is expected to do. But the alternatives to tort are not doing an obviously superior job, at least not across the board. So what we do is hedge our bets. Tort itself is a mixed system, simultaneously pursuing deterrence, compensation, and justice goals. And tort is part of two larger systems that are themselves mixed and that attempt, respectively, to promote safety and to provide compensation for the consequences of injury, illness, and death. We maintain these overlapping approaches in the hope that they will do a better job together than any individual component could do alone.

This is not a ringing recommendation of the tort system, however, and that is the public policy predicament that tort poses. Tort is not an impressively effective system of deterrence or compensation but we are far from being able to rely exclusively on the alternatives to tort to do all or even a large part of its work. The argument for wholly abolishing product manufacturers' liability for injuries caused by defective products, for example, would be very weak. It would be imprudent policy to rely entirely on government regulation and the marketplace to produce safe products. Similarly, leaving loss insurance as an exclusive source of compensation for injury victims would leave some victims with even less adequate compensation than they receive now. Complete abolition of liability for injuries caused by defective products would make sense only if a system that had some capacity to deter unsafe conduct and to provide compensation were substituted for tort. Workers' compensation accomplished both goals in one domain a century ago; 40 years ago auto no-fault was envisioned as a similar solution to the auto accident problem, but for reasons I will discuss in Chapter 3, that did not occur; and as yet we have no technically feasible, analogous no-fault alternatives to tort in such fields as products liability and medical malpractice.

We are left, therefore, with a tort system whose operation is frustrating for many and wholly unsatisfactory for some. For several decades now a series of proposals for interstitial reform of tort doctrine have figured in public debate. The puzzle is that, although many have been enacted, for the most part they have neither reduced frustration with the tort system nor eliminated the widespread sense that the system is unsatisfactory. One of the objectives of this book is to show that the way tort and insurance interact provides part of the solution of this puzzle. The tort system came to be what it is over a long period of time and in part because of the interaction of tort and insurance. As long as the many structural features of this interaction are in place, we will have a tort system whose character makes it more difficult to reform from within than might be supposed.

Yet there is little reason to think that we would find it either desirable or feasible to change the kinds of structural features that my analysis will suggest are fundamental to the way the tort system interacts with insurance. For example, we would not prohibit or place severe limitations on the amount of liability insurance that could be purchased to protect any given policyholder against tort liability; we would not cut back on health and disability insurance in order to contain the inflationary effect of these forms of coverage on tort awards; we could not keep the courts from considering the availability of insurance to potential defendants as the courts fashion new liability rules; we would not preclude liability insurers from setting up their policies to give them the right to defend and settle claims against their policyholders; we would not and almost certainly could not eliminate the contingent-fee system that places little if any burden on plaintiffs who bring doubtful claims and gives plaintiffs' attorneys such strong incentives to bring claims, especially against insured defendants; and although the amounts liability insurers offer to settle tort suits depend on the anticipated actions of jurors, who understand how frequently defendants are insured, we would not and could not amend the U.S. Constitution, or the constitutions of all 50 states, to abolish the right to a trial by jury in civil cases.

In taking stock of the situation that these fundamental features of the interaction of tort and insurance have generated, what has occurred in the last year, or even in the last five years, is far less important than what has occurred over the long term, and what we can expect to occur over the long term in the future. Short-term developments in the tort system tend to be the result of local, sometimes idiosyncratic forces. Long-term developments, however, are more often the product of structure and of larger, more likely enduring forces. Moreover, data about the functioning of the tort system is hard to come by, and its reliability is sometimes uncertain. We can be much more confident looking at data about what has happened over a period of decades than about what has happened during the last two or three years. Consequently, my focus will be the long term, with relatively little concern for the most recent, possibly temporary, developments in the system.

Finally, it is worth noting that much of this book is directed at analyzing the history and economics of the interaction of insurance and tort law. Yet I am neither a historian nor an economist. Perhaps the best thing I can say in my defense is that someone needed to address this largely unanalyzed subject. At least I can take the first step in the effort to shed some light on the subject. If the insights I develop and the conclusions I reach seem contestable, then they can be taken as informed hypotheses worthy of further investigation, rather than as contentions that I have spoken the last word on these matters. If what I have to say opens up further examination of the subject, then at least one goal of the book will have been achieved.

—1—

The Dawn of a New Era

We tend today to think of tort liability and liability insurance as inextricably linked together. Indeed, given the scope of liability that individuals and organizations now face and have faced for decades, it is difficult to imagine tort liability existing without there also being insurance against it. Potential defendants' financial vulnerability would be too great, and many deserving victims would go uncompensated, if there were no liability insurance.

In fact, however, tort liability existed long before there was such a thing as liability insurance. We know without question that there was civil liability for certain forms of accidental personal injury and property damage in medieval England. By the fifteenth century, for example, a limited version of liability in tort (then called "trespass") had evolved from even earlier beginnings and was being regularly imposed.[1] Yet liability insurance was not introduced in England or the United States until more than four hundred years later, in the 1880s.

Before this time, as I will explain below, it was against public policy to insure against tort liability. Insurance against liability for even negligently caused harm, it was thought, would unduly encourage irresponsible behavior. But then, in the industrializing economy of the late nineteenth century, the incidence of accidental injury began to explode; tort claims became much more common; and compensating victims was slowly recognized as an independent and important function of tort law. As a consequence, the demand for liability insurance increased. Only when this increased demand became strong enough to put pressure on the public policy that prohibited insuring against tort liability did the courts come to have a more positive view of liability insurance.

After this point was reached, change came quickly. In the courts, where

14

public policy was expressed in legal doctrine, there was a transformation. Liability insurance went from being frowned upon to being viewed with favor. Previously criticized on the ground that it was a method of avoiding moral responsibility, liability insurance was now recognized as socially desirable, because it helped to assure that accident victims would be compensated for their injuries.

As a consequence, a robust market developed for the new form of coverage. In the 25 years that followed the introduction of liability insurance, demand for the new product grew. And almost inevitably, because it was the liability insurer's money that was at stake, the insurer not only provided insurance against liability but also furnished the policyholder with a defense against lawsuits, and decided whether and when to settle them. The entire claims process was thus placed under the insurer's control. That arrangement would prove to have profound implications for the modern relationship between tort liability and insurance. Because of its control over the process, the liability insurer would become the public face of the tort system, and the intermediary through which virtually everything associated with the making of a tort claim flowed.

This chapter tells the story of these early years in the development of liability insurance. I begin by examining the eighteenth- and nineteenth-century public policy prohibiting insurance against losses caused by negligence, and explore the way that policy eroded as the nineteenth century progressed. I then show how the erosion of this public policy and the eventual validation of the new form of coverage in the courts reflected an intellectual shift that laid the groundwork for the modern tort system, with its heavy reliance on liability insurance as a source of protection for defendants and compensation for plaintiffs. The story concludes on the eve of the enactment of workers' compensation in 1910, with a rudimentary system of liability insurance in place. At this point the criticisms that would eventually be leveled against liability insurers were already in the early stage of development.

Moral Hazard and Nineteenth-Century Insurance

The dominant forms of insurance during the nineteenth century were marine and fire insurance. They first emerged in the United States in the eighteenth century and grew thereafter, with fire insurance overtaking marine insurance in importance just before the Civil War. Along with life insurance, which also became much more prominent around midcentury, these forms of insurance are what we now call "first-party" insurance. That is, they cover the policyholder against the risk of suffering a loss of his or her own. In contrast, liability insurance is often called "third-party" insurance; it covers the policyholder against the risk of incurring liability for causing a loss suffered by someone else. In these arrangements, the insured policyholder is the "first" party, the insurer is the "second" party, and (where liability insurance is involved) the party suffering a loss and suing the policyholder is the "third" party.

One of the characteristic problems facing any insurer, whether in first-party or third-party insurance, is "moral hazard"—the tendency of a policyholder to exercise less care to avoid suffering a loss than he would exercise if he were not insured. Because of moral hazard, the very sale of an insurer's product increases the risk that the policyholder, and therefore the insurer, will suffer a loss. From early on, insurers developed methods of combating moral hazard in first-party insurance. Coverage was always precluded when the insured intentionally caused a loss. And many insurers required that the policyholder have an "insurable interest" in the insured subject matter. These insurers would not sell insurance on the life of someone who was a complete stranger to the policyholder, and they would not sell insurance on property in which the policyholder had no interest. For a few decades in the 1700s in England, insurers actually did sell some such insurance, but with undesirable consequences. There was gambling on strangers' lives, and there may have been more nefarious doings as well. Eventually Parliament prohibited such sales of insurance by adopting a legal requirement that policyholders have an insurable interest in the insured subject matter. Throughout the United States the same rule has long prevailed. Insurance sold to someone without an insurable interest in the insured subject matter is invalid.

In first-party insurance the presence of an insurable interest is a proxy for situations in which moral hazard is minimized. When the policyholder insures his own life or property, or the life or property of others on whom he depends, he already has an incentive to preserve the subject matter that is insured. Even if the incentive to avoid suffering a loss is marginally diminished in these situations once there is insurance, the insurer can combat this incentive by declining to insure the full value of what is insured, so that the insured continues to have some financial interest in avoiding loss.

In contrast, it is more difficult for an insurer to combat moral hazard in liability insurance. In this field the insured has no underlying self-interest in taking care to avoid causing injury to other people or property. And since there is in principle no ceiling on the amount of liability that may be incurred for injuring others, it is more difficult for the insurer to combat moral hazard by placing an appropriate limit on the amount of liability insurance it is willing to sell to any given policyholder. There may be a limit that prudence dictates, but nothing more. A deductible may have something of this effect indirectly, by making the policyholder a total self-insurer as to comparatively small losses and a partial self-insurer as to others. However, whenever potential losses are a substantial multiple of the deductible amount, the insured self-insures little of the risk in question, and the deductible has only a limited impact on moral hazard.

At common law, liability insurance was therefore understood to be against public policy, because it was thought to create excessive moral hazard. A person insured against liability would be discouraged from exercising care to avoid injuring others. It was in this context that nineteenth-century tort law operated. There was no liability insurance, but compared to today there were also substantial limits on the scope of liability that people and businesses faced. A variety of doctrines based on proximate cause, the absence of duty, the status of the parties, and the plaintiff's own conduct placed formal obstacles in the path of anyone seeking to recover damages in tort. A good deal of the history of tort law in the twentieth century involves the slow removal of these obstacles, and the expansion of liability for personal injury or property damage whenever the defendant failed to exercise reasonable care under all the circumstances.

It is commonplace these days for scholars and commentators to note the narrow scope of nineteenth-century tort liability but to ignore the absence of insurance against the tort liabilities that did exist. I think that this most often occurs because tort scholars and teachers are simply unaware of the origins of liability insurance. The torts casebooks from which generations of law students have learned the subject, for example, often include the opinion in *Ryan v. New York Central R.R.* to illustrate the strength of the nineteenth-century limits on the scope of tort liability.[2] The case actually is emblematic of the scholarly blind spot regarding insurance, because in fact what was really going on in *Ryan* cannot be understood without appreciating the history of liability insurance.

Ryan was decided by the New York Court of Appeals in 1866 and involved what was for that era a routine set of facts. Sparks from a passing locomotive set fire to the railroad's own woodshed. The fire spread from the burning shed to the plaintiff's property, located 130 feet away. The plaintiff sued the railroad for negligence, seeking damages for the destruction of his house by fire. The question before the court was whether the railroad could be held liable even though the sparks had not come directly from its engine, but instead indirectly, from the burning shed. At that time the risk that fire would spread from one property to another was a common one. The implications of the issue posed in *Ryan* were therefore significant.

The court in *Ryan* held that the destruction of the plaintiff's property—the second building to catch fire as a result of the railroad's conduct—was not the "natural and expected result" of the destruction of the first building. Under the circumstances, the risk of damage to the plaintiff's property was too "remote." The railroad's negligent conduct therefore was not the proximate cause of the plaintiff's loss, and the railroad was not liable. As anyone familiar with tort law knows, however, these were legal conclusions—labels more than reasons—and certainly not statements of empirical fact. The one thing that was "natural and expected" in the nineteenth century, at least in common parlance, was that when one building caught fire, other buildings near it often would catch fire as well. In fact, the doctrine of "public necessity" permitted the authorities to tear down a building in the line of fire, precisely in order to prevent the spread of fire in this manner.[3]

What, then, was really going on in *Ryan*? The case has been a poster child for a long-running dispute over the extent to which tort law in the nineteenth century largely served economically powerful interests, subsidizing industrial and commercial growth at the expense of the individuals who suffered accidental physical harm.[4] Lawrence Friedman, for example, cited *Ryan* as a prime example of the way the courts "worked to limit damages" because "capital had to be spared for its necessary work."[5] Disputing the idea that nineteenth-century tort law subsidized industry, Peter Karsten argued that the approach the *Ryan* court took to the particular issue it addressed was very much in the minority, and that nineteenth-century judges were in general far more friendly to plaintiffs in tort cases than subsidy proponents believe.[6]

What many of the participants in this dispute often have not sufficiently appreciated, and sometimes have completely ignored, however, is the significance of the further explanation the *Ryan* court offered for its decision: "A man may insure his own house, or his own furniture, but he cannot insure his neighbor's building or furniture, for the reason that he has no interest in them. To hold that the owner must not only meet his own loss by fire, but that he must guarantee the security of his neighbors on both sides, and to an unlimited extent, would be to create a liability which would be the destruction of civilized society."

The court obviously considered it significant that the railroad could not have bought insurance on neighboring property, in effect insuring itself against liability for damaging that property. Holding a party responsible for starting a fire for the spread of the fire beyond the first building it destroyed could therefore create what the court considered "a liability that would be the destruction of all civilized society." The railroads probably could have passed on the cost of liability to their customer base even without liability insurance. But the rule in *Ryan* protected not only large enterprises such as the railroads but also smaller enterprises and individuals with few assets and no means of spreading the risk of liability to a large customer base.

Whether the availability of liability insurance actually would have changed the outcome in *Ryan* is uncertain. Neither Friedman, nor Karsten, nor the others who have weighed in on the *Ryan* issue, however, have recognized that in 1866 that was impossible. Liability insurance would not be introduced in this country for another 20 years. Once it did become available, it would enable small enterprises and ordinary individuals who would come to face substantial tort liabilities to insure against them. Such insurance would also enable the railroads and other industries that faced the risk of enormous liability to spread that risk and to pass the cost of their insurance on to their customers. And after that, the one-building rule adopted in *Ryan* would disappear.

The question, then, is why it took so long for liability insurance to come on the scene. How can it be that as late as the second half of the nineteenth century, after tort liability had been a fixture in the common law for hundreds of years, there still was no such thing as insurance against liability in tort? How can liability insurance, which is today so closely intertwined with modern tort liability, have taken so long to develop? The answers lie both in economic history and in a web of legal doctrines that prohibited insuring against tort liability.

The Evolving Legal Status of Insurance

In one sense the absence of liability insurance until late in the nineteenth century is no puzzle at all. Until then there was no substantial need for it. In an agrarian society, personal injuries often occurred on family farms, where most potential defendants were close relatives whom the victim either could not lawfully sue or had no interest in suing. And until the advent of the railroads, transportation accidents were sporadic and often comparatively minor. Collisions involving horses and horse-drawn carriages produced fewer and less severe injuries than those involving heavy locomotives. There were therefore not enough economically significant potential defendants with substantial liability exposure to create a demand for liability insurance.

Further, until the middle of the nineteenth century there was no general-purpose tort of negligence. Liability for accidental personal injury was imposed only if it fell into a recognized set of limited categories. Blackstone's *Commentaries* (1765), for example, contain almost no discussion of tort liability of any sort. Even after negligence did emerge as a separate and independent basis for imposing liability around the middle of the nineteenth century, there were limits on its scope. For example, employment-related accidental injuries were subject to existing defenses such as contributory negligence and assumption of risk. And a new defense, the fellow-servant rule (discussed below), was developed in the 1840s to further limit the scope of an employer's liability. Only when the accident rate increased after the Civil War and the doctrinal limitations on employer liability began to erode did a demand for liability insurance arise.

Still, before the accident rate increased and the expansion of tort liability was sufficiently in prospect to create a significant demand for liability insurance, deep within the doctrinal structure of the common law of the eighteenth and nineteenth centuries there was also ambivalence about insurance. On the one hand, it was a lawful transaction that produced social benefits. On the other hand, it created moral hazard—it could encourage careless or even intentionally wrongful behavior. Insurance also seemed a bit like gambling, which was legally disfavored. Because the main reflections of this ambivalence eventually disappeared from insurance law, the doctrines that addressed the tensions within that body of law have been largely forgotten. But after liability insurance was introduced, and before its validity could be confirmed, these doctrines had to be confronted and dismantled.

The core issue was whether insurance against losses caused by the policyholder's own negligence was valid.[7] The courts struggled throughout the century with different versions of this issue, first in connection with first-party insurance, and ultimately in connection with liability insurance. For example, suppose that a shipowner failed to equip his vessel with proper rigging, or a property owner was careless in using a wood-burning stove. If these parties were covered by marine or fire insurance, the question was whether they could recover insurance benefits when they suffered a loss resulting from their own failure to take sufficient care to protect their property. It was in instances such as these that the tension between insurance seen as a social good and insurance seen as an encouragement of morally suspect behavior was manifested.

First-Party Insurance and Negligently Caused Loss

The tension is best illustrated by an example from marine insurance. The principal coverage marine insurance policies provided was found in an insuring agreement that protected the policyholder against losses caused by "perils of the sea." This phrase was a term of art among the shipowners and men of means who frequented Lloyd's Coffee House in London in the seventeenth and eighteenth centuries. In that setting, marine insurance was bought and sold by these individuals, who sometimes served as insurers, and sometimes as policyholders. But as with many terms of art, this one was vague at its boundaries. The meaning of the phrase "perils of the sea" was partly a question of the intent and expectations of the parties to marine insurance contracts, and partly a question of legal policy governing the legitimate scope of these contracts.

The doctrinal vehicle that addressed the issue was a defense to a claim for insurance coverage that was based on what was known as "barratry." The barratry defense precluded the recovery of insurance for losses caused by the misfeasance of the policyholder. These losses were not considered to result from the "perils of the sea" and therefore did not fall within the insuring agreement of the typical marine insurance policy. There was no doubt that the defense applied to losses resulting from deliberate wrongdoing by the policyholder, but how far beyond these forms of wrongdoing the defense extended—perhaps to losses caused by mere negligence—was an evolving issue in the world of nineteenth-century American insurance law. The express question in cases that raised the issue was how language that literally was sufficiently general to be interpreted as insuring against losses caused by negligence ("perils of the sea") should actually be interpreted. But the implicit question was whether encouraging, or at least tolerating, insurance against losses that resulted from the negligent conduct of the policyholder or its agents was to be permitted.[8] Until well into the nineteenth century the answer seems to have been that such insurance was invalid.[9]

As the middle of the century approached, however, the attitudes that supported the barratry defense, and therefore the defense itself, were evolving. Not only marine but also fire insurers increasingly found that the defense of barratry was denied to them when they sought to avoid coverage obligations on the ground that the policyholder's negligence had caused an otherwise-insured loss.[10] The decline of the barratry defense often was not accompanied by any explicit recognition that there had been a shift in policy. Rather, marine and fire insurance policies that did not expressly exclude coverage of losses caused by the policyholder's negligence were now simply understood to cover, respectively, what they said they did: loss of ships and cargo, and destruction of property by fire. As a consequence of this somewhat formalistic way of addressing the issue, there was little or no discussion in the opinions of why the conflicting values and causal notions that had come together in the barratry defense were now being reconciled in favor of, rather than against, the validity of first-party insurance for losses caused by negligence.

Liability Waivers and Indemnity Agreements

As long as the barratry defense applied to first-party insurance, the concern about moral hazard underlying that defense made third-party insurance even more objectionable. Because of the greater moral hazard that would have been associated with such liability insurance, it seemed self-evident that insurance of this sort would be improper, although the question rarely arose directly.[11]

Once the barratry defense was put to rest, conceptual and public policy space for the eventual emergence of liability insurance was created. Before that could happen, however, there had to be a significant reason for there to be liability insurance. As I noted earlier, the demand for this form of insurance, even if it had been valid, was minimal before, and well into, the nineteenth century. The quintessential tort actions of the first half of the nineteenth century in the United States remained those of a rural society, even as the country was beginning to transform itself into an urban, industrialized nation. Typical tort suits for accidental injury involved milldams, horses and the carriages they pulled, farm and residential fires, and in the classic case, a dogfight.[12]

By midcentury, however, the one major exception involved the railroads. They were causing an increasing number of accidental injuries. And in contrast to virtually all other potential victims of accidental injury, the tort rights of a railroad's passengers, as well as those who shipped their goods on railroads, were comparatively broad. This exceptional treatment was the historical product of a body of rules governing the liabilities of what were called "common carriers." Common carriers were the operators of stagecoaches, inns, and the like, who owed their customers more than merely reasonable care. They had long been held to have a high duty of care to their customers— something approaching, though not quite as exacting as, strict liability. When railroads came into being, the rule was applied to them as well.

The idea behind this rule was that the customers of common carriers were in a position of involuntary dependency, being away from home in necessitous circumstances, and therefore typically without the ability to negotiate contract terms governing the services provided them. Often for practical purposes the common carrier had what amounted to a monopoly. As a consequence of the natural advantage the common carriers' position gave them, the law provided that they owed their customers a high duty of care in return. Even as the railroads became more powerful and garnered certain kinds of favorable legal treatment, the rule demanding that they exercise a high duty of care to their customers was maintained. It was in this connection that the courts would next confront the common law's ambivalence about insurance against losses caused by the policyholder's negligence.

By the 1870s the railroads had become a major economic force. In many settings they had the economic power to dictate both prices and the terms on which they would transport passengers and carry goods. The common carrier's common law high duty of care, however, was etched in stone; the courts simply were not inclined to alter that duty. But this was the era of freedom of contract. Even if the law of torts could not be modified, it might be circumvented by contract. And that is precisely what the railroads often attempted to do.

The method they used was to contract out of their high duty of care by requiring the passenger or shipper of goods to waive their right to recover from the railroad for injury or damage suffered in the course of passage, or to agree in advance to "indemnify" the railroad against any liability that the railroad might have for injury or damage. Since the railroad's liability would have been to the very party providing the indemnification, the latter device was nothing but a waiver of liability with another name. By means of these liability waivers and indemnification agreements, the railroads attempted to supplant tort law's high duty of care with a contract providing that the railroads had no duty of care whatsoever.

There was a long-running dispute about the extent to which common carriers such as railroads were permitted to contract out of their common law high duty of care in this way.[13] Uncertainty about the validity of these kinds of contracts reflected the same concern about moral hazard that was at the foundation of the barratry defense.[14] The demise of the barratry defense enabled first-party policyholders to recover for the consequences of their negligence from their own insurers. In contrast, liability waivers and indemnification agreements enabled railroads and other common carriers to avoid liability for their negligence. The former promoted compensation for loss, whereas the latter restricted it.

This distinction made a big difference. The dominant rule, even late into the nineteenth century, was that both liability waivers and indemnification agreements, at least insofar as they relieved the common carriers of liability for negligence, were invalid. Thus, although the barratry defense of the policyholder's negligence was dying out in first-party insurance, despite the moral hazard the defense had combated, liability waivers by common carriers were still invalid, precisely because of the moral hazard that they created.

The *Phoenix* Doctrine

Even as these differing strains of thought were coexisting uncomfortably within tort and insurance law, another insurance device that created moral hazard came under scrutiny in the Supreme Court of the United States. In that era the Supreme Court still made general common law decisions, as it would until the decision in *Erie R.R. v. Tompkins* in 1938.[15] A ruling by the Court with implications for the validity of a new form of insurance would therefore command considerable attention. As often happens, that ruling came indirectly. But it turned out to be very significant nonetheless, for it marked a turning point in the law's attitude toward the moral hazard created by insurance and insurance-like devices.

In 1886, just a few months before the first liability insurance company would be established in this country, the case of *Phoenix Ins. Co. of Brooklyn v. Erie & Western Transportation Co.* came before the Supreme Court.[16] A marine insurer had paid a shipper for loss of its goods while in transit, and then sued the common carrier of the goods—a company operating steamships on the Great Lakes—for reimbursement of what the insurer had paid the shipper. The common carrier's defense to the insurer's claim was that because the shipping contract gave the carrier "the benefit of the shipper's insurance," the insurer had no right against the carrier.

Like the liability waivers and indemnity agreements with common carriers whose validity had been litigated for decades, this was probably another instance in which the carrier had dictated the terms of the transaction, this time by demanding that the shipper provide it with insurance that would pay for a loss of the goods while they were in the common carriers' custody. That way the common carrier would not have to pay the shipper for a loss or, if it paid, could recover it from the shipper's insurer.[17] The carrier in *Phoenix* argued that, because it was in effect an insured party under the shipper's insurance policy, the insurer had no right to sue it for the loss.

The insurer responded that the provision in the shipping contract giving the carrier the benefit of the shipper's insurance was against public policy and therefore invalid, because it amounted to insuring the carrier against liability for its own negligence. Since the carrier was not legally entitled to have the benefit of the shipper's insurance, this argument went, the carrier was not insured, and the insurer could sue the carrier.

The Court in *Phoenix* therefore had to decide which doctrine had the greater gravitational pull in this situation: the rule prohibiting liability waivers and indemnity agreements between common carriers and their passengers and shippers or the rule (abolishing the barratry defense) that permitted the owner of property to recover insurance for a loss even when it had been caused by the owner's own negligence. The Court concluded that there was a closer analogy between what had been done in *Phoenix* and the now-legitimate purchase of insurance covering loss resulting from a property owner's own negligence. "As the carrier might lawfully himself obtain insurance against the loss of goods by the usual perils, though occasioned by his own negligence," the Court reasoned, "he may lawfully stipulate with the owner to be allowed the benefit of insurance voluntarily obtained by the latter."[18]

Now the fact that formally this arrangement involved insurance and not a liability waiver or indemnification agreement did not make the moral hazard it entailed disappear. A common carrier given the benefit of a shipper's insurance had less incentive to protect the goods it was carrying than a carrier that was not given the benefit of such insurance. The question, therefore, was why this form of insurance was permitted, notwithstanding the moral hazard it entailed, even while liability waivers and indemnity agreements were not. The Court explained the basis for the distinction in a memorable phrase that would heavily influence courts subsequently addressing whether liability insurance itself was valid: "By obtaining insurance," the Court said, the insured (in this case the carrier) "does not diminish his responsibility to the owners of the goods, but rather increases his means of meeting that responsibility."[19]

The point was that an increase of moral hazard could be tolerated if the result was to help ensure that injured parties were compensated. Liability waivers and indemnity agreements restricted compensation at the same time they increased moral hazard. In contrast, allowing a carrier to insure property in its custody against loss caused by the carrier's own negligence, or providing that carrier with the benefit of a shipper's insurance, did not deprive anyone of compensation; these devices merely shifted the risk of loss to an insurance company.

All *Phoenix* did literally, of course, was to hold that the barratry defense of the policyholder's negligence was abolished under marine insurance policies, not only when the claim was made by the named insured but also when the insurer sued a party given the benefit of that insurance by contract. *Phoenix* itself did not involve liability insurance, and the particular dispute in *Phoenix* concerned what amounted to indirect insurance against liability for damage to property, not direct or even indirect insurance against liability for personal injury.

However, because liability insurance as we now know it, and challenges to this new form of insurance, were to come on the scene within months of the decision in *Phoenix*, its implications were historic. In *Phoenix*, what previously had been at most implicit in the decisions abolishing the barratry defense had now become explicit. Ensuring the compensation of victims by making insurance available to parties responsible for negligently caused loss was a positive value that could overcome the law's concern about moral hazard. *Phoenix* offered a compensation justification for permitting insurance against losses resulting from negligence that could apply even in the face of the moral hazard that liability insurance would create.

The Rise and Validation of Liability Insurance

In the decades following the Civil War, the quickened pace of industrialization, the growth of railroads and streetcar lines, and the dispersal of a growing population across greater distances increased the opportunities for injury to occur in people's jobs and daily lives. An increasing number of accidents placed increased pressure on the tort system to provide redress for those injuries. Meanwhile, attitudes toward the fundamental causes and social responsibility for accidents themselves were beginning to change. An older conception of accidental injury as the product of fate or bad luck was slowly being replaced by a conception that assigned causal responsibility to individual behavior, including the behavior of business enterprises that created the conditions in which injury occurred.[20]

The Threat of Employer Liability

As industrialization and mechanized transportation accelerated, many accidents involved the employees of new industrial and transportation enterprises themselves. In response to both the increasing number of on-the-job injuries and to the evolution of attitudes about the causes of accidents, the common law of employers' liability began to change in fits and starts. The principal changes involved the "fellow-servant" rule. In general an employer is "vicariously" liable for torts committed by its employees within the scope of their employment, even if the employer itself has not been negligent. Thus, if an employee negligently injured a customer or bystander, the employer (as well as the employee) would be liable to that party. However, under the fellow-servant rule, which was introduced in the 1840s and spread quickly thereafter, the employer was not vicariously liable to one employee for a tort committed by another employee, even if the tort was committed within the scope of employment.[21] Only if the employer was negligent in its own right could an injured employee recover from the employer. The idea underlying this rule was that, in accepting employment, employees assumed the risk that they would be injured by their fellow employees.

Over time a variety of common law exceptions to the fellow-servant rule affording more room for suit were created. For example, some courts began to hold that under some circumstances the employer had a nondelegable duty to furnish a safe workplace, which included providing nonnegligent employees; others developed a "vice-principal" doctrine that rendered the fellow-servant rule inapplicable to the negligence of an employee's supervisor; and still others held that the rule did not apply when an employee was injured by an employee who worked in a "different department" of the same company or business.[22]

As the labor movement gained strength, it put its muscle behind additional, legislative reform of employer liability law. Statutory exceptions to the fellow-servant rule applicable only to railroads were enacted in a number of states between 1855 and 1874, for example.[23] By the 1880s, labor was targeting not just the railroads alone, but was seeking legislation to limit or overturn restrictions on employers' tort liability generally. Eventually more than two dozen states would adopt employers' liability acts that modified the fellow-servant rule and the contributory negligence defense.[24] England's fellow-servant rule was modified by statute in a similar way in 1880.

Employers' Liability Insurance

The enactment of legislation expanding employers' liability on both sides of the Atlantic marked a tipping point. Following the enactment of the new English rule, a company that offered insurance against the new liabilities of employers, the Employers' Liability Assurance Corporation, Ltd., was established.[25] In view of the employers' liability legislation that also had been enacted or was in prospect on the other side of the Atlantic, Employers' Liability Assurance apparently saw the United States as a potential market as well. While the Massachusetts legislature was considering the adoption of employers' liability legislation in the spring of 1886, Employers' Liability Assurance opened an office in Boston and sold its first policy.

Just a few months later, 26 textile manufacturers and community leaders from the Boston area convened, and decided to form their own mutual company to provide themselves with liability insurance.[26] To distinguish this company from their English rival, they named it the American Mutual Liability Insurance Company. Appropriately, the new form of coverage that was developed to deal with employers' expanding tort liability was called "Employers' Liability" insurance, and that was the only form of liability it covered.[27] An employers' liability act that expanded the scope of employers' liability was then enacted in Massachusetts in 1887, simultaneously spurring demand for the new coverage.[28]

Within a couple of years, the two original Boston liability insurers were joined by other companies selling liability insurance, both in Massachusetts and elsewhere. But even while a market for the new form of insurance was developing, the validity of the new product was still open to question. The *Phoenix* case had implied that liability insurance would be valid, but it certainly had not directly held that public policy permitted insuring against tort liability.

As in *Phoenix*, the first cases raising the issue involved common carriers. By this time, common carriers such as trolley companies, railroads, and steamships were disproportionately likely to be involved in tort suits, and therefore likely to be among the first defendants who would seek to take advantage of their newly purchased liability insurance policies. In addition, because common carriers had a high duty of care to their passengers and to those whose goods they transported, it was in connection with the purchase of liability insurance by this particular kind of enterprise that a challenge to the validity of liability insurance had the greatest chance of succeeding. If common carriers, and other enterprises whose conduct was as affected by the public interest could validly purchase insurance that risked diminishing their incentive to comply with their common law duty, then other enterprises whose conduct was less affected by the public interest would surely be permitted to purchase liability insurance. The opposition to liability insurance was thus likely to make its strongest arguments in cases involving common carriers.

Ten years after liability insurance was first introduced in Boston, the Court of Appeals of Maryland rejected what appears to have been the first challenge to liability insurance, relying on prior decisions that fire and marine insurance could validly apply to losses resulting from the policyholder's negligence. The court extensively cited the *Phoenix* doctrine as authority for its decision. In upholding the validity of the new form of insurance, the court completely dismissed the contention that the "inevitable tendency or effect" of liability insurance would be "to induce less vigilance or to promote greater carelessness" on the part of the policyholder.

Liability insurance, the court said, does not in any way relax the carrier's duty of care and vigilance to the public. This is because insurance is "at best limited and partial" and because the policyholder will "endeavor to reduce the sum total of his insurance to a minimum figure, and thereby diminish the amount of the annual premium rate charged him for it," which will "always depend in a large measure, if not entirely, upon the prudence, care, and skill with which his affairs are managed and conducted. Such a carrier has, consequently, exactly the same motive or incentive to protect the public and the individual from injury that he would have if he should become his own insurer."[29] A year later the Supreme Court of New Jersey reached the same result, employing similar reasoning and also quoting *Phoenix*.[30]

This was hardly a convincing refutation of the claim that liability insurance would not promote moral hazard at all. But these courts did not take the position they did merely because they rejected the moral hazard attack on liability insurance. Rather, like the U.S. Supreme Court in *Phoenix* before them, they emphasized as a ground for their decisions the fact that liability insurance helped to ensure the compensation of those who were injured by the policyholder's actions. The Maryland Court of Appeals noted that "the result of the insurance is to furnish him [the policyholder] the means to make compensation" and that insurance made "more certain his ability to respond in damages for personal injuries caused by his carelessness and neglect."[31] In the words of the *Phoenix* Court that were repeatedly quoted in the cases rejecting attacks on liability insurance, such insurance increased the policyholder's "means of meeting" its responsibility—that is, of paying compensation for negligently caused injuries.

The new doctrine validating liability insurance was accepted virtually without objection, first in the 1890s and then as the years went on. The only vigorous judicial criticism I have located came a decade later in *Breeden v. Frankfort Marine,* in which the Supreme Court of Missouri applied the *Phoenix* doctrine to liability insurance in the face of an extensive dissent that expressly took issue with that doctrine.[32] The dissent simply could not accept what it took to be the premise of the doctrine, that liability insurance does not undermine accident prevention, arguing that "when a carrier knows that a third person [the liability insurer] is required to furnish the means from his own pocket with which to pay for the injuries done by his negligence to the passenger, then that consideration has a direct and potent influence in encouraging negligence on the part of the carrier."[33]

The *Breeden* dissent, however, was the dying gasp of an older point of view. That view saw the common carrier's "responsibility" as lying in its duty to exercise care to avoid causing personal injury. In contrast, the newer point of view saw responsibility differently. When the *Phoenix* Court said that, by purchasing liability insurance, the policyholder does not diminish his responsibility, "but rather increases his means of meeting that responsibility," it did not conceive of "responsibility" as the obligation to exercise reasonable care to avoid causing injury. If insurance increases the policyholder's "means of meeting" his "responsibility," then the responsibility in question cannot be the obligation not to be negligent. Whatever one thinks about whether being insured has a *negative* impact on safety, the Court could not have been saying that insurance had a *positive* safety impact. With the exception of occasional loss management services provided to policyholders, liability insurance then, as now, did not "increase" the policyholder's "means" of preventing the occurrence of accidents resulting from negligence.

Liability insurance does, however, increase the policyholder's means of paying for the costs of his negligence. Because this was the increased means of meeting responsibility to which the *Phoenix* doctrine was referring, the very idea of responsibility had begun to evolve, from "responsibility" to avoid negligently injuring others toward "responsibility" to compensate for negligently caused injury when it occurred. Liability insurance functioned in this intellectual evolution as a vehicle for ensuring compensation to the injured. And since, rightly or wrongly, the courts also understood liability insurance to be compatible with accident prevention, the seeds of the modern functioning of liability insurance had been planted.

Thus, the courts accepted liability insurance, and confirmed its validity, because employers were increasingly in need of protection against liability and because changing notions of responsibility no longer led to the conclusion that insuring against liability for negligence violated public policy. In addition, evolving notions about the nature of risk may have implicitly contributed to the new judicial attitude. Morton Horwitz has attributed the increased acceptance of all forms of insurance as the nineteenth century proceeded to the rise of an actuarial consciousness during this period.[34] And it may well be that at this time there was a transformation in the understanding of both insurance and the events it covers. On the older view, insurance was just one of many forms of indemnity, in which risk was merely transferred from one party to another. With the transfer of risk came the undesirable removal of responsibility from the party who was transferring it. On the other hand, once insurance began to be seen not only as a risk *transfer* but also as a risk-*spreading* mechanism, in which the insurer is the vehicle by which the law of averages can be enlisted to protect both insurer and insured, it would have been much easier to view the insurance transaction as a means of economic planning and stabilization rather than as a device for avoiding common law responsibilities.

Nevertheless, the judicial opinions upholding the validity of liability insurance do not themselves contain any evidence that the actuarial conception of insurance affected the courts' reasoning or conclusions. It is true that by the dawn of the twentieth century the courts were universally rejecting the contention that liability insurance would so undermine safety incentives that this new form of insurance was against public policy. And the courts had come to see the benefit of liability insurance as a means of ensuring that the policyholder would be able to compensate those it tortiously injured—as a means of "meeting that responsibility" rather than shirking it. The courts rejecting attacks on liability insurance consistently emphasized the fact that those purchasing liability insurance were not relieving themselves of any obligation to those they injured. The Maryland Court of Appeals noted, for example: "Notwithstanding such insurance, the carrier remains liable to the owner or shipper of the goods, and by insuring them he merely contracts, as in every other instance of a insurance, with some one else for reimbursement of such loss."[35]

But there is nothing in these opinions to suggest that the courts were thinking in anything other than two-party terms. The common carrier had a responsibility to compensate those injured by its negligence, and liability insurance helped to assure that such compensation would be available. There was no reference to the fact that other similarly situated common carriers would also be purchasing insurance and would in effect be participating in a common risk pool, or to the possibility that shipping costs would rise and that customers as a group might therefore be indirectly footing the bill for the carrier's liability insurance.

In short, the courts were not yet speaking about the loss-spreading effects of liability insurance. In their reasoning there were no other policyholders in the background, no risk-spreading benefits being taken into account. For these courts, liability insurance appeared for all intents and purposes to have the same character as an ordinary indemnity that transferred financial responsibility from one free-standing party to another. It would take another step in the evolution of thinking about liability insurance before the courts understood insurance not merely as risk transfer but also as risk spreading. Risk-spreading considerations would not be brought fully into play until there were deliberations about the adoption of workers' compensation in the first decade of the twentieth century.

Liability to the Public and the Emergence of Insurer Control of Litigation

Even before the validation of liability insurance by the courts, the new form of coverage had begun to spread. The Fidelity and Casualty Company of New York established a liability department in 1888 and began to write Employers' Liability insurance.[36] Travelers first wrote Employers' Liability insurance in 1889.[37] Over time others followed—Aetna, for example, began writing liability insurance in 1902—and a broader market for liability insurance began to develop. By 1909 there were 27 liability insurance companies, enough to warrant publication of a manual to assist in establishing rate classes and fixing premiums. That year these insurers' total premium revenue for liability insurance was just over $21 million. With an average loss ratio (measured by comparing premiums to losses paid) of 43.2 percent, they paid about $9 million per year in claims.[38] Typical policy limits (i.e., the maximum amount payable under the policy) were $5,000 for injury to one person and $10,000 for injury to two or more persons. The average claim payment was still small—roughly $25 for each claim made, and $500 for each claim that resulted in a lawsuit.[39]

Coverage of Liability to the Public

After a time the policies became more varied and were written to address the particular risks arising out of the policyholder's business, with different bases for setting premiums.[40] More important, once liability insurance was established, insurers began to branch out beyond the core Employers' Liability insurance policies with which they began. The first major addition came because of recognition that businesses faced the threat of liability not only to their employees but also to members of the public at-large. Before the turn of the twentieth century, a "public liability" feature was therefore being added to the policies.

Exactly how widespread liability insurance was, and what percentage of claims were covered by insurance, is not entirely clear, but some extrapolation from the available data is possible. Data filed by 9 of the 27 liability insurers doing business in 1908 indicated that they had paid or reserved for 1.9 million claims during the 10 previous years. About one-third of the industry thus paid about two hundred thousand claims per year.[41] We can extrapolate from this figure to an estimate of about six hundred thousand paid claims per year that were covered by liability insurance. Case studies of the period suggest that work-related tort claims comprised, very roughly, 20 percent of all tort claims filed.[42] By this measure, liability insurers paid about 120,000 work-related tort claims per year during this period, out of a total of about two million work-related injuries and deaths per year. The remaining 480,000 claims liability insurers paid they paid to members of the public rather than to the employees of policyholders.

The addition of a public liability feature to the standard liability insurance policy resulted from, and in turn undoubtedly added to, the increasing incidence of tort suits by members of the public as the end of the nineteenth century approached. No national or even statewide data exists on the overall incidence of tort liability during this period. But there are a number of useful studies of rates of suit in particular locations. These studies suggest that the number of tort suits increased substantially between about 1870 and 1910, especially in urban areas. For example, in 1880 in Boston and its surrounding counties there were a total of 120 suits alleging negligently caused personal injury. By 1900, however, just 20 years later, there were 3,300 such lawsuits.[43] A study of litigation in Manhattan during roughly the same period tells a similar, if not quite so dramatic, story. In 1870, 13 tort suits for personal injury were filed in the Supreme Court of the City of New York. By 1900 the number had increased to 112, and by 1910 to 595.[44]

In less urban and in rural areas the increase in tort claims was not as pronounced but still was noticeable. From 1880 to 1900 in Alameda County, California, 340 personal injury lawsuits were filed.[45] But between 1901 and 1910—less than half as many years—there were 335 such suits.[46] Tort suits (including but not limited to personal injury actions) in three rural West Virginia counties increased from a total of 66 between 1872 and 1880 to a total of 292 between 1901 and 1910.[47]

A portion of each of these increases—in some instances a major portion—was inevitably a reflection of the population growth that took place in these areas during the periods in question. The population of Boston increased by 35 percent between 1880 and 1900.[48] Manhattan grew from a population of 950,000 in 1870 to 2,750,000 in 1910.[49] The population of Alameda County nearly quadrupled between 1880 and 1910.[50] And in the 40 years between 1870 and 1910, the population of the three West Virginia counties that were the subject of the aforementioned study increased 480 percent.

But the role increased population played in the rise of lawsuits and liability insurance is not this simple. The late nineteenth- and early twentieth-century population increases in Boston and Manhattan, for example, cannot fully account for the increases in lawsuits in these cities. An increase in the kinds of activities that resulted in lawsuits, and not increased population alone, is probably the most important responsible factor. Population growth increases the number of potential plaintiffs and defendants proportionately; but increased development and industrialization tend to increase the potential liability of certain identifiable defendants, such as railroads, trolley companies, and coal mines, disproportionately.

It is no surprise, therefore, that certain categories of defendants appear repeatedly in the litigation case studies. The conventional wisdom is that railroad accidents dominated late nineteenth-century tort law, and railroads were definitely repeat defendants in this era. In Alameda County between 1901 and 1910, over 40 percent of the personal injury suits were against common carriers, many of whom would have been railroads.[51] In turn-of-the-century Boston, 5 percent of all personal injury suits were against railroads.[52] In New York City that figure was 9 percent in 1890, though it had dropped to 3 percent in 1910.[53]

A different kind of common carrier, however, dominated tort suits in the cities. For example, in Boston in 1880 there were only a dozen suits alleging negligent operation of a horsecar. In 1900, after an electric streetcar system had been introduced, there were 1,400 suits alleging negligent operation of this new method of urban transportation.[54] In New York City, streetcar accidents comprised 25 percent of all personal injury suits in 1890, and in 1910 still comprised 15 percent of them.[55] Data for Alameda County during the period 1880–1900 shows that there were 94 railroad cases and 110 streetcar cases, comprising 60 percent of all personal injury suits.[56] The new technology of urban transportation, operating in the congested streets of the cities, obviously produced a good deal of injury.

The Insurer's Role: Defending and Settling Claims

Liability insurers not only paid the judgments and settlements in many of these cases—by my earlier estimate, more than five hundred thousand claims per year. In addition, liability insurance policies obligated the insurer to provide the insured with a defense against lawsuits alleging liability that would be covered by the policy if the suit was successful. This duty to defend was included in policies soon after the introduction of liability insurance, and as nearly as I can determine, in many instances from the very beginning. A policy a prominent insurer issued in 1895, for example, provided for such a duty to defend.[57] This coverage was provided "outside" of the policy limits—that is, the costs the insurer expended on defense did not erode the amount of coverage provided.[58] The language of the Aetna policy at the turn of the twentieth century is typical. This policy provided: "If suit is brought against the assured to enforce a claim for damages covered by this policy he shall immediately forward to the company every summons or other process as soon as the same shall have been served on him, and the company will, at its own cost, defend such suit in the name and on behalf of the assured."[59] Thus, once a policy was in force, its coverage of the cost of defense was unlimited.

Although the fact that policies provided a "free" defense to every policy-holder was an added benefit of purchasing liability insurance, taking charge of and defending suits against their policyholders was the means by which liability insurers controlled litigation. Insurers could hardly afford to permit their policyholders to determine how to litigate cases or whether to settle. Otherwise, policyholders would be deciding how to spend their insurers' money. A liability insurance policy would have the potential to be like a broken slot machine, paying for the policyholder's defense and settlements without limit. So liability insurance policies not only provided for a duty to defend. For control over the defense to be meaningful for insurers, they also had to control the decision whether to litigate or settle. Consequently, the policies afforded the insurer the privilege to settle or to decline to settle claims. Indeed, policies expressly excluded coverage of settlements reached by the policyholder without the insurer's consent.

The duty to defend, then, together with the allied provision affording the insurer the privilege to decide whether or not to settle a case, put liability insurers in charge of litigation against their policyholders. The insurer decided how to defend, what positions to take, and whether and how much to offer in settlement. The policyholder also had an express obligation under the policy to cooperate in the insurer's defense of the case. Failure to cooperate in the defense constituted breach of a policy condition and was a ground for the insurer's voiding the policy. And if the insurer did decide not to settle and then lost the case, the policyholder's premiums for the following year might increase on account of the insurer's additional defense expenditures and/or payments to successful plaintiffs.

Liability insurers were thus the real parties in interest and were very much in control of the lawsuits they were involved in. And because of this role, insurers' interests were not always perfectly aligned with those of the policyholders they insured. Liability insurers were the classic repeat players, with reputations at stake among plaintiffs' attorneys regarding the insurers' toughness, and with a portfolio of claims to manage. One policyholder might want a case settled in order to avoid adverse publicity; because of its right to control litigation, however, the insurer could nevertheless decide to take the case to trial. Another policyholder might be opposed in principle to settling what it considered a groundless claim; but the insurer's dispassionate financial calculation could lead it to settle such a claim nonetheless.

In short, a liability insurer did not simply stand in the wings, waiting to be called on if liability was imposed on the policyholder. Whenever the policyholder was covered by liability insurance, the tort system looked and acted like a liability insurance system, with the liability insurer at the center of the dispute. Only when a case actually went to trial was the liability insurer's role formally ignored, via the rule that any mention of the fact that the defendant was insured was a ground for a mistrial. The jury, it was thought, would be prejudiced in favor of the plaintiff once it knew that the defendant would not have to pay a judgment out of its own pocket. But this rule was increasingly a pointless legal dance, as over time juries came to assume that many if not most defendants had insurance.

In retrospect it seems virtually inevitable that liability insurance policies would have been structured so as to place the insurer in control of litigation. Any other arrangement would have been difficult, if not impossible, to administer. If policyholders had been left to control litigation, then insurers would have needed to devise a method of limiting their policyholders' incentive to overspend in defending certain claims and to settle other claims that should have been resisted. But there was, and still is, no easy way of combating such incentives. This is why most contemporary liability insurance policies still impose a duty to defend on the insurer, but also give it the right to settle. For example, it would have been cumbersome for the early liability insurers to leave policyholders in charge of litigation but to carefully experience-rate premiums in subsequent policy years in order to give policyholders an incentive to optimize the cost of defense and settlement in the current policy year. Although they sometimes experience-rated premiums in a rough-and-ready manner, in the early years insurers had little statistical data on which to base refined calculations. And even if doing this had been statistically feasible, serious experience-rating for small policyholders could easily have defeated the whole point of their buying insurance—to protect against the risk of the rare but costly lawsuit.

Eventually, something resembling what we might now call "managed legal care" could have developed, with insurer-specified reimbursement rules constraining policyholders' freedom to litigate and settle, but an approach such as that would have been a long time coming. The simpler and more efficient approach was for the insurers to assume control of the defense and settlement of claims for which they had ultimate financial responsibility under their policies.

By the early decades of the twentieth century, then, the building blocks of the modern relationship among plaintiffs, defendants, and defendants' liability insurers were in place. When liability insurers were involved in tort suits, their involvement influenced both the defense and settlement of suits. Although policyholders were the nominal defendants, it was the liability insurers whose money was effectively at stake. Liability insurance policies therefore gave insurers the right to make crucial litigation decisions.

Over time, liability insurers' presence in tort suits would come very nearly to be constitutive of the system's character. Not only would the insurers' involvement affect the procedure and operation of the system; the availability of insurance as a source of compensation would influence the substantive evolution of tort law. Much of the scope of modern tort liability eventually would be justified in at least some quarters as a method of gaining access to defendants' liability insurance. In a very real sense, tort would become insurance.

—2—

The Original Tort Reform: Workers' Compensation

By the turn of the twentieth century, liability insurance had become an established ingredient of the U.S. tort system. The principal function of this form of insurance was to cover employers' liability to their employees, although liability insurance had by then also been extended to cover the policyholder's liability to the public at-large. However, employees' tort rights and consequently their prospects for receiving compensation for injuries suffered on the job were still limited. The employers' liability acts adopted in some states had relaxed certain common law limitations on an employer's liability, but had not by any means eliminated these limitations. The employee who contemplated bringing a tort suit against his employer still faced a steep uphill legal battle.

Not only could employees expect little compensation from their employers if they were injured, most employees had little if any insurance of their own to call on for protection against the economic consequences of injury. The typical worker had minimal life insurance and no disability or medical insurance. As a result, the probability that a worker who was injured on the job would be adequately compensated for his or her lost wages or medical costs, from any source or combination of sources, was low.

Just 20 years later, there had been a transformation in the law governing workplace injury, and with that transformation the injured worker's prospects had brightened. The vast majority of states had enacted workers' compensation acts, called "workmen's" compensation at the time. These acts abolished employers' tort liability and employees' tort rights, but substituted for tort an administrative system of virtually automatic compensation for workplace injuries. In effect, workers' compensation insured workers against the risks of workplace injury, by providing them with prompt compensation of at least some of their lost wages and medical costs. No longer were employees at the mercy of a tort system that had promised substantial compensation to the very few injured employees who were entitled to recover in tort, but at the same time provided no compensation to the far greater number of employees who had no such prospects.

Workers' compensation was the original tort reform, and still is the most fundamental tort reform ever undertaken. Moreover, the issues that workers' compensation confronted at the time of its enactment, and in many ways still confronts, provide a general template for the analysis of virtually any significant contemporary tort reform proposal. It was in debates about workers' compensation that the first sustained, though comparatively primitive, arguments about risk spreading and enterprise liability were made. And it was in fashioning this alternative to tort that three of the principal concerns of any significant tort reform—compensation, deterrence, and administrative costs—were first seriously confronted.

The Turn-of-the-Century Flaws in the Status Quo

Despite employers' increasing concern about the threat of liability to their employees, at the turn of the twentieth century tort liability was still a wholly inadequate method of ensuring compensation for injured employees. The *Phoenix* doctrine, which I discussed in Chapter 1, may have proclaimed the value of insurance as a means by which a defendant could satisfy tort responsibility to its victims. But as long as the scope of an employers' legal responsibility for employment-related injuries was very limited, liability insurance would remain a correspondingly limited source of compensation for injured employees.

To deal with the problem of workplace injuries, Germany and England had enacted workers' compensation programs late in the nineteenth century. These programs required employers to pay the costs of injuries suffered by their employees, regardless of whether either party was negligent. By the turn of the twentieth century, the enactment of similar programs in the United States had been placed on the political agenda. But the political support that would lead to the enactment of workers' compensation, state by state, took considerable time to develop.

Samuel Gompers, head of the American Federation of Labor and perhaps the most prominent labor leader of the time, opposed workers' compensation for much of the first decade of the twentieth century. He believed that programs that made employees dependent on management for their welfare would ultimately undermine the strength of the labor movement. More than a decade later Gompers would oppose government-sponsored national health insurance for a similar reason. He favored generous social welfare programs but wanted them controlled and administered by labor, not by management or government. So Gompers and the national labor movement held out for reforming tort liability to make it more easily imposed and more generous, rather than replacing tort, even while the labor movement in many individual states and its Progressive Era allies had begun militating for workers' compensation. Eventually Gompers relented and threw his support to workers' compensation.

The support of organized labor alone, however, would not have been sufficient to secure the enactment of the new program. Far from being a pure triumph of labor's effort to obtain progressive legislation over its business adversaries, the enactment of workers' compensation was the product of mutual self-interest on the part of labor and a substantial subset of American business that wished to displace the way the existing tort and insurance systems were operating during the first two decades of the twentieth century.

There were three flaws in these systems. First, the tort rules governing employers' liability severely impeded the compensation of injured employees. Losses therefore went uncompensated, producing hardship and economic disruption. Second, and partly for this reason, the tort system did not do enough to prevent accidental injury in the workplace. Limited liability on the part of employers generated limited incentives for them to make the workplace safer. Third, the administrative costs of the tort system, as well as the administrative costs of the liability insurance that often accompanied tort, were unduly high. In addition, the administrative costs of the insurance that workers might purchase themselves were high; as a consequence, for practical purposes workers could not purchase adequate amounts of their own insurance against the risk of suffering personal injury. Workers' compensation was a response to each of these flaws.

Undercompensation in Tort

A worker had two potential sources of injury compensation: tort, and first-party insurance that he had purchased for himself. But neither was adequate.

The tort law of the late nineteenth and early twentieth centuries was stacked against the injured worker. He could not recover damages from his employer unless he proved that the employer was negligent itself, or was legally responsible for another employee's negligent act or omission that caused the injured employee harm. An employer could be held "vicariously liable" to third parties for the negligence of an employee even if the employer was not himself negligent. But under the "fellow-servant rule," with only a few exceptions, vicarious liability did not apply to injuries suffered by one employee through the negligence of another employee of the same employer. The employer was exempted from vicarious liability in this situation. In addition, even if an injured employee could prove the employer's own negligence—in supplying an unsafe piece of equipment, for example—the employee could not recover if he was either contributorily negligent, or had assumed the risk that he would be injured, by knowingly taking the risk posed by dangerous conditions on the job. The fellow-servant rule, contributory negligence, and assumption of risk—"the unholy trinity" of defenses, as they were sometimes called—made it extremely difficult for injured workers to recover in tort for their injuries. And because it was difficult for a worker to succeed in a tort suit, comparatively few such suits were brought.

For example, a study of late nineteenth- and early twentieth-century tort litigation in New York City found that there were no personal injury suits alleging work-related injuries filed in 1870; 24 such suits (constituting 21 percent of all personal injury cases) filed in 1890; and 160 suits (constituting 27 percent of all personal injury cases) filed in 1910.[1] Other studies of litigation during this period yielded analogous findings.[2] The increasing rate of suit as the decades progressed may have reflected the relaxation of limitations on employees' tort rights that had began to occur, slowly and in very small steps, in the decades following the Civil War. But the increased rate of suit does not begin to reflect the full amount of workplace injury that was occurring during the same periods; there were probably several hundred times as many accidents as there were suits.

The accident rate was examined in one of the seminal documents in the field, New York's Wainwright Commission Report, which made the findings that supported the enactment of the earliest noteworthy workers' compensation statute, adopted in New York in 1910. The commission held 11 days of hearings around the state in late 1909 and early 1910. It heard testimony from 106 witnesses and produced a 470-page transcript of this testimony. A study conducted for the commission found that over 15,000 work-related injuries had been reported to the Commissioner of Labor of the State of New York during each of the preceding three years. In 1909, for example,

252 work-related deaths, 3,739 serious or permanent injuries, and 12,839 other injuries had been reported.[3] Yet even these figures undoubtedly understated the frequency of injury, since the reporting requirement that produced this data was not easily enforceable. The enormous disproportion between the nearly 17,000 work-related injuries and deaths that occurred statewide in that year and the 160 suits filed in New York City the following year—even discounting for the fact that the population of the state as whole at that time was just about twice that of New York City—is evident.

Nor was there a process of presuit compensation that can explain this disproportion. Rather, victims mostly went uncompensated or radically undercompensated. There were a number of major studies of the scope of compensation paid to the victims of on-the-job injury or death during the early 1900s, similar to and including that conducted by the Wainwright Commission. In these studies, the percentage of cases in which families of fatal accident victims received no compensation at all from their employers was a weighted average of 44.5 percent. The mean ratio of compensation to annual earnings in these fatality cases was .56, which produced sums that obviously would not have provided adequate long-term support for families that had lost a breadwinner. Even focusing only on the group of families that did receive some compensation, typically the ratio of compensation to annual income ranged from about .6 to about 1.5 percent of annual earnings.[4] The data on compensation paid to the victims of nonfatal accidents is similar. About 40 percent of victims in these studies received no compensation. Of the 60 percent of the victims in the different studies who did receive compensation, the average percentage of their out-of-pocket losses that was compensated ranged widely, from 24 percent to 140 percent.[5]

One of the most prominent works addressing this problem was Crystal Eastman's classic study of industrial accident compensation in Pittsburgh. Eastman was a reform-minded activist and lawyer from New York City. She demonstrated that among Pittsburgh workers there was a dramatic gap between the losses they suffered and the amounts they recovered in tort, if they recovered anything at all, and recommended the adoption of workers' compensation as a substitute for tort. Eastman found that in 222 instances for which there was information involving the workplace death of a married man in Pittsburgh during a 12-month period in 1906–1907, 164 dependent families recovered $500 or less, 59 of whom recovered nothing. Only 8 families received more than $2,000. Thus, only 48, or just over 20 percent, recovered more than $500 for the death of a breadwinner.[6] The national average annual wage at that point was about $750 per year.[7] The vast majority of families, then, received less than one year's wages for the death of a breadwinner. Tort thus provided hopelessly inadequate compensation for the death of a breadwinner.

Compensation from First-Party Insurance

If workers had possessed more insurance themselves, the failure of the tort system to protect them more vigorously might have been of less concern. Instead, the compensating wage differentials that tended to pay workers in comparatively dangerous employments higher wages might have been considered an acceptable alternative.[8] But such differentials would have been far less desirable to risk-averse employees than insurance against the losses that would arise out of nearly inevitable work-related injuries. It is commonplace now to think of compensating wage differentials and first-party insurance as opposite sides of the same coin. Either workers in hazardous employments receive higher wages that can then be used at their option to purchase their own insurance, or employers pay lower wages than they otherwise would pay but provide more insurance to such workers as part of their compensation package.

This was not how the market worked at the turn of the century, however, because of obstacles to the purchase of efficient insurance by workers. Life insurance was the most prevalent form of insurance that workers purchased, but even that coverage usually was purchased in only very limited amounts. In 1904 there were over 15 million "industrial life insurance" policies in force, but they provided an average of only $142 in benefits per policy.[9] This form of coverage was colloquially known as "burial insurance," because that was about all the average amount of insurance could provide. Premiums for these policies usually were collected from workers door-to-door each week; and as we will see below, administrative costs for this form of coverage were extremely high.

Accident insurance protecting the policyholder against injury resulting from "external, violent, and accidental means" was also available, but it was purchased in even more smaller amounts. Just $19 million in accident insurance premiums (as compared to about $3 billion in industrial life insurance premiums a few years earlier) was collected in 1911.[10] And workers had virtually no medical insurance—a form of coverage that would not become widely available until many decades later.

The last significant form of coverage available to workers was disability insurance paid for lost wages. This insurance was available from fraternal societies—organizations of worker mutual support that had grown up in the latter half of the nineteenth century.[11] Exactly how much disability insurance coverage they provided even at the peak of their operation is unclear. But the societies began to decline in importance around the turn of the century.

The lack of adequate life, accident, and disability insurance for workers was partly the result of the limited funds at their disposal. Adequate insurance would have been a luxury that most workers could not afford. But there were structural features of the insurance market that also stood in the way. The enormously greater amount spent on industrial life insurance than on various forms of insurance against loss of income for injured workers—more than one hundred times as much—suggests that other factors were also preventing the purchase of adequate amounts of insurance against income loss.

The most satisfactory explanation, I think, lies in a combination of two potential threats to any insurance regime: adverse selection and moral hazard. Each contributed to the limited amount of income-loss insurance that was available to injured workers. Adverse selection is the disproportionate tendency of those who know that they face an above-average risk of suffering a loss to seek insurance against that loss. An insurer that simply charged all policyholders an average premium would likely find that it experienced higher losses than it had projected, because of adverse selection. The insurer can then raise premiums to the new projected average, but the increase in premiums may cause those who are at a comparatively lower risk of suffering a loss to purchase less insurance, and those who are at higher risk to purchase more insurance, thus increasing the average amount of loss and restarting the entire process again. Eventually, either insurance cannot function at all in the face of such adverse selection, or an equilibrium is reached in which comparatively low-risk policyholders buy less insurance than they would otherwise like to buy because they are in effect being overcharged.

In order to combat adverse selection effectively, an accident or disability insurer has to be able to determine the comparative probability that different applicants will suffer a loss—in this case, lost income due to accident. Around and shortly after the turn of the twentieth century, this determination would have depended in heavy measure on the degree of danger posed in the applicant's workplace. If the insurer could not differentiate among applicants along this dimension, it could be subject to adverse selection by those who knew that they were working in comparatively dangerous jobs. The commercial insurers of the time did employ crude distinctions aimed at combating this effect, but they could not do so in refined fashion, because they had only crude data. They knew something about the differences in injury rates in different industries, but very little about the differences across employers within the same industry. This limitation on the information at insurers' disposal restricted the amounts of insurance they were willing to sell to many applicants, and increased the cost of the coverage they were willing to sell. This is part of the explanation, I think, for the very limited amounts of commercial disability and accident insurance that were sold at the time.

In contrast, the fraternal societies of the late nineteenth and early twentieth centuries could rely on member solidarity to deal with adverse selection. All members paid the same sums in order to be eligible for benefits, on the theory that the ethic of mutual support would enable them to maintain membership. The level-premium approach meant that the young, and those working in comparatively safe jobs, subsidized the old and those working in more dangerous jobs. As people aged, they in turn would be subsidized, as would those who shifted to more dangerous jobs. For a while the attractions of membership in fraternal societies were strong enough to help maintain the insurance function in the face of these two forms of cross-subsidization. But eventually the prospect that low-risk members would end up paying excess sums in order to ensure that there was coverage for high-risk members caused these societies to lose their ability to function.[12] Lower-risk potential members declined to join, and the societies, as well as the insurance they provided, withered away.

In addition to the problem of adverse selection, disability and other forms of income loss insurance would have faced a particular form of moral hazard. Classic moral hazard is the tendency of those who are insured to use less care to avoid a loss than they would use if they were uninsured. Disability insurance may have entailed some such *ex ante* moral hazard, but probably not much. Suffering a disabling injury was not an enticing prospect, even when the lost income resulting from the disability was partially insured. But more than any other form of coverage, disability insurance was subject to severe *ex post* moral hazard—in this instance, the tendency to stay out of work, once one was injured, for longer than an uninsured worker would. Even today a worker who has been injured and whose income is being partially replaced has less incentive to return to work than one who is not insured. In the days of long hours and often brutal working conditions of a century or more ago, *ex post* moral hazard would have been an even more serious challenge for insurers considering the sale of disability insurance.

There are two ways for an insurer to address this kind of *ex post* moral hazard. The first way is to limit the amount of income replacement the insurer provides. The lower the percentage of lost income that insurance replaces, the greater the policyholder's incentive to return to work. But this approach is in some sense self-defeating, since it results in only partial insurance. The second way to address *ex post* moral hazard is to monitor the ability of injured workers to return to work. This is an expensive proposition for a commercial insurer, however. As a result, disability insurance is more expensive than it would be in the absence of moral hazard, either because the insurer incurs the high cost of monitoring the ability of injured workers to return to work or because the insurer does not incur that cost but instead pays some claims that should not in fact be paid. Either way, disability insurance is more costly than it might otherwise be, and therefore less of it is sold.

In contrast to commercial insurers, the fraternal societies had members who probably lived near and could therefore easily observe the behavior of injured members on a virtually round-the-clock basis. This basically cost-free monitoring reduced the cost to these societies of detecting malingering, and thereby reduced the cost of coverage. It may well be that this superior ability of fraternal societies to combat *ex post* moral hazard was what made them able to function effectively for several decades even in the face of potential adverse selection.

To sum up my analysis of the compensation issue, then, neither tort nor first-party insurance were effective methods of compensating the victims of workplace accidents as the first decade of the twentieth century neared its end. Given the amount of workplace injury that occurred, workers brought strikingly few suits against their employers for injuries caused by these accidents, and the damages that were recovered in settlement or at trial were, on average, insufficient to compensate for the losses suffered. Workers' own life, accident, and disability insurance also was inadequate to protect them and their families against the consequences of workplace accidents, in part because of adverse selection and moral hazard afflicting the market for these forms of insurance. Consequently, rather than receiving adequate compensation for their losses through tort or through their own insurance, most workers shouldered a major portion of the losses resulting from work-related accidents themselves. The result was that workplace injuries and deaths produced enough destitution to generate not only legal but also social problems.

Accident Prevention

The picture we have of the accident prevention effects of the tort system at the turn of the twentieth century is uncertain, largely because the available data is thin. There can be little doubt that the tort system as it actually operated created far less incentive for employers to reduce workplace accidents than a more robust liability regime would have created. Employers bore only a portion of the costs of these accidents, and probably only a small portion. Their interest in accident reduction would have been limited accordingly. On the other hand, employees' own incentive to take steps that would reduce the risk of accidents would accordingly have been higher, because they had little prospect of recovery in tort or under their own insurance for most of the costs of accidents they suffered. The question is whether more tort liability on the part of employers would have increased employers' prevention of accidents to a greater degree than prevention would have been reduced as a result of employees' taking less care. The temptation is to say a priori that net accident prevention would have increased if there had been more tort liability, both because employers were strategically better placed than employees to influence the causes of accidents and because employees' instinct for self-protection would have tended to maintain their incentives to avoid involvement in accidents even if tort liability and insurance had been more robust.

Unfortunately, there is only a little data to confirm this conclusion. A few studies suggest that the enactment of employers' liability acts expanding employer liability in the last few decades of the nineteenth century increased accident prevention. Promoting such deterrence, however, was not seen as a principal reason for these expansions of tort liability. Rather, providing compensation to those injured by wrongdoing was the goal of these reforms. Deterrence theory as we now understand it is largely a twentieth-century concept, and in many ways a mid- to late twentieth-century concept.[13] It is therefore no surprise that, as we will see shortly, increased accident prevention was not a major of goal of most of those who attacked the tort system and proposed substituting a workers' compensation system for tort. Of those who were at least somewhat prominent, only John R. Commons, of the newly founded American Association for Labor Legislation, seems to have viewed workers' compensation as a method of promoting accident prevention in a major way. And his views on this score emerged mainly after the worker's compensation movement had begun to bear fruit.[14]

Crystal Eastman's 1910 book, for example, focused heavily on the causes of industrial accidents and the need of workers for compensation. Although the study contained discussions of accident prevention, for the most part they identified only generic categories of employer negligence whose elimination would reduce accident rates. At only a few points in Eastman's book was there any intimation that imposing liability on the employer for all accidents, whether or not they resulted from negligence, would enhance accident prevention.[15]

This seeming underemphasis on accident prevention was the result not only of the reformers' overwhelming concern with ensuring compensation for the consequences of accidents when they did occur. Their experience with the tort system would not have made them confident that the threat of liability, even the nearly automatic liability of workers' compensation, would translate directly into more effective loss prevention. Employers could be expected to insure against workers' compensation liability, and insurance would dilute their incentive to prevent accidents. It is true that even before the enactment of workers' compensation, the insurers writing Employers' Liability insurance had understood that, in theory, varying premiums in accordance with factors that policyholders could control might influence accident prevention. As early as the turn of the twentieth century, for example, the Travelers Insurance Company was inspecting the premises of its liability insurance policyholders and giving them reductions in premiums for complying with safety standards. But Travelers' own company history recounted the difficulties it encountered in getting policyholders to make safety changes. This history quoted one of the early inspectors as saying, "'We enjoyed little cooperation and much downright antagonism. The boss had no interest in the elimination of the danger, and the workers themselves had become so used to conditions that they resisted change.'"[16]

It was in this context that New York's Wainwright Commission Report emphasized the inadequacies of the compensation workers received under the tort system, the absence of significant sources of insurance to which employees had access on their own, the waste and delay entailed in the system, and the antagonism between employees and employers that the system produced. Although there was also passing reference in the Report to the potential of a workers' compensation system to reduce the incidence of accidents, the Report noted at the outset that the Commission had not yet been able to address the causes and prevention of accidents, promising to address these issues in a subsequent Report. A Report that recommends the enactment of workers' compensation before it has had the chance even to address the causes and prevention of accidents must be understood to be concerned primarily with other issues.

In short, although the failure of the tort system to promote accident prevention effectively was probably a given in the minds of the proponents of workers' compensation, remedying this failure was not a major goal of workers' compensation proposals. If abolishing tort liability for workplace accidents achieved that result, all the better. But it was achieving greater compensation of workers' losses that preoccupied these reformers.

Administrative Costs

The tort and insurance systems of the early twentieth century were remarkably cost-ineffective methods of deterring accidents and of compensating victims, both from the standpoint of the critics of the time and when viewed a century later. Court delays were endemic. Even though there was little of the time-consuming pretrial discovery that now occurs, it still was not unusual for a simple negligence claim to take several years to come to trial.

More significant, the proportion of total expenditures that made their way into the pockets of victims was comparatively small. For example, for every dollar of premium revenue collected by casualty (mostly liability insurers) and miscellaneous insurers in 1909, these companies paid only 36 cents to policyholders.[17] The Wainwright Commission found almost identical data on the premium-to-claim-payment ratio (what would now be called the loss ratio) of liability insurers doing business in New York during the years 1906–1908—that ratio was 36.34 percent. In contrast, today's loss ratio in commercial liability insurance is much higher—insurers now pay a much higher percentage of premiums for losses and consume less on administrative expenses and profit. For the period 1995–2004, for example, the U.S. commercial liability insurance loss ratio was over 73 percent.[18]

Even discounting for the greater investment income now earned by commercial insurers, which can offset greater claim payouts per dollar of premium received, the difference is striking. The Wainwright Commission further found that on average about 26 percent of the employee's gross recovery was paid for counsel fees. The employee then received an actual net recovery of less than 30 percent of the total premiums paid for liability insurance.[19]

Nor were employers entirely happy about this state of affairs. Many felt that in fighting cases and refusing to settle in order to maximize their profits, liability insurers often denied injured employees compensation that they deserved and generated unnecessary animosity in the workplace. There were a few large companies—International Harvester and U.S. Steel most prominently—who instituted their own voluntary compensation programs as an alternative.[20]

The picture is little better when one looks at the efficiency of the insurance that employees were able to purchase themselves. Industrial life, or "burial" insurance—by far the dominant form of life insurance purchased by blue-collar workers—was very costly to administer and consequently paid a low percentage of premiums in actual death benefits. Louis D. Brandeis, later a Justice of the U.S. Supreme Court but long before that a Progressive Era reformer, made calculations about the cost of industrial life insurance in an article he published in 1906, proposing the alternative of "savings bank" life insurance. Brandeis found that the Metropolitan Life Insurance Company, which sold 49 percent of all industrial life insurance, incurred management expenses of 42 percent of its premium receipts for industrial life policies. Obviously, this high an administrative expense left a smaller portion of premiums (and of income earned on that portion) available to pay as death benefits. In stark contrast, Brandeis showed that the administrative cost of maintaining a bank savings account that would finance burial expenses, into which deposits also could be made weekly, was 1.47 percent—not even one-tenth of the cost of administering commercial life insurance.[21]

Industrial life insurance involved such high administrative expense for two reasons. First, premiums were paid weekly, and typically were collected door-to-door. Weekly accounting and collection expenses were therefore comparatively high. Second, there was an exceedingly high lapse rate. More than one-third of the policies lapsed due to nonpayment within three months of sale, and more than half lapsed within a year.[22] Since the initial cost of selling and setting up a policy was incurred whether the policy lapsed shortly after sale or was maintained for many years, the higher the lapse rate, the more of these initial costs had to be spread among the remaining policyholders. Accident and disability (often then called "sickness") insurance was no more efficient. In 1908 the ratio of losses paid to premiums in these lines was 39 percent.[23] How much of this was the result of inefficient administration and how much was actual profiteering is unclear. In 1905 a prolonged investigation of the life insurance industry in New York, under the famous Armstrong Committee, certainly uncovered an enormous amount of corrupt administration.[24]

What is clear, however, is that life, accident, and disability insurance were not a good buy for the employee—considerably less than half of what policyholders paid for insurance coverage was actually returned to them in benefits. Thus, not only was the tort system largely a failure as a method of compensating the victims of workplace accidents; the system of first-party insurance that employees could purchase for their own protection was little better.

Replacing Tort

Momentum for tort reform of one type or another began to build around the turn of the twentieth century. Employers recognized the threat that legislation relaxing or completely eliminating restrictions on employers' tort liability would be demanded by workers, and perhaps enacted by state legislatures. By 1910, for example, 23 states and the federal government had enacted employers' liability acts that modified the common law restrictions on employers' liability in some way. Many of these laws were weak and only slightly limited employers' defenses to tort claims. But this was a period of increasing unionization. Between 1900 and 1910, union membership more than doubled. As labor increasingly gained political power, more tort reform could be expected.

At the same time, cultural and social changes were occurring that could also be expected to have an impact on the legal setting in which employers' potential liability operated. There was, for example, a continuing evolution in the way the causes of accidents were perceived. Contributory negligence, assumption of risk, and the fellow-servant rule—the unholy trinity of defenses to the employers' tort liability—were not merely arbitrary doctrinal categories. These defenses also were the reflection of a nineteenth-century legal ideology of individual responsibility. From the standpoint of tort law, workers who suffered injury on the job were often perceived as ignorant, selfish, or reckless. They were entirely in control of their own fate, it was thought, and did not have to work at jobs that were too dangerous for them. Limits on the amount of work available, less-than-perfect mobility, and the necessity of sometimes choosing between working in a hazardous job and having nothing to feed one's family were all ignored. In this view, accidents resulting from workplace conditions of which the victim had been aware were the victim's own responsibility, and arguably the victim's own fault. There was nothing the law of torts should do to protect such a victim.

However, as Lawrence Friedman suggests, the law of torts was never "a perfect instrument of oppression," and it was growing less oppressive as the twentieth century began.[25] It came to be understood that the market for labor was imperfect. Employees could not simply switch jobs if they didn't like their working conditions, and in the twentieth-century factory it was management rather than skilled tradesmen that controlled these conditions. Ideas about the causes of accidents thus evolved.[26] The emerging ideology of the Progressive Era made it possible for more people to see workplace injury as a social problem that needed to be solved rather than as a matter of worker responsibility embedded in a web of legal rights to be untangled by the courts through the application of tort doctrine.

Thus, the increasing threat of substantial employer tort liability and changing conceptions of the causes of workplace injury were mutually reinforcing. Of course, change of both sorts may have been prerequisites to tort reform, but concrete political change was quite another matter. There is substantial literature that attempts to explain the politics of workers' compensation and to identify the forces and interests that made its enactment possible.[27] Clearly, workers' compensation was not a simple triumph of labor over business during an era when labor power was increasing. Nor, as I will indicate below, did workers' compensation always accomplish a major, immediate redistribution of wealth. The details vary from state to state, but on the whole the adoption of workers' compensation was the product of coalitions of labor and at least a substantial portion of the business community. Businessmen saw that if workers' compensation were not enacted, tort liability might expand and create a less desirable form of liability exposure. In the meantime, the absence of an acceptable method of compensating employees for workplace injury would produce labor–management antagonism that was not good for business.

Workers' compensation was designed to remedy this problem by ensuring that compensation for work-related injury was automatically available. Quoting Lloyd George's admonition that "the price of the product should bear the blood of the workingman," the proponents of the new system recognized that this would be achieved through what would amount to an insurance regime. In enumerating the requirements that she believed a workers' compensation law must satisfy, for example, Crystal Eastman said that "it must shift a considerable share of the burden of each accident from the family immediately affected to the business, and thus to the whole body of consumers."[28] Similarly, at its outset the Wainwright Commission Report indicated that "just as employers now fix their selling price with reference to the costs of replacing and repairing machinery, so we would have them make an element of the price of the product the cost of relieving injured workers of hazardous industry."[29] And addressing the cost of the proposed system, the Report argued: "If the bridge builder in the State of New York must pay more to his employees in the shape of damages or compensation for injuries, that additional cost will be reflected in the total cost of building the bridges, just as would a rise in wages or a rise in the cost of materials; but when the law is known the bridge-builder and the house builder will make his contracts accordingly and his prices accordingly, and no man will be deprived or property or unduly mulcted. The community at large will then support the injured workman by compensation through the employer in the first instance, rather than through increased taxes for charity."[30]

These statements marked the early stages of a new way of analyzing liability issues. Eastman and the Wainwright Commission (of which she was a member) had begun to recognize that imposing liability on employers could have loss-spreading benefits that reached beyond the immediate parties to a claim. Liability, even if it was workers' compensation rather than tort liability, could perform an insuring function. And if the responsible party was a business enterprise, then it was "enterprise liability"—a term whose origin John Witt attributes to the new manager class that was emerging at the time—that would accomplish this insuring.[31]

Thus, the proponents of workers' compensation counted loss spreading through enterprise-based liability as one of the benefits that would be generated by the new system. These benefits did not by any means occupy first place in the rationale that the proponents of workers' compensation deployed in favor of reform. The assumption that accident costs would be spread to consumers was never extensively analyzed, and the benefits of the broad spreading of costs that would result were not identified as one of the major arguments in favor of moving to the new system that was proposed. But the arguments were there nonetheless.

In addition, although these considerations did not figure as prominently in the debate about workers' compensation as they might have, their presence in the debate was implicit recognition that employees themselves had little access of their own to loss-spreading devices. Workers had little insurance themselves, and little ability to obtain it. Lack of insurance not only meant that workers had no source of compensation independent of tort; the desperate circumstances that resulted also put workers at a disadvantage within the tort system. They did not have the staying power that access to insurance of some of their losses would have given them in the event that they brought suit. The few employees who did make tort claims for their injuries would therefore have felt considerable pressure to compromise their claims against the employer in order to obtain enough money just to maintain themselves and their families while they were still out of work.

State by state and year by year—though rapidly—the politics and arguments in favor of workers' compensation prevailed. Between 1910 and 1920, 43 states adopted workers' compensation.[32] And none of this could have happened without liability insurance. As we will see below, although a few large employers self-insured against their workers' compensation obligations, the vast majority of employers purchased insurance against their new liabilities. The new form of insurance that the *Phoenix* doctrine had validated just 25 years earlier now not only was commonplace but also was an essential component of tort reform. It was simply assumed, and correctly, that liability insurance would be the means by which most employers would make themselves capable of shouldering their workers' compensation liabilities.

The first statutes enacted in each state tended to be limited and tentative. Over time, however, the scope of compensation provided was expanded. The foothold of the approach was slowly solidified. The system now exists in every state.

The Basic Scheme

Workers' compensation was and still is comprised of three prongs. The first prong created immunity from tort liability for the employer. In its mature form, there is complete immunity. Some early versions gave the employee the option of suing in tort or electing workers' compensation. Technically a few states still preserve this option for employees to elect at the outset of their employment, but virtually no one opts out of workers' compensation. For all practical purposes workers' compensation schemes involve automatic tort immunity for the employer, except for injuries resulting from an employer's intent to cause harm or behavior nearly as blameworthy. Other early versions limited their application to certain "dangerous" employments; within a few years these restrictions also were eliminated in most states.

The second prong of workers' compensation was the imposition of a new form of liability. Under workers' compensation the employer is liable for injury or death "arising out of or in the course of employment." Under this standard, the employer is liable without regard to his negligence; workers' compensation imposes strict liability. The unholy trinity of defenses that so impeded an employee's right to recover in tort were completely eliminated. The employer's only defense to a claim that would otherwise be covered was that the employee had engaged in "wanton and wilfull misconduct"—in effect, that the employee had injured himself on purpose.

The third prong involved a substantial reduction in the compensation that was awarded to the injured employee. The damages recoverable in tort had consisted of full payment of past and future lost wages and medical expenses, plus compensation for the pain and suffering associated with the injury. For death, recovery in tort was limited by statute in many states to the economic losses suffered by the workers' survivors, and in some states was subject also to a monetary cap (often applicable only to suits against railroads) that varied, but was about $5,000 at the time.[33]

In contrast, workers' compensation paid only medical expenses and lost wages, but nothing for pain and suffering. Eventually comparatively modest lump sums also were paid for designated permanent injuries such as loss of a limb, loss of an eye, and so forth. But worker's compensation covered at most two-thirds of the employee's weekly lost wages. In the early statutes the first two or three weeks of wage loss also were excluded, and loss was payable only for a maximum number of weeks, typically lasting several years but then terminating. Early on there also were often very low ceilings on covered medical costs—$100 or $200 was typical. Death benefits were payable as lost wages, subject to a limit on the percentage of weekly wages that was recoverable and subject to a maximum number of weeks during which payment was made—again, usually several years. All these payments were made periodically rather than in a single lump sum, as they would have been in tort.

Workers' compensation was thus a tradeoff of certain employee rights for others, and of certain employer obligations for others. Employees gained a much-broadened and liberalized compensable event, which afforded them the right to compensation on the occurrence of any on-the-job injury. But the amount of compensation employees received was substantially lower than they could, in theory, have recovered in a successful negligence suit against the employer. Conversely, employers were relieved of liability for full damages in those comparatively infrequent instances in which they would previously have been liable in tort, in return for being automatically responsible for paying smaller amounts to a much larger group of accident victims, including many whose injuries were not caused by anyone's negligence.

The Impact of the New System

These were the three formal changes that workers' compensation made in the rules governing liability and compensation. However, not only how the new system actually operated in practice with respect to the new rules but also how other features of the employer-employee relationship adjusted to these rule changes, is revealing.

Average payments to households of accident victims for both fatal and nonfatal accidents increased between 75 and 200 percent under workers' compensation. For fatal accidents, more than 90 percent of families received some compensation, whereas the aggregate figure in the studies that had looked at tort compensation shortly before workers' compensation was enacted was only 55 percent. The average amount of compensation for those receiving some payment for fatal accidents rose from about one year's annual earnings under tort to between 1.9 and 8.2 times annual earnings under workers' compensation. For both fatal and nonfatal injuries, workers' compensation produced average compensation that was between 1.7 and 4 times as great as what could have been expected in tort. By 1920, workers' compensation was providing at least three times as much total compensation as tort would have provided if workers' compensation had not been enacted.[34]

These measures of the impact of the new system on the incidence of compensation, however, omit something important. They are, so to speak, gross rather than net figures. At the same time that workers' compensation was producing a clear increase in compensation paid to injured workers, there was another factor that was partially offsetting this increase in workers' overall wealth. For workers in some industries, workers' compensation had a depressing effect on their real wages over time. This effect was manifested mainly in nonunionized industries, and amounted to between 1 and 2 percent of the wages they would otherwise have been expected to earn in the absence of workers' compensation. Since the total cost of workers' compensation during its early years amounted to between 2 and 2.5 percent of payroll, this meant that many workers paid the majority of the cost of workers' compensation benefits themselves, in the form of forgone wages and reduced-wage increases.[35]

This evidence of a significant amount of cost pass-through to employees suggests that workers' compensation was simultaneously addressing not just one but two problems. The first problem involved features of the tort system that had made it so difficult for employees to recover compensation from employers for workplace accidents. Workers' compensation addressed that problem by broadening and liberalizing the compensable event and thereby making compensation more widely and frequently available to injured workers.

The second problem that workers' compensation turned out to address, however, was more subtle. The new system was helping to remedy some of the flaws in the first-party insurance markets that had prevented workers from purchasing their own insurance against the risk of suffering workplace injury or death. The mandatory, and admittedly somewhat paternalistic, character of workers' compensation solved the adverse selection problem that had plagued the various forms of income loss insurance and, to a lesser extent, life insurance, that were available to individual purchasers. Because all employees were automatically covered by workers' compensation, there was no threat from an unidentifiable group of high-risk applicants who were disproportionately likely to seek coverage. As a consequence, the cost of providing compensation was correspondingly lower, and more of it could be provided than was available through the private insurance markets. The new workers' compensation system did not provide this substitute for worker-purchased insurance free of charge, but it did provide it. By passing on a portion of the cost of workers' compensation to workers, the new system was in effect requiring employees to purchase more insurance themselves, at lower cost, than they had previously purchased voluntarily.

Like the disability insurance that workers previously had found it diffi-cult to purchase, however, workers' compensation was subject to *ex post* moral hazard. Like disability insurance, workers' compensation pays bene-fits on a periodic basis. Periodic payment has considerable advantages over the single-recovery approach that prevailed (and still prevails) in tort. But because it is essentially an insurance program, workers' compensation must continually combat a phenomenon that any program paying insurance benefits on a periodic basis faces. The beneficiaries of periodic-payment programs such as workers' compensation, health insurance, and disability insurance receive benefits as long as they consume health care or are out of work as the result of a compensable event. The resulting *ex post* moral haz-ard that is generated by periodic payment programs produces a continuing tension between benefit levels and costs. As time went on this feature of the workers' compensation system would contribute to its problems.

The new system not only expanded compensation but also had an im-pact on accident prevention. It is interesting that the accident prevention effects of the adoption of workers' compensation seem to have been mixed, probably at least in part because of the cost pass-through effect. On the face of it one would think that, in straightforward fashion, workers' compensa-tion would have increased employers' incentives to invest in preventing accidents that could be avoided at lower cost than the additional compen-sation costs that workers' compensation generated. Certainly some studies show that early in its existence workers' compensation produced a decline in accidental injury and death.[36] Studies of the contemporary effect of workers' compensation show a similar effect.[37]

But not all industries showed a decline in accidents after the adoption of workers' compensation. This varied, depending mainly on whether an in-dustry was unionized. In nonunionized industries the advent of workers' compensation had little or no impact on accident reduction, probably be-cause employers in these industries were able to pass through the cost of the new program to their employees in the form of reduced real wages. Because these employers were not internalizing the additional cost of liability, their accident prevention incentives do not seem to have been affected.

A recent study of the coal industry at the time, for example, has found that the presence of workers' compensation was associated with a 20 per-cent *increase* in fatal accidents.[38] Part of the explanation appears to be that a greater share of the costs of compensation were passed through to coal miners than to workers in most other industries, and that mine owners therefore had no additional accident prevention incentive, and perhaps less, because of the elimination of tort liability.

This could explain the absence of a decrease in the accident rate, but not the increase in accidents that occurred. The explanation for the increase may be that the greater availability of compensation exacerbated coal miners' *ex ante* moral hazard, especially with respect to certain safety measures over which only they had control, and whose use impeded the tonnage of coal that they mined. Because tonnage mined was the basis of miners' wages, the availability of workers' compensation may have caused coal miners themselves to be less careful in order to increase their earnings.[39]

Finally, the available data on administrative costs shows workers' compensation to have been substantially more efficient than tort. We saw earlier that on the eve of the adoption of workers' compensation, Employers' Liability insurance had paid out about 36 percent of premiums in compensation. Initially workers' compensation paid out about 55 percent of its premiums as compensation, but by 1925 the figure had risen to 68 percent of premiums.[40] The new system was substantially more cost-effective in this respect than the old one.

Nonetheless, at the outset there was controversy about permitting commercial insurance companies to sell workers' compensation insurance. The commercial insurers, after all, had sold the liability insurance that permitted them to control the defense and settlement of tort suits against employers. These insurers had refused to settle claims for what the workers and the unions considered adequate compensation for their injuries. The unions therefore tended to favor state-run workers' compensation insurance as an alternative to profit-making by the commercial insurers, and some employers agreed. The commercial insurers' argument against a government monopoly was of course that competition in the private marketplace would keep premiums lower than they would be if there were a state monopoly, and that a state-sponsored company could itself prove to be inefficient in administering claims.

The political compromises that were struck varied from state to state. Seven states established state-sponsored monopolies on the sale of workers' compensation; 10 established state-sponsored insurers to compete with the commercial insurers; and the remaining two dozen states permitted the private market to provide insurance exclusively. To this day, six states still have state-run funds that are the exclusive source of coverage, and fourteen states have state-run insurance programs that compete with commercial insurers.[41] This mixed public-private insurance approach contrasts with the systems of many other countries, in which the compensation of workplace injury is now subsumed in their social welfare systems. The heavy use of employer-purchased insurance, and especially private insurance, by U.S. workers' compensation reflects the way our system has chosen only to partially socialize the cost of workplace injury, and to continue internalizing part of this cost to individual employers.

The Legacy of Reform

The workers' compensation system has been in place for nearly a century now. It has had time to mature fully and for both its lessons and its problems to emerge rather clearly. With the perspective provided by nearly a century of experience, three features of workers' compensation are especially significant for the inquiry I undertake in subsequent chapters. First, workers' compensation was the first liability regime that was developed expressly to provide a viable source of recovery for victims. Tort did not provide such a source of recovery, because so few suits could be successful. Workers' own insurance was meager, at least in part because of the flaws in the first-party insurance market. By broadening the set of events that were compensable, workers' compensation eliminated the tort law restrictions on the right to recovery. Preserving the employer's liability, however, ensured that there was a responsible party obligated to pay for the expanded right to compensation. Tort liability was abolished, but employer liability was preserved. In one form or another, this sort of search for a viable source of recovery would influence the development of tort liability for most of the twentieth century. And liability insurance would be a means through which much of this expanded liability would be financed.

Second, workers' compensation marked the clear emergence within policy debates of the concepts of loss spreading and enterprise liability. The *Phoenix* doctrine, which I discussed in Chapter 1, had been premised on the notion that insurance helps a policyholder meet his responsibility of compensating those whom it has injured or whose property he has damaged. But the logic of this doctrine did not depend on the loss-spreading power of insurance. A two-party indemnity agreement that did not involve the pooling of multiple risks would have performed the same compensation-ensuring function and would have been valid for the same reason as liability insurance.

Although the principal concern of the workers' compensation reformers also was not loss spreading, but ensuring compensation through the imposition of liability for all workplace injuries on employers, the reformers recognized the loss-spreading effect of what they proposed. The slogan "the price of the product should bear the blood of the workingman" was not only a call for putting the cost of injuries into the price of the products they made. Because prices are paid by large numbers of purchasers, the slogan was also an implicit argument for the principle of insurance—the notion that it is better for a large number of people to suffer a small loss than for one person to suffer a larger loss. And it was the employer—a business enterprise—that was to be the vehicle through which losses were spread. Workers' compensation thus introduced into thinking about tort and its reform the first important references to loss spreading as a desirable function of liability regimes and of enterprise liability as a means of performing this function. The loss-spreading idea would come to dominate much of the thinking about tort liability for the next half century.

Finally, the workers' compensation experience reveals the intermediating role that insurance tends to play in liability regimes. In the pre–workers' compensation era, liability insurers were the object of considerable criticism by employers for the way they conducted many employers' defenses against employee tort suits. Employees' claims were vigorously defended and claims that even employers thought were valid were not paid. Although some of this criticism probably ought to be discounted as hypocrisy on the part of those employers who simultaneously benefited from the system, the fact that so many employers supported workers' compensation suggests that a good deal of the criticism from employers was genuine. The way liability insurance operated in practice influenced employer support for the abolition of tort liability and the substitution of a compensation program that would be potentially more expensive for employers.

This state of affairs was ameliorated, but by no means eliminated, by the enactment of workers' compensation. In most states employers were required to post a bond, to provide other proof of their ability to pay workers' compensation benefits on their own, or to purchase workers' compensation insurance. Most employers—and virtually all small employers—chose to purchase the insurance. By the early 1930s, for example, 99 percent of the employers in Pennsylvania who were subject to workers' compensation purchased insurance rather than self-insuring, although self-insured benefits constituted 42 percent of all compensation paid in Pennsylvania.[42] In

New York, self-insured employers paid 19 percent of all benefits.[43] Clearly what happened was that a comparatively few large employers in each state decided to self-insure, but most employers, and certainly most medium-sized and small employers, bought insurance.

Insurers therefore became involved with all but the largest employers. Insurers who had a large book of business in a state sometimes performed safety inspections that figured in their premium calculations. The Hartford Steam Boiler Inspection and Insurance Company's historic practice of inspecting steam boilers provided a model for this approach.[44] But inspections had to be cost-effective before insurers were willing to perform them; small employers were therefore often exempted, because the premiums they paid did not warrant insurers' incurring the cost of inspection. Similarly, when it was feasible, premiums might also vary with the employer's actual accident experience. This "merit rating," as it was called, tended to provide employers with accident prevention incentives, although interindustry rating probably was more refined than intraindustry rating.[45] All employers in hazardous industries paid higher workers' compensation premiums than those in comparatively safe industries, but there was less differentiation among employers within a hazardous industry than might have been ideal. But as with inspections, experience-rating of individual employers could take place only when an employer was large enough for its experience to be statistically meaningful. Even by the mid-1930s, less than 10 percent of all risks were experience-rated.[46]

Insurance Premiums as a Barometer of the System's Health

Over time the system became bureaucratized. Disputes in most states were handled by administrative boards rather than in courts of law. Benefit levels were increased periodically but rarely kept pace with inflation and often provided only partial compensation to injured workers for lost wages. Nor did the system handle occupational disease (which was often excluded from coverage altogether) or subjective injury (back pain or stress, for example) terribly well. Proving causation in these cases was far more difficult than in cases involving more tangible, visible harm. For all these reasons, to an important extent the problem of virtually no compensation in tort had been replaced by the problem of undercompensation in workers' compensation.

Further, since insurers were so heavily involved in the system, the cost and functioning of workers' compensation insurance became the lens through which the merits of the system were debated. But that lens was not transparent. Over the decades, the extent to which insurers' operating practices and profits are responsible for the cost of workers' compensation has been a perennial issue. From almost the beginning (1919), the National Council on Compensation Insurance (NCCI), a private organization formed by the insurers, has been involved in collecting data and preparing workers' compensation rates for private insurers. These rates have then been presented for approval to state insurance commissioners—the administrative officials charged under state law with regulating rates. The rigorousness of this process of regulating workers' compensation rates, like the process of rate regulation generally, has varied enormously.

In addition, the workers' compensation insurers' handling of the claims process has been the subject of criticism. As early as the 1920s, for example, the differences among the benefits paid and the speed of claim processing by commercial insurers, state insurers, and self-insurers were the subject of investigation, though with no definitive results.[47] And in New York during the early 1930s there was a prolonged controversy over insurers' hiring of physicians whose testimony was charged with being biased against compensation.[48] This same pattern recurred for decades. Insurers, and the employers they insured, were accused of setting up a system that was biased against its beneficiaries.

By the mid-1950s, liberal critics of the system were suggesting that benefits were so inadequate that they should either be raised substantially or serious-injury and fatality claimants should be given the option of suing the employer for negligence in tort.[49] It was not until 1972, however, that a National Commission recognized the severity of the problem and recommended that the states enact substantial benefit increases.[50] These were enacted in many states, and between that time and the early 1990s total benefits paid increased several hundred percent in nominal dollars. Unsurprisingly, workers' compensation insurance premiums also increased substantially. In reaction to these premium increases the pendulum then swung back the other way, and there was benefit-level retrenchment in many states.

The Central Tension

This brief history of postenactment workers' compensation reveals that the central tension in workers' compensation has long been how to provide satisfactory levels of compensation at tolerable cost. Since for most employers the cost of workers' compensation is measured by the cost of their workers' compensation insurance, insurance costs are often the focal point of controversy. These costs can be contained in the long run only by limiting benefits, by greater accident prevention, by more efficient administration, or by some combination of all three.

Increases in benefit levels put the greatest pressure on the system's political equilibrium. Modern workers' compensation faces the same problems of *ex post* moral hazard that we saw afflict disability insurance in the period before workers' compensation was enacted, but in a sense, to an even greater degree. Not only is a portion of the workers' wages paid while he is out of work but his medical expenses are paid as well, and the payment of medical expenses exacerbates moral hazard. The fact that a worker has continued to incur medical expenses provides some evidence of his continued inability to work, and therefore also of his continued entitlement to be paid lost wages. So employees have an incentive to continue to receive medical care in order to support their claims for lost wages.

Thus, unless workers' compensation insurance effectively manages the cost of medical care, it finds that the cost of both the wage loss and medical expense components of the program escalate. Yet it has been difficult for workers' compensation insurers to manage medical costs effectively. Many states allow workers to select their own treating physician; and unlike virtually every other form of health insurance, in workers' compensation there are no deductibles or coinsurance applicable to medical expenses the worker incurs. Rather (sometimes after a waiting period of one or two weeks), there is 100 percent coverage. All this creates substantial upward pressure on medical costs.

These problems converged in California and a number of other states in the first few years of this century. Workers' compensation costs in California, for example, rose from $9 billion in 1995 to $29 billion in 2003. Nor was this largely the result of a booming economy in which more wages were being paid. Rather, the cost of workers' compensation insurance during this period rose from $2.61 per $100 of payroll to $5.81 per $100 of payroll. At the same time, the injury rate fell by about 33 percent, and California's per-unit price of medical costs remained one of the lowest in the nation. Medical costs per workers' compensation claim, however, rose 250 percent during this period.[51]

Clearly, a major driver of the increase in California's workers' compensation costs was an increase in the amount of medical care that injured workers were receiving. This was also true nationally, where medical benefits comprised 49 percent of all workers' compensation payments in 1993 but that share rose to 55 percent by 2003.[52] In California the problem was even more severe.[53] Part of the explanation for what appears to have been a significantly greater than average utilization of workers' compensation–based medical services in California was the enactment of statutes in the 1990s that limited employers' ability to control health-care utilization. Another part was the longstanding problem of dealing with awards for permanent partial disability, which were paid to workers who were permanently injured but also were able to do some work. Legislation enacted in 2004 addressed both problems. Employers may now direct employees to approved networks of physicians. And a variety of devices addressed permanent partial disability, including an automatic 15 percent reduction in benefits if the employer offers an employee modified-continued work.[54]

But the political factors that generated this reform are unlikely to be stable. It is no surprise that workers' compensation is rarely in political equilibrium. Either employees complain that benefits levels are inadequate and benefit restrictions unduly constraining, or employers are critical of the high cost of workers' compensation insurance premiums and seek relief through reforms that limit benefits in one way or another. The very nature of workers' compensation makes conflict over its scope and generosity inevitable. When periodic payments are a structural feature of the system, either increases in benefit payments or cost-containment efforts will always be putting pressure on the other. The more nearly adequate the benefits provided, the greater the aggravation of *ex post* moral hazard; the more effectively costs are controlled, the more severe must be the restriction of benefits to levels lower than would otherwise be optimal. The pendulum has continued to swing between cost increases and benefit controls, and will always do so.

The Nonexclusive Remedy

Workers' compensation was originally conceived as an exclusive remedy, precluding suit in tort. But a major consequence of the decades-long tension between controlling costs and providing adequate benefit levels has been for workers to seek ways of supplementing their workers' compensation awards. Ironically, this search has led them back to the tort system.

Although workers' compensation statutes immunize employers from tort liability for work-related injury, they do not immunize third parties. An employee who is injured on the job is therefore free to sue the manufacturer of a product that caused her injury, as well as any other individuals or entities—including drivers of automobiles—whose activities may have contributed to a work-related injury. But the workers' compensation benefits that the employee has received must be repaid to the employer or its insurer out of the employee's tort recovery or settlement with a third party.

This structure gives the employee an incentive to bring a tort action only where his recovery has the potential to exceed the amount of his workers' compensation benefits by a significant margin. Since workers' compensation does not pay damages for pain and suffering, in effect these employee tort suits against third-party defendants are a search for a substantial payment for the employee's pain and suffering. The result is that tort suits brought by employees injured on the job are often high-stakes affairs. Although only 10 percent of all tort suits arise out of workplace injuries, over 60 percent of all tort recoveries in excess of $100,000 involve these injuries.[55]

There is a double irony to this arrangement. First, it enables workers' compensation, a program designed to remove workplace injury litigation from the tort system, to serve instead as an avenue of entry into the tort liability arena. Workers' compensation benefits give employees access to capital, thereby providing them with staying power they would not otherwise have in tort suits against third parties. For practical purposes, workers' compensation makes limited-recourse loans to employees, requiring that the loans be repaid only in the event of a tort recovery from a third party. What was originally envisioned as an exclusive remedy that was an alternative to tort has turned out to create traction for the employee within the tort system itself. Pain and suffering damages have been eliminated where a workers' injury is not caused by the negligence of a third party, but they are preserved otherwise, because employees may recover them from these third parties.

The second irony is that this relationship between workers' compensation and tort provides employers with reimbursement for the cost of workers' compensation benefits, thereby potentially undermining employers' accident-prevention incentives by externalizing the cost of workers' benefits to third parties. Whenever the employee is successful in a tort suit against a third party, the price of the employer's product does not bear the blood of the workingman. Instead that blood is on the price of a third-party's product or activity.

The original theory of workers' compensation, that in general it is the employer who is in the best position to insure and guard against the risk of work-related injury, has thus been compromised. A solution might be for workers' compensation to return to its origins by raising benefit levels and, once benefit levels were adequate, prohibiting employees' tort suits against third parties. But that would channel more costs through employers, and would therefore be a politically unpopular move for legislatures. And that approach would risk reducing third parties' accident prevention incentives, leaving only contracts between employers and these third parties, where they exist, to create such incentives.

Some commentators have proposed that, to counteract this effect, employers could be permitted to bring negligence or products liability suits in the nature of subrogation actions against third parties for the amount of benefits paid to their employee. Further, the employer's right of recovery in such actions could be made subject to a reduction for the employer's own negligence. These actions would effectively be between the employer's workers' compensation insurer and the third party's liability insurer, and the liquidated sum paid as benefits by the employer would be at stake rather than the amount of the employee's pain and suffering. The suits would therefore be less expensive to resolve than the current suits by employees against third parties.[56] But this arrangement still would incur some litigation costs, simply in order to accomplish a transfer of funds from one set of insurers to another set. And the arrangement still would be complex, would involve the tort system in worker injury claims, and would somewhat dilute employers' incentives.

In the end, then, workers' compensation—the first tort reform—has been unable to escape tort entirely. Employees' search for a source of full recovery has led them beyond workers' compensation and back into tort. And neither tort nor workers' compensation has been able to muster the means to return to the exclusive-remedy structure originally envisioned by workers' compensation, or to devise a relationship among workers' compensation, tort, and insurance that harmonizes their operations. Until this occurs, workers' compensation is unlikely to be completely faithful to its original promise.

—3—

Drivers, Lawyers, and Insurers:
A Costly Combination

In the United States we spend over $110 billion per year for insurance against liability for auto accidents. This expenditure dwarfs what we spend on any other kind of liability insurance. It is twice what we spend on workers' compensation insurance, more than five times what we spend on medical malpractice insurance, and at least seven times what we spend on products liability insurance.

Each year in this country there are over 6.3 million reported auto accidents, with nearly 2 million involving personal injury. Auto liability is now big business. It is also the field where the modern tort process came into its own. It was in auto liability where an active plaintiffs' bar first arose, and it was in auto liability where a system that relies heavily on settlements negotiated between plaintiffs' lawyers and liability insurers first developed. Auto liability established a negotiation and settlement pattern that persists to this day in most areas of tort liability.[1]

The most controversial period for auto liability occurred between 1960 and 1980. During these years the auto liability and auto insurance systems received substantial public criticism, as well as sustained attention from legal scholars and reformers. During this period the auto no-fault movement arose and had some initial success. But for a variety of reasons that I will identify, this movement was then halted in its tracks.

With the demise of the no-fault movement, the cost of auto insurance became the perennial focus of concern in this field. The sheer amount of money we spend on auto insurance—not only $110 billion a year for liability insurance, but an additional $70 billion for first-party insurance against damage caused by collision and other forms of physical damage to the policyholder's own vehicle—makes this inevitable. The cost of auto insurance is partly the product of the sheer number of vehicles and miles we drive each year, often in urban areas where vehicle density and road conditions virtually guarantee that there will be frequent accidents. But this cost is also the result of a system that, while it is routinized and bureaucratic, nonetheless relies on lawyers for both plaintiffs and defendants to resolve a significant portion of all claims. Legal and administrative costs therefore account for more than half of all the system's expenditures. Less than half of every dollar spent on auto insurance finds its way into the pockets of auto accident victims.

But despite its economic significance, auto liability itself is not the five-hundred-pound gorilla that we might expect it to be in debates about tort liability and its reform. With only a few exceptions, over the past 25 years tort law's contribution to the high cost of auto liability insurance has received little scrutiny or attention from the proponents of tort reform. In my view this lack of reform attention has been the product of several factors: the routinization of auto liability; the absence of a discrete group of defendants who face substantial auto liability and whose interests therefore warrant investing in reform efforts; and the fact that auto liability has been the beneficiary of generally applicable reforms of the law of damages sought by product manufacturers and physicians in order to address their own perceived liability problems. How auto liability came to occupy this position is the subject of this chapter.

The Rise of the Auto Compensation Problem

The first automobiles came on the scene very late in the nineteenth century. During their early years they were almost a novelty. In 1900 there were only eight thousand vehicles being operated in the entire country. Then came an explosion in their number. By 1915 there were 2 million cars; by 1920 there were 9 million; and by 1930 there were 23 million cars on the road—a tenfold increase in just the 15 years between 1915 and 1930.

With this exponential growth in the number of vehicles in operation came a corresponding increase in the accident rate. In the early years there were few real highways. Some streets and roads were paved but many were not. A great deal more driving took place in the warm months of the year than in the winter, both because roads were often impassable in winter and because canvas or cloth roofs, when a car had a roof at all, were the norm until the late 1920s. Roads were not constructed in anticipation of the high speeds that cars were able to attain beginning in the 1920s; signage and intersection controls were limited; driving skills were often low; and cars themselves were not designed to tolerate impact to the degree that they are now.

Viewed by today's standards, there was carnage on the roads.[2] Over 30,000 people were killed in auto accidents in 1930. This was 30 percent of all the accidental deaths that occurred that year. Today, there are about 44,000 auto-related fatalities per year, constituting about 40 percent of all accidental deaths. But the effective fatality rate from driving in 1930 was nearly 20 times higher than it is today. In 1930 there were 28 deaths for every 100 million miles driven; today the rate is 1.46 deaths per 100 million miles.

Almost immediately after automobiles appeared, insurers began to sell coverage against auto liability. At first, coverage was provided under what was called a "teams" policy, which insured against liability arising from the operation of horse-drawn coaches and wagons. Beginning in 1905, however, a separate auto policy became available. By 1921, the first year in which the *Statistical Abstract of the United States* contained a separate entry, premiums for auto liability insurance totaled $64 million and losses of $29 million were paid.[3] As a benchmark for comparison, in that same year workers' compensation premiums totaled $99 million and losses of $56 million were paid. But by 1930 auto liability insurance had outpaced workers' compensation, and the figures had crossed; premiums for auto insurance were now $189 million and for workers' compensation were $150 million.[4] Even late in the 1920s, however, barely 25 percent of all drivers were insured, though the figure may have approached 50 percent in some cities.[5]

Automobiles first came into use during the height of the negligence era. At the turn of the twentieth century there were small pockets of strict liability for injury or damage caused by "ultrahazardous" activities that were both uncommon and highly dangerous. But the early slow-moving cars were far from being candidates for this category of liability. From the beginning, therefore, auto liability was governed by a negligence regime. By the time motor vehicles could attain speeds that made them dangerous, they were also very common, and in any event application of the negligence regime to auto accidents was firmly established. An accident victim therefore could not recover without proving a driver's negligence, and even then a victim could not recover if he or she was contributorily negligent.

In addition, beginning in the late 1920s more than half the states enacted "guest statutes" requiring that a passenger prove gross negligence in a suit against the driver of the vehicle in which he had been riding. The apparent rationale behind these statutes was that because the driver had engaged in a generous undertaking, his duty should be less onerous than if he had risked harming a stranger.[6] Whatever their stated rationale and however unpersuasive it may been, there can be no question that one effect of the guest statutes was to help to limit collusive suits, in which an insured driver would acknowledge his negligence in order to make it possible for his passenger to obtain compensation from the driver's insurance company. How successful these statutes were in achieving this aim is unclear, since fabricating a story that would support a finding of gross negligence is not much more difficult than lying about negligence. The received wisdom is that the insurance industry helped to secure this legislation, in order to minimize its exposure to collusive claims. This theory seems plausible, though the available evidence supporting it is thin.[7] But there can be no doubt that, at the very least, the guest statutes did benefit the insurance industry and that once the statutes were enacted, insurers supported them.

The result of this combination of the negligence standard, incomplete liability insurance, and the guest statutes was that only a small fraction of auto accident victims recovered compensation in tort. Since most people at the time also had no health or disability insurance of their own, there was a substantial compensation gap. Over the years a variety of methods of closing this gap were proposed, and some were adopted. The earliest was the development of what came to be called "financial responsibility" laws. These laws required a driver who was involved in an accident, if he was to retain driving privileges, to post a bond or show other evidence of his financial ability to pay future claims. Submitting proof that the driver had purchased liability insurance was the typical way to satisfy the financial responsibility requirement. But this approach only helped to ensure that a driver would have sufficient financial means to compensate the victims of future accidents; financial responsibility laws did nothing to solve the compensation problem posed by the accident that had given rise to the driver's financial obligation to begin with. In 1925, Connecticut was the first state to enact a financial responsibility law. By 1932, 18 states had enacted such laws, and other states followed this approach in the decades to come.

A more direct and effective approach to the compensation problem would have been compulsory auto liability insurance. This would not have solved the problem of proving negligence or of the applicability of guest statutes to some claims, but it would at least have made the defendant's liability insurance available to any successful plaintiff. Financial responsibility laws effectively made insurance available only to the victims of a drivers' second accident, but not his first. By 1927, however, only Massachusetts had enacted generally applicable compulsory auto liability insurance legislation (though most states had such a requirement for common carriers), and not until the 1960s would more than a handful of states begin to adopt compulsory insurance requirements. Today, 47 states have compulsory liability insurance laws; three retain the financial responsibility approach.

The reason for the prolonged delay in adopting what is now a nearly universal requirement is that the insurance industry opposed making auto liability insurance compulsory. At first glance this stance may seem perplexing, as one might think that insurers would have favored this. Expanding demand for an industry's product would seem to be something the industry would support. For example, if brushing one's teeth three times a day were required by law, the makers of toothpaste would certainly seem to benefit. It would be surprising, therefore, if the makers of toothpaste opposed a tooth-brushing requirement. Similarly, requiring all drivers to have liability insurance would have substantially multiplied demand for the auto insurers' product. But the insurers' opposition to such a requirement is an early example of a phenomenon that recurred throughout the century. The industry has not only opposed compulsory insurance but (as we will see in Chapters 4 and 5) has supported tort reforms that decrease the scope of tort liability and damages and also thereby reduce the demand for its product and its potential revenue.

In the case of compulsory insurance, insurers were concerned about its long-term effect on their freedom of action and, ultimately, on their profitability. Initially, premium revenues would rise if all drivers were required to buy liability insurance. The insurers believed, however, that a compulsory insurance requirement would lead government regulators to force insurers to cover high-risk drivers whom they did not want to insure, and they worried that they would be prevented from charging such drivers sufficiently high premiums. The result of making auto liability insurance compulsory would then ultimately be that the insurers would be forced to insure a portion of their policyholders at a loss.

This is exactly what seems to have happened in Massachusetts after it became the first state to make auto insurance compulsory. Auto insurers' losses in Massachusetts for each of the policy years from 1927 through 1931 were between 15 and 30 percent higher than what the Commissioner of Insurance had permitted them to anticipate in their rates. The consequence was increased premium volume, followed by decreased profits.[8] The Massachusetts experience was sobering confirmation of the insurers' concerns. The compulsory insurance movement therefore made little headway in the face of intensified insurance industry opposition, even as auto accidents became increasingly frequent and the shortfall in compensation for auto victims became more evident.

The Columbia Plan

In this setting, in 1932 a group of reform-oriented scholars, lawyers, and judges operating under the auspices of Columbia University produced a proposal for auto liability and insurance reform that came to be known as the Columbia Plan.[9] The Plan envisioned the mandatory purchase of automobile liability insurance by all owners of motor vehicles. But it went further than merely requiring the purchase of liability insurance. The Plan would have filled a remaining portion of the compensation gap by making it unnecessary for a victim to prove negligence in order to recover damages. Under the Plan a driver involved in an auto accident was to be held strictly liable for personal injuries caused by his driving. In a two-car collision each driver would be liable for the other's injuries; all involved drivers would be jointly and severally liable to nondriver victims.

The Plan was clearly and expressly based on the workers' compensation model. Not only did it recommend imposing strict liability for auto accidents on those causing the accidents but as in the case of workers' compensation, in order to avoid massive increases in the cost of insurance, the Plan recommended a reduction of compensation to accompany the expansion of liability, through the adoption of a benefit schedule that was modeled on workers' compensation. There were to be no damages for pain and suffering, and there were limits on the recovery of economic costs such as medical expenses and lost wages. Like the New York Wainwright Commission Report that ushered in workers' compensation, the Columbia Plan marshaled an extensive array of statistics in support of the proposition that there was a substantial accident problem resulting in inadequate compensation of victims.

Perhaps the Plan's most telling finding concerned the role liability insurance played in ensuring compensation for victims. If the other driver involved in an accident was not insured, a victim had only a 25 percent chance of receiving some payment for his injuries. On the other hand, when the other driver was insured, some payment was received in 85 percent of the cases.[10] Interestingly, however, despite its emphasis on the amount of injury associated with the automobile, the Plan paid little attention to its potential impact on accident levels. On the contrary, it concluded that "compulsory insurance has no demonstrable effect on accident frequency" and that "if . . . the fear of personal injury will not restrain careless driving, it is not to be supposed that the fear of having to pay money will do so."[11] Like the proponents of workers' compensation a generation before, the authors of the Columbia Plan were more interested in ensuring compensation for victims than in reducing the need for compensation by encouraging the prevention of accidents.

The Columbia Plan was never enacted by any state. The depression brought other much more pressing economic problems to the forefront of public policy and put auto liability reform far down on the list of priorities. And of course, for the reasons I suggested earlier, the insurance industry opposed any form of compulsory insurance, including the form the Columbia Plan proposed. More important, however, there was no consensus that auto accidents were sufficiently similar to workplace injuries to warrant treating them in the same way. The debates that followed the debut of the Plan revealed that the relationships between drivers and passengers, between drivers and pedestrians, and especially between drivers and other drivers often were not seen as sufficiently analogous to the relationship between employers and employees to garner a consensus in favor of adopting a strict liability approach modeled on workers' compensation.

Although the Plan itself was devoid of any reference to the loss spreading that would result from the compulsory liability insurance it proposed, supporters of the Plan made it clear that this was one of its advantages. The mandatory insurance requirement was a method of rendering individual drivers analogous to employers in workers' compensation. Just as each employer was expected to pass the cost of workers' compensation on to its customers, by purchasing auto liability insurance each driver would pass along the cost of the injuries he or she caused to a pool composed of other drivers. The cost of injuries would thereby be collectivized.

For supporters of the Plan, auto liability insurance was a way of financing the proposed strict liability obligation to pay compensation that otherwise could not have been financed. Liability insurance placed both injurers and most victims in the same risk pool, spreading the cost of accidents among them.[12] Compulsory liability insurance not only made strict liability feasible; the availability of such insurance also made it desirable. For the Plan's critics, on the other hand, imposing strict liability on drivers was not justified, and mandating insurance against strict liability could not make it so. The loss spreading that would be produced by compulsory auto insurance was desirable only for losses that it made sense to spread. The question was whether an auto liability regime should function as a method of ensuring compensation for all injuries that would inevitably result from the use of automobiles. And in the critics' view the answer was no.[13]

The core of the debate about the Columbia Plan was therefore about much more than automobile accidents. It was about the general theory of strict liability. Proponents of the Plan saw the liability it would have created as justified on loss-spreading and victim compensation grounds. Critics, however, thought that something more was required to justify the imposition of strict liability. In the case of workers' compensation, strict liability could be justified by the nature of the relationship between employer and employee, including the employer's control over conditions in the workplace. But in the critics' view, strict liability for auto-related injuries could not be justified, because there was no analogous disparity between the position of drivers and those they injured.

Further thinking about the different settings in which strict liability might operate would eventually be generalized and developed into the theory of strict enterprise liability that began to emerge around this time. Still missing at this point, however, was a clearer recognition of the different functions that strict liability, including strict enterprise liability, might serve. The proponents of the Columbia Plan clearly understood that strict auto liability would circumvent certain of the problems auto victims faced in proving negligence. And they also recognized that, through a compulsory insurance requirement, strict auto liability would promote loss spreading. But because they doubted that the threat of auto liability, whether based on negligence or strict liability, had much impact on driving behavior, the Plan's proponents did not incorporate the deterrence function into their thinking about auto liability reform. As we saw in Chapter 2, the proponents of workers' compensation also were uncertain about that system's potential accident prevention effects. In contrast, deterrence theory would ultimately have a major impact on enterprise liability thinking, and would in some ways help to mark out the domain in which enterprise liability operated. But that would not happen for several decades, and it would happen outside the field of auto liability.

Victim Compensation and the Evolution
of the Standard Auto Liability Policy

Because of the objections to the strict liability feature of the Columbia Plan, its compulsory insurance feature received comparatively little separate attention. And as I noted earlier, the insurance industry was successful in opposing compulsory insurance for the next three decades. Nonetheless, during the same period, insurance against liability for negligent driving, which tort law did impose, became increasingly popular. Financial responsibility laws were slowly enacted, and their practical effect was similar to what the insurance industry opposed, since the way that most vehicle owners satisfied the financial responsibility requirement was by providing proof that they were covered by liability insurance. As of 1950, 44 states had enacted financial responsibility laws.[14] And by 1963 over 80 percent of all drivers in these states were covered by auto liability insurance.[15]

Expanding the Scope of Coverage

The scope of coverage expanded during each decade as well.[16] For example, the earliest policies excluded coverage of liability arising out of the insured's failure to observe traffic laws. As these laws proliferated, however, virtually any accident would have involved at least a potential violation, and the exclusion was quickly eliminated. The early policies also were so narrowly drawn that they covered liability for operation of the vehicle, but not for loss arising when the vehicle was parked. That restriction was soon eliminated. And some of the early auto policies were written on an indemnity basis—they paid the insured only after the insured had paid the plaintiff. The policies therefore provided no protection to the insured or his victim if the insured was forced into bankruptcy by a judgment against him. By the 1920s a combination of legislation, judicial decisions, and competition among insurers to provide more attractive coverage converted the surviving indemnity-only policies into a universal "pay on behalf of the insured" insurance obligation that applied whether or not the insured was capable of satisfying a judgment out of his own funds. Similarly, for decades the standard policies covered liability for "bodily injury." If the use of an automobile caused illness—for example, through exposure to gasoline or exhaust—there was no coverage. In 1947 the policy was expanded to fill this gap by including coverage of liability for "bodily injury, sickness or disease."

These expansions in the scope of coverage not only afforded increasingly broad protection to policyholders; they also helped ensure that accident victims would be compensated. In the typical commercial setting a business named as a defendant in a tort suit would likely be capable of satisfying most judgments against it, whether or not it had purchased liability insurance. This was emphatically not the case, however, in auto liability. The ordinary individual defendant in an auto liability suit would have no means of fully satisfying a judgment if he or she were not insured. Consequently, as the scope of coverage provided by the standard auto liability insurance policy expanded, the prospect that the victims of auto accidents would receive compensation also rose.

It was here that the legacy of the *Phoenix* doctrine that I discussed in Chapter 1 had its strongest impact. Concerned about the increasing incidence of auto injuries, both the courts and regulators came to understand that insurance protected not only the policyholder but also his victim. Expansions in the scope of coverage, and therefore in the availability of an insured source of recovery for victims, were increasingly encouraged by both regulatory and judicial authority.

By far the most important expansions in coverage of auto liability over the years were additions to the parties who were insured under auto policies. Originally only the "named insured"—the owner of the vehicle—was covered. Soon coverage was extended to all members of the named insured's household. In 1918, what has come to be known as the "omnibus" clause (anglicized from the Latin "for all") was added. The clause provides coverage of liability incurred by anyone operating the insured vehicle with permission. In short order a "drive other cars" (DOC) provision was developed to provide coverage to any insured (i.e., the named insured or members of his household) who was driving another vehicle with permission of the insured. And in 1941 the standard policy was amended to make it clear that when both clauses applied (because both the owner and the driver were insured), the sum of the two policies' coverage was available if necessary.

The importance of the omnibus and DOC clauses would be hard to exaggerate. The addition of the omnibus clause meant that anyone driving an insured vehicle with permission was insured against liability for that driving. And the addition of the DOC clause meant that anyone who had insurance and drove another vehicle was insured against liability for that driving, even if the owner of the vehicle was not himself insured. After these clauses were introduced, liability insurance ran both with any insured vehicle and with any insured driver. The clauses thereby filled a potentially substantial insurance and compensation gap.

The courts were an especially active force in promoting victim compensation through the expansive interpretation of liability insurance policy provisions. For example, as drafted, the omnibus and DOC clauses applied only when the borrower of the vehicle was driving "with the permission of the named insured." Many courts were liberal in their interpretation of the word "permission," however, holding among other things that the owner's permittee could give permission to a second permittee. Often there was additional flexibility regarding the scope of permission, such as when the permittee made a particular use of the vehicle that had not been expressly authorized.[17] There was also considerable flexibility as to what constituted injury "arising out of the ownership, operation, or use" of the insured motor vehicle, which was the touchstone of coverage.[18] Each time the courts held that there was insurance in a borderline situation, they ensured not only that the driver was covered but also that the victim would have a source of recovery if his claim were successful.

Medical Payments Coverage

In addition to both the express expansion of auto liability insurance and the expansive judicial interpretations of policy language, over time the standard auto policy was transformed into a combination of additional coverages. In 1941, first-party medical expense coverage became available as part of the standard policy. This made it possible for the named insured to ensure limited compensation to injured parties, whether passengers or drivers borrowing the car with permission, without the necessity of a lawsuit. This coverage was applicable without regard to negligence, and thus filled another compensation gap, especially where guest statutes required proof of the owner's gross negligence as a prerequisite to recovery in tort. But the new medical payments coverage still left the named insured and residents of his household without coverage of medical expenses. In 1953, this coverage was made available for purchase by any insured who had also purchased based basic medical payments coverage for his nonfamily passengers.

Medical payments coverage never became economically significant. It was sold only in small amounts, and in any event did not cover lost wages or pain and suffering. But in the era before health insurance was widespread, this form of coverage made it possible for auto accident victims to receive modest compensation for their medical expenses without the necessity of bringing a lawsuit, and provided this compensation even when there was no cause of action in tort. In this sense medical payments coverage served as a placeholder for what would eventually become no-fault insurance, a more expansive form of coverage of both medical expenses and lost wages that also would not require a lawsuit in order to obtain compensation.

Uninsured Motorists Coverage

The last expansion of the voluntary insurance market that would fill a significant compensation gap came in the form of uninsured motorist (UM) coverage. This type of coverage had a political midwife. In 1953, the insurance industry vigorously opposed and defeated an effort to adopt a compulsory auto liability insurance in New York. The following year, in a threat to support a renewed effort to enact this legislation if the industry did not respond positively, the newly elected Governor's Superintendent of Insurance requested that the insurance industry propose an alternative to compulsory liability insurance that would solve the problem of uninsured drivers.[19]

The solution the industry proposed was insurance that would protect auto victims against the risk that they would have a claim against a driver who was uninsured and therefore unable to pay the claim. Thus, vehicle owners would buy their own insurance, and their own insurers would pay them, if they had valid claims against other drivers that could not be collected. There would be no need to sue and obtain a judgment against an uninsured driver. Proof that a judgment could have been secured would be sufficient, and disputes over that issue would be arbitrated. By offering this UM insurance, insurers avoided what they feared would be the regulatory intrusions that would flow from compulsory auto liability insurance. And drivers who wished to buy UM coverage filled yet another gap in the fabric of their protection against auto injuries.

Uninsured motorist coverage spread in the voluntary market, and when the states finally began to enact compulsory liability insurance laws a decade later, many also required that drivers purchase UM coverage. The remainder required that such coverage at least be offered to any applicant for liability insurance, often also providing that UM coverage would automatically be part of any policy unless the applicant specifically declined to purchase it.

The Postwar Picture

As the veterans returned from World War II, they needed housing, much of which was built in new suburbs. This led to more road and highway construction, including the interstate highway system, construction of which began in 1956. The housing and highway construction boom led not only to more cars but also to more insurance. Premium volume in the late 1940s for all forms of auto coverage had been about $600 million. Ten years later, that figure had increased more than sevenfold, to $4.4 billion.[20]

By the mid-1950s the industry's statistical sophistication, the amount of driving, and the incidence of accidents all had increased to the point where basing premium rates partly on driving records could be sensibly done. For more than 50 years, premiums had been based predominately on three factors: the territory where the insured vehicle was driven, the type of vehicle insured, and the age of the principal driver of that vehicle. Earlier efforts at adding an experience-rating factor based on the driver's accident record had been unsuccessful, largely because statistical data on which to base this approach was unreliable or nonexistent.[21] But this time experience-rating stuck.

Experience-rating, however, has a limited reach. The average driver is involved in an accident once every 10–12 years. So those who have not been in an accident are not necessarily above-average drivers, and those who have been involved in an accident are not necessarily below average. Experience-rating is therefore in a sense a statistical compromise. It is an effort to achieve the impossible goal of measuring each individual driver's probability of being involved in an accident. Over time the approach that has developed has been to surcharge the premiums of those involved in an accident for several years after the accident, because those involved in one accident have an increased probability of being involved in a second, those involved in a second have an increased probability of being involved in a third, and so on.

Whether or not differential premiums influence driving behavior, at the margin they probably influence aggregate family driving levels. The decision whether to purchase a second or third family car, for example, is likely to be influenced by the cost of insuring that additional car, which is affected at the margin by the family's recent driving history. And even if experience-rating had no impact on driving behavior or driving levels, since it came into use in the 1950s it has had the political effect of reducing what might be regarded as the objectionable cross-subsidization of high-risk drivers by apparently lower-risk drivers.

By the late 1950s, then, all the pieces of the standard combination auto insurance policy as it now exists, as well as the way it is priced, were in place. The policy provided broad coverage against tort liability, insured the owner against damage to his own vehicle, provided modest medical payments coverage to the owner, driver, and passengers, and insured them against the risk that they would be injured by the negligence of an uninsured driver. And that insurance was the principal source of what became the routine and bureaucratic system of auto compensation.

The Trial Bar and the Claims Process

At just about the point when the standard combination auto insurance policy had fully matured, a steady increase in claims and insurance costs began to occur. The number of auto liability lawsuits increased about 50 percent between 1955 and 1970, for example.[22] Similarly, in 1955, auto liability insurance premiums totaled $2.4 billion; by 1960 that figure had risen to $3.8 billion; by 1965, $5.4 billion; and by 1970, $8.9 billion.[23]

Part of the explanation for these changes was the changing driving environment of the time; the more vehicles there are on the road, and the greater the density of population, the more auto accidents will occur. But these environmental changes cannot begin to explain the size of the increases in lawsuits and insurance costs that occurred during this period. Rather, two other factors appear to me to have been most responsible. The first was the increasing power and effectiveness of the plaintiffs' trial bar. Plaintiffs' lawyers became better at what they did, and payouts therefore increased. The second factor was the enormous increase in health-care spending that took place during this period. Since medical expenses are a major component of tort recoveries, this increase in health-care spending had a very substantial affect on the value of claims and on the amounts paid in judgment and settlement. Neither factor, of course, could have had the influence it did were it not for the availability of auto liability insurance.

The Professionalization of the Trial Bar

Even before liability insurance became compulsory in most states between 1965 and 1980, the expansion of the standard auto liability insurance policy had made it possible for auto litigation to become a viable specialty for trial lawyers. As the Columbia Plan had made clear, few uninsured drivers were capable of satisfying a significant judgment against them. But as early as the 1920s, a driver covered by a liability insurance policy with standard coverage of $5,000 was a worthwhile target.

There had long been a plaintiffs' bar. The term "ambulance chasing" was common at least as early as the late nineteenth century. Despite the tremendous increase in the number of auto accidents during the 1920s, however, the depression of the 1930s and the practical limitations on driving during World War II helped suppress levels of auto litigation until after the war.

The end of the war and the return of the veterans changed all this. When the war ended in 1945, there were 25 million automobiles registered in the United States. By 1955 that number had more than doubled, to 52 million. And by 1965 the number had increased to 75 million.[24] In 1945 the states constructed 15,000 miles of new roads. Each year from 1950 through 1960, they built more than 50,000 miles of new roads. Federal highways built during these years increased from 3,000 new miles in 1945 to over 20,000 new miles of highways each year from 1952 through 1962.[25] New suburban housing, increased shopping, more commuting, and more driving on the new roads and highways produced an increase in the frequency of auto accidents and the opportunity for litigation.

The lawyers who handled this litigation had much in common, and they established an organization to further their common interests. The National Association of Claimants' Compensation Attorneys (NACCA), was formed in 1946. It was the predecessor of what became the Association of Trial Lawyers of America (ATLA), recently renamed the American Association for Justice. A sense of the organization's focus can be gleaned from the activities held just prior to its annual conventions, where there were programs designed to improve its members' knowledge and skills. The 1954 program, for example, included presentations on "Use of Medical Photographs in Evidence," "Use of Mortality Tables," and, most significantly for my purposes, "Has the Defendant Liability Insurance, and the Amount?"[26]

The central figure in these NACCA gatherings was Melvin Belli, the self-styled "King of Torts."[27] The reports of the NACCA proceedings show Belli seeming to be almost everywhere, conducting what were called Belli Seminars, offering frequent comments on other lawyers' presentations, and serving single-handedly as the moderator of virtually all of the numerous practical sessions. He was a combination father figure, teacher, and role model for the plaintiffs' lawyers who sought to learn his secrets and achieve successes like his.

Belli was a San Francisco lawyer who had pioneered the use of innovative methods of enhancing the size of damage awards in tort cases. Obtaining increasingly larger verdicts was not only in the obvious interest of plaintiffs but also benefited members of the plaintiffs' bar, who had long practiced under a contingent-fee system. The plaintiff paid his or her lawyer only if the defendant paid the plaintiff, and then only a percentage of the recovery. This system made it possible for plaintiffs without any other way of paying a lawyer to bring suit. If they lost, they paid nothing; they paid their lawyers only if they won. By maintaining a portfolio of cases and charging a high enough percentage in successful cases, plaintiff's attorneys could afford to take not only routine cases but also those that had a high potential payoff but a comparatively low probability of success.

The centerpiece of Belli's strategy for enhancing awards was the "per diem" method of proving damages. This method began by obtaining a ruling from the trial judge that Belli was entitled to use a blackboard to illustrate his argument. With audiovisual and computer-assisted demonstrative evidence as common as they are today, it is difficult to imagine that there was a time when trials consisted almost entirely of talk and printed documents. Not all courts permitted the use of a blackboard, although over time more did. Belli asked the jurors to imagine how much money they would accept for suffering the injury for which the plaintiff was seeking compensation. "What would *you* take for a fractured wrist, ladies and gentlemen? If I placed three one-thousand dollar bills and a sledge hammer upon this jury box and suggested that I would allow you to pick up those three one-thousand dollar bills if you would first allow me to crack your right wrist with that sledge hammer, tell me truthfully, would you allow me to do it?"[28]

Having secured the jurors' implicit agreement that a particular lump sum was insufficient compensation, Belli would tell them what sum he thought was adequate, and then persuade them of its adequacy by using the blackboard to divide up the period the plaintiff suffered from his injury into minutes, hours, and then days, multiplying a "small" amount of compensation per day times the total number of days that the plaintiff suffered, or could be expect to suffer, from his injury. Compensation of 1 cent per second for the plaintiff's pain and suffering became $315,000 per year—a virtually unprecedented award in the 1950s. To make sure that his colleagues appreciated not only his technique but also the magnitude of the damages he believed they should be seeking, Belli published accounts of the cases that secured the largest awards each year, calling them "adequate" awards.[29] Belli's seminars marked the beginning of the networking and mutual self-education among plaintiffs' attorneys that are so characteristic of the litigation that now is the hallmark of the modern tort system. Networking got its start in the postwar world of auto litigation.

Although plaintiffs' attorneys were the first to coordinate effectively, it was not long before the defense bar recognized that it was facing an increasingly organized and aggressive set of adversaries. In 1957 the first volume of a journal that was intended to help defense counsel in their battles with the plaintiffs' bar, the *Defense Law Journal,* was published. A preface by the editor proclaimed: "Verdicts in astronomical amounts, often entirely disproportionate to the loss sustained continue to be a threat," and the lead article was entitled "The Defense Cannot Rest." An article of over 80 pages, entitled "The True Adequate Award," constituted a direct attack on Melvin Belli. The article contained sections on "Verdicts Held Excessive" and "Verdicts for Less Than $50,000."[30] Subsequent volumes included updated versions of this article.

This mobilization of the plaintiff's and defense bars is reminiscent of the old joke about the only lawyer in a small town who had difficulty making a living until a second lawyer opened up a practice in the same town. Then they both thrived. By the end of the 1950s, personal injury litigation—with auto cases leading the way—had become a distinct and profitable specialty for both plaintiffs' and defense lawyers. And it was auto injury cases that dominated the dockets. For plaintiffs' lawyers, auto accidents occurred frequently enough to provide a steady source of cases.

The rise of auto insurance provided a ready source of recovery in these cases. Indeed, given the meager assets of most drivers, there was little reason for a plaintiffs' attorney to bring a lawsuit unless the potential defendant had liability insurance. And there was little point in seeking damages in excess of the amount of insurance that covered the defendant. For all practical purposes, then, the scope of tort liability for auto accidents was defined by the liability insurance that covered the defendant.

The Influence of Health-Care Costs

Partly because of what was simultaneously occurring in the field of health care, however, the value of an auto injury case would begin to increase substantially as the 1950s ended. Very roughly, medical expenses and lost wages comprise about half of the typical tort plaintiff's damages recovery. The other half is comprised of damages for noneconomic loss, or pain and suffering. In a number of different ways after about 1960, increases in the amount of the medical expense component of tort recoveries expanded the typical tort award.

First, the cost of medical care increased faster than the general rate of inflation. The average annual increase in the consumer price index during the 1950s was 2.1 percent; during the 1960s, it was 2.7 percent; and during the 1970s, it was 2.7 percent. During the same decades, however, on average the cost of medical care increased at an annual rate of 4.0 percent, 4.3 percent, and 8.2 percent, respectively.[31] On the basis of these increases alone, the average tort recovery could be expected to increase significantly more than the general rate of inflation.

Second, not only the cost of medical care increased during this period. In addition, the amount of medical care that was consumed increased exponentially. National personal health-care expenditures doubled between 1950 and 1960; tripled between 1960 and 1970; and more than tripled again between 1970 and 1980.[32] In 1955 the U.S. expenditure on health care constituted 4.4 percent of gross domestic product; by 1965, that figure was 6.1 percent; by 1975, 8.3 percent; and by 1980, 9.1 percent.[33] The ability of the health-care system to treat illness and injury, and therefore the cost of treatment, was increasing rapidly during this period. For this reason, the amount of medical care and the medical expenses incurred by the typical auto accident victim also increased at the same time.

Third, beginning around 1960, private health insurance became increasingly common for the American middle class. This form of insurance was becoming a standard fringe benefit of employment. And in 1965 the federal government adopted the Medicare and Medicaid programs, extending health-care insurance to virtually the entire population over the age of 65 and providing a certain amount of medical care to the very poor. In 1960, benefits paid by private health insurance had been just under $6 billion. By 1970 the figure was $15 billion; by 1980, $68 billion—over 11 times the amount of benefits that had been paid 20 years earlier.[34] Medicare had added another $7 billion in expenditures by 1970 (benefits paid were a sizable portion of this sum) and $37 billion by 1980, none of which had been available before 1965.[35]

Prior to this time, most tort victims had minimal or no access to health insurance. Tort victims did not know before they received a settlement or went to trial how much, if anything, they would receive. Consequently, the possibility of recovery in tort probably did not measurably increase victims' consumption of medical services. With the advent of widespread health insurance, however, this whole picture changed, and tort was afflicted with a version of the *ex post* moral hazard problem that afflicts all periodically paid health and disability insurance. An accident victim could now consume whatever medical services his or her insurance covered, without fear of being left with the entire bill for these services. A major portion, in many cases nearly all of that bill, would be paid by a private or public health insurer. As a consequence, the plaintiff's attorney could encourage him to obtain medical treatment without concern for his financial circumstances. The result would be no disadvantage to the plaintiff, plus an even greater recovery in tort if his lawsuit were successful.

Finally, in addition to increases in the medical expense component of tort recoveries that were generated by the developments I have just described, increased medical expenses had a multiplier effect on total tort recoveries. In settling routine cases, and even in larger cases that are not routine, the victim's medical expenses were used (and often still are used) as a baseline for the computation of a settlement offer. A total offer was calculated as some multiple (three or four times, for example) of these expenses.[36] A rule of thumb of this sort is an inexpensive and fairly uniform way for insurance claims adjustors and defense attorneys to calculate damages. The approach is also used because, other things being equal, the greater the victims' medical expenses, the greater his pain and suffering is likely to be, and the more damages a jury would be likely to award at trial. As a consequence, as the typical auto accident victim's medical expenses increased beginning in the late 1950s, typical settlements and verdicts increased by a multiple of that increase. The steady rise in auto liability insurance costs in the decades that followed was in part a reflection of these increases.

Flaws in the System

Even as auto insurance costs increased, many of the same problems the Columbia Plan had identified three decades earlier continued to plague the system. Delay, inequity, and undercompensation led the list. The dynamics of the relationship among plaintiffs' lawyers, defense lawyers, and auto liability insurance played a role in all three of these problems.

Delay

As the number of auto liability suits increased, the time between loss and ultimate payment lengthened. This was not only a function of the limited number of judges available to try cases, though that was a contributing factor. In addition, liability insurers themselves were caught between two conflicting incentives. On the one hand, it has long been understood that the longer a claim goes unpaid, the greater the claimant's dissatisfaction and the higher the payment the claimant is likely to demand to settle the case. In this sense insurers benefited by resolving claims quickly. Moreover, it was the natural bureaucratic incentive of claims adjusters and other insurance company personnel to close claims expeditiously even at the cost of paying extra in order to do so.[37] Their job was to process claims; they were not doing their job if claims were left open. Both of these factors promoted prompt processing and settlement of claims.

On the other hand, insurers earn income on invested premiums. The longer they can hold those premiums without paying claims, the more income insurers earn on their investments. Consequently, liability insurers themselves had conflicting incentives about expediting the payment of claims. The net effect of these conflicting incentives was (and still is) reflected in insurers' practice of expeditiously disposing of comparatively small claims by paying more than they are "worth" but delaying the settlement of large claims.

A second reason for the slow processing of claims was that the incentives of both plaintiffs' and defense counsel tended to promote delay. It is true that the more quickly a plaintiff's lawyer moves a case to settlement or trial, the more quickly the lawyer gets a contingent fee. But plaintiffs' lawyers also have an incentive to maintain a large portfolio of cases. The larger the portfolio, the less variance there is in aggregate outcomes and the more predictable and steady is the flow of cash from contingent fees. The larger the portfolio, however, the more cases there are in the pipeline at any given time and the longer it will take for the lawyer with finite time to resolve any given case through trial or settlement. The busier the lawyer, the longer the line of cases to be resolved, and the longer the period of time between filing the claim and resolving it.

Defense lawyers hired by liability insurers had a different kind of incentive but delay was also its consequence. Liability insurers pay defense counsel by the hour. But the rates insurers pay tend to be below the market average. Much of the work is routine; and because defending cases for insurers provides a steady source of revenue, it is worthwhile for law firms to discount their rates for this kind of work. As a consequence, however, the natural incentive of some defense counsel probably is to extend cases in order to produce more revenue. And although it is in liability insurers' interest to limit the number of unnecessary hours that defense counsel invests in a case, the insurer also may wish to delay settlement, especially during periods when investment returns on retained premiums are favorable. Paying for some arguably unessential billed hours here or there—an additional deposition that takes several months to schedule and complete, for example—may facilitate delay.

By the late 1960s, the problem of delay had become severe in many urban areas. In Chicago, for example, there was a civil case backlog of 69 months. There were similar waiting periods in other cities as well. Over time, the market for the services of plaintiffs' and defendants' attorneys adjusted to take account of these forces. Eventually additional judges were appointed, law school enrollments increased, and a new equilibrium was reached. But at the same time that auto litigation was increasing, so were other forms of tort litigation. It therefore took the market longer to adjust than might otherwise have been expected. In the meantime the consequence of the interacting incentives of liability insurers and counsel for both sides was that, as the incidence of auto accidents and claims increased, the time between the making of a claim and ultimate payment also increased.

It is ironic that in the face of these forces promoting delay, most cases never went to trial anyway. The whole system had become routine and bureaucratic, and trials were a rarity. One of the most respected studies of the mid-1960s focused on auto claims made in the state of Michigan during 1958. The study found that less than 1 percent of all auto accident victims were involved in cases that went to trial, and that substantially all of these involved serious injuries. Small claims virtually never went to trial. But 95 percent of even the victims with serious injuries never went to trial either.[38] For all but a few victims, liability insurance had created an administrative compensation system that was nonetheless operated by lawyers, whose costly services inflated what drivers had to pay for that insurance.

Inequity

Because almost all claims were settled, the system operated mainly through negotiation, and it favored certain categories of victims over others. The dynamics of the claim process produced differential treatment of small and large claims. It was not in the interest of liability insurers or plaintiffs' attorneys to make a substantial investment in comparatively small claims. Counsel fees would exceed what it cost to pay the plaintiff to settle. These claims therefore had what came to be called "nuisance value." The result was that many such claims were resolved with minimal negotiation, often before a plaintiff's attorney became involved at all.

The public stance of the insurers was that claims were not paid merely because it was cheaper to pay than to contest them. And it is true that it was in an insurer's interest to establish a reputation for toughness, and that the internal dynamics of the company bureaucracy would not permit indiscriminate payment. Indeed, in 1960 the Defense Research Institute published a monograph entitled "The Revolt against Whiplash," containing nine articles by both physicians and lawyers designed to stiffen the defense community's willingness to contest hard-to-verify "whiplash" claims for cervical sprains.[39] But internal company rules of thumb for determining whether a claim was valid did evolve. The classic rule was that the driver who "rear-ended" another car was liable virtually without further inquiry. Rules of thumb for valuing claims also developed, based largely on the amount of medical expenses incurred by the claimant. As I noted earlier, a claim typically was "worth" a multiple of the claimant's medical expenses—three, four, or five times these expenses, depending on the jurisdiction and the era. Rather than being the individualized process it purported to be, for the ordinary victim with small losses, tort looked a lot like insurance that tended to ignore individual differences in claims.

Large claims, however, were often worth contesting. In contrast to nuisance claims, the ability of the plaintiff or his attorney to extract a favorable settlement depended more on the merits of the case and the prospect of obtaining a large verdict before a jury than on the insurer's desire to close the claim. In addition, plaintiffs were risk-averse, since they had only one claim, whereas the defendant's liability insurer was a repeat player. It had a portfolio of claims and was therefore more nearly risk neutral.[40] For this reason as well, in connection with large claims the settlement process favored the insurer.

Finally, other things being equal, the more seriously injured the claimant, the greater the likelihood that his claim was worth more than the amount of liability insurance covering the defendant. Yet most drivers had little means of paying the portion of a settlement or judgment in excess of the amount of liability insurance covering them. Even when the insurer was willing to pay its entire policy limits in settlement, the seriously injured claimant might be left with no means of recovering the full amount of his or her losses. In actual practice, then, the amount of liability insurance the defendant had purchased determined the maximum amount of damages that were available for injuries caused by negligent driving, regardless of what the law of torts said on paper.

Undercompensation

Even apart from its differential treatment of small and large claims, in a number of other ways the system failed as a mechanism for compensating auto accident victims, as it had failed from the beginning. Only victims injured by the negligence of a third party had rights of recovery. Victims of nonnegligent accidents had no claim. And victims of single-party accidents such as those who lost control of their vehicles and collided with stationary objects had no claim. They were left to claim coverage from their more modest auto medical payments coverage or from any health or disability insurance that covered them independently, and they received no compensation from any of these sources for their pain and suffering. Even the victims of third-party negligence could recover only if the victim was not guilty of contributory negligence himself. Although in practice this rule probably was applied to reduce rather than preclude payment, this meant that the contributorily negligent victim was undercompensated. And until the 1970s liability insurance was not compulsory in many states; not all negligent defendants were insured or (if they were) had enough insurance to cover liability for a substantial claim.

The consequence of these gaps was that most victims received little or no compensation in tort. In the Michigan study, for example, 63 percent of all auto accident victims received no tort compensation, and only 3 percent received $3,000 or more. Just over 55 percent of all the dollars paid in tort went to this 3 percent of all victims.[41] Moreover, there was a considerable gap between the amount paid in tort and the amount of loss—even just economic loss—incurred by victims. The aggregate economic loss of the victims in the Michigan study was $178 million, of which tort paid only $46 million.[42] And the gap was greatest for seriously injured victims, even considering both the tort and the nontort compensation they received. Of victims with economic losses of less than $1,000, 64 percent recovered more than 75 percent of their economic losses from all sources of compensation, including tort. But only 8 percent of those with losses of more than $25,000 recovered 75 percent or more of their economic losses, from all sources combined.[43]

Other studies at the time yielded similar results.[44] And a systematic national study by the Rand Corporation several decades later confirmed that these patterns persisted over a long period of time. This study found that only one-third of all auto accident victims received compensation in tort, and that tort payments accounted for only 22 percent of compensation for victims' economic losses.[45] It was in the context of these patterns of under-compensation that there occurred a revival of the auto liability reform movement that had been quiet since the Columbia Plan had been shelved in the early 1930s.

The No-Fault Movement

The Columbia Plan had proposed a strict liability approach to auto accidents modeled on workers' compensation. In a two-car accident, each driver was to be strictly liable to the other. Although eliminating negligence from the picture in this way would have solved some of the problems with the existing system, this approach would have been awkward. Each injured driver or passenger would have been forced to deal with the other driver's liability insurer. Many of the problems associated with the liability insurance negotiation-and-settlement system would therefore have been replicated by a strict liability approach.

The great innovation of the movement that began in the 1960s was to propose moving from a third-party, or strict liability, approach to a first-party, or no-fault, approach.[46] This approach was developed by Robert Keeton and Jeffrey O'Connell in a 1965 book that became the blueprint for legislation that was in the forefront of debate in the ensuing years.[47] Their book never used the term "no-fault." But in the course of debate over a bill proposing the Keeton-O'Connell plan that was introduced in the Massachusetts legislature in 1967 by a young legislator named Michael Dukakis, a Boston newspaper coined the term "no-fault," and the term stuck.

Auto no-fault had two prongs. First, there would be either limited or complete immunity from tort liability for negligent driving. Second, in place of liability, each vehicle owner would purchase her own insurance against economic losses associated with auto-related injury. This insurance would cover the owner, those driving the vehicle with the owner's permission, passengers in the vehicle, and pedestrians injured by the operation of the insured vehicle. Compensation would be paid regardless of negligence. In effect, the medical payments coverage that was sold with many policies would be made broader and deeper and would become the centerpiece of coverage. The dollar amount of coverage would be substantial, and not only medical expenses but also lost wages resulting from auto accidents would be covered. There would be no coverage of noneconomic losses for pain and suffering. Each driver and her passengers would look only to their own insurance for compensation of their economic losses. And in single-car accidents, compensation would be paid even though there was no other party responsible for the loss.

Critics of no-fault attacked the proposal on a number of grounds. Doing away with the tort rights of even victims with minimal injuries was objectionable, they argued. Moreover, in their view, eliminating or reducing the tort rights of those with more than minimal injuries was wholly unacceptable. These critics argued that relieving negligent drivers of liability would undermine the deterrent effect of the threat of tort liability. They also asserted that it was unfair to deprive victims of compensation for their pain and suffering.

Apart from the substantive merits of the issue, there were practical political implications involved in the no-fault debate. Eliminating or limiting tort liability would deprive the plaintiffs' bar of a major source of income. The organized plaintiffs' bar—which by the late 1960s had become an important political force in some states—could be expected to oppose no-fault for this reason. In addition, the plaintiffs' bar thought that the enactment of even a watered-down version of no-fault would be the camel's nose under the political tent that could facilitate even more objectionable tort reforms. As we will see in the next two chapters, by the 1970s, when auto no-fault was being seriously debated around the country, both medical malpractice and products liability were also becoming controversial. Claim frequency and severity were increasing in both fields, and proposals for reforms that would limit these forms of liability were surfacing. Because plaintiffs' attorneys did not want the enactment of auto no-fault to serve as a precedent for future tort reform in these other fields, or to encourage those who supported reform, the plaintiffs' bar opposed legislative limitation on auto victims' tort rights even more vigorously than they would have otherwise.

In the wake of this political opposition, compromises similar to what

Keeton and O'Connell had proposed were reached in the states where no-fault was enacted. There would be a limited abolition of tort liability, but seriously injured victims would still be able to sue in tort. Small claimants would be left to their no-fault insurance alone; those with claims above a "threshold" would retain their right to sue in tort and to recover pain and suffering damages, as well as any economic loss in excess of their no-fault coverage.

The no-fault statutes that were actually enacted by 16 states in the 1970s employed two different kinds of thresholds, one "monetary" and the other "verbal." The former required that the claimant incur a specified amount of medical expense in order to surpass the threshold; the latter required "serious" injury, typically defined (among other things) as hard tissue injury other than a simple fracture, and loss of use of a limb.

Only a small percentage of potential claims could satisfy the verbal thresholds. The monetary thresholds that had to be exceeded before a tort suit could be brought varied enormously, however, and the variation reflected significant operational differences among no-fault plans. In some states, monetary thresholds as low as $500 in medical expenses permitted most claimants to sue in tort. In contrast, states with thresholds as high as $5,000 in medical expenses precluded suit by all but a small percentage of the claimants who could previously have brought lawsuits.

Variations in the amount of no-fault insurance that the statutes required also were significant. Some states required the purchase of only $2,000 of no-fault insurance, whereas a few required $50,000 or more. Even when a threshold was satisfied, the larger the amount of no-fault coverage that was available to a claimant, the less likely he would be to sue, because no-fault benefits were always deducted from tort recoveries. A claimant whose economic expenses had been paid in full by no-fault, for example, could recover in tort only for pain and suffering.

Thus, a requirement that $2,000 in no-fault insurance be purchased did little more than remove very small claims from the system. Many of these claims, however, would have been settled even in the absence of no-fault. The shift to no-fault merely reduced the value of these claims and shifted the locus of compensation from another driver's insurer to one's own. Requiring the purchase of higher amounts of no-fault insurance would have discouraged even more claimants from suing, but would have been in tension with the underlying legislative compromise designed to permit the plaintiffs' bar to retain its high-value tort cases.

Moreover, as the principal academic critics of auto no-fault, Walter Blum and Harry Kalven, noted at the time, requiring the purchase of higher amounts of no-fault insurance could have produced a highly undesirable income-regressive premium structure.[48] Because no-fault insurance covered not only medical expenses but also lost wages, when middle- and upper-income policyholders suffered a loss it was likely to be greater than the loss suffered by comparatively low-income policyholders. To avoid a regressive cross-subsidy running from low- to higher-income policyholders, either premiums for high amounts of coverage would have to be calibrated to the policyholder's income, or relatively low ceilings would have to be placed on the amount of weekly wage loss that was reimbursable by no-fault coverage.

Calibrating premiums to income in order to avoid regressivity would have been too cumbersome. But limiting regressivity by placing low ceilings on the amount of required no-fault insurance raised a different question. Why require middle- and upper-income policyholders to purchase insurance against small amounts of medical expenses and lost wages that was likely to duplicate the health and disability insurance that they already had, or could have purchased voluntarily if they had wished? One not very attractive answer was that no-fault was a disguised way of requiring low-income drivers to purchase small amounts of medical and wage-loss insurance, because these low-income drivers were much less likely than middle- and upper-income drivers to have other sources of such coverage. In this sense no-fault was a paternalistic device that forced the poor to buy insurance that they either would not or could not have purchased otherwise.

Another reason that high-limits no-fault insurance often was not required, however, is that no-fault plans were not written on a clean slate. Rather, they were produced as alternatives to the tort system, and their features were constructed to address dissatisfactions with particular aspects of tort. If small claims were receiving a disproportionate share of the compensation dollar because of their nuisance value, then relatively low thresholds and small required amounts of no-fault insurance would address this problem. But if the problem were also perceived to involve undercompensation of the small percentage of claims that involved serious injury, then mandating the purchase of higher amounts of no-fault insurance would help to address that problem.

In the case of both the low and high no-fault insurance states, then, the tort system was the reference point for reform. No one seemed to be thinking about abolishing or limiting tort liability and then simply allowing people to purchase the broad-based health and wage-loss insurance they needed or wanted, although that was another plausible alternative. Rather, the shape of the tort system tended both to inhibit the imagination of reformers and to constrain the political feasibility of the alternatives to tort.

In the early 1970s there were battles over no-fault in nearly all states. The plaintiffs' bar mobilized to oppose no-fault; as time went on, some insurers tended to favor it, although their support often was lukewarm, and other insurers and trade organizations opposed it. Sometimes emotions ran high over the issue. Plaintiffs' lawyers brought the victims of auto accidents in wheelchairs to the rooms where legislative hearings were held and pleaded that these victims' rights not be limited. And the rhetoric of debate occasionally got out of hand. A special committee of the American Bar Association's Section on Negligence, Insurance, and Compensation opposed no-fault, for example, partly on the ground that "the principle of liability for fault is derived from the religious belief that each of us is responsible to his God for his own conduct."[49]

During this time the consumer movement was picking up strength, however, and the media, often captivated by the idea of no-fault reform, both supported and publicized it. Jeffrey O'Connell recalled often arriving at the airports of a number of state capitals the day before he was scheduled to testify before legislative committees considering no-fault and finding local television reporters there to meet him with their cameras. That evening he would see a story about no-fault on the evening news, and more public support for the idea would be generated.

When the dust settled, 16 states had adopted some version of the approach. Four states have since repealed their no-fault legislation. Interestingly, these states had adopted the lowest dollar thresholds of any of the no-fault states, and as a result their statutes had produced the least impact. And Kentucky, New Jersey, and Pennsylvania have modified their legislation to adopt "choice" plans that in various ways make tort "elective" rather than mandatory. A number of other states enacted statutes that made medical payments coverage mandatory, thus creating what has sometimes been given the misleading name "add-on" no-fault. In these states, tort liability is fully preserved. A limited version of no-fault coverage is simply added on to every liability insurance policy.

Since 1976, however, not a single state has adopted a true no-fault plan. The idea arose, was adopted and firmly planted in about a dozen states, and then ground to a halt, all in the space of decade. Nonetheless, like workers' compensation, auto no-fault remains a model for thinking about reform of other areas of tort law, such as medical malpractice and products liability. The reasons for no-fault's failure to thrive are therefore worth examining, not only in their own right but also for what they can tell us about the prospects for similar reform in these other areas.

The Demise of an "Incontestable" Idea

In the period before it became clear that no-fault was not going to sweep the country, the soon-to-be Senator Daniel Patrick Moynihan called no-fault "the one incontestably successful reform of the 1960s."[50] Moynihan, it turned out, was dead wrong. The explanation for his error sheds light not only on this field but also on the nature of the evolving relationship between tort and insurance during the last quarter of the twentieth century.

Four factors were especially influential in making it possible for the political opposition to no-fault to prevail. First, the states that adopted auto no-fault did so toward the end of a distinct legal era. For the 50 years running roughly from the mid-1930s to the mid-1980s, first legal scholars, and eventually the courts, became increasingly disenchanted with the negligence system. For a while it looked like the negligence system might even be totally dismantled and replaced by strict liability. But that era was coming to an end at the very moment when the debates about no-fault became most intense. What happened to no-fault was a harbinger of what would happen all across the tort system.

During the period when negligence came into academic disrepute, legal scholars developed the theory of strict enterprise liability, proposing that businesses be held liable for their activities without regard to negligence, and especially for harm caused by their products. The courts followed suit and adopted strict liability for product defects in the 1960s. By 1970, other fields seemed ripe for a similar transformation. But the trajectory of strict liability had become completely flat by the early 1980s, for both political and economic reasons. The conservative revolution had resulted in the appointment of judges who opposed enterprise liability. And the liability insurance "crises" in the mid-1970s and mid-1980s highlighted the cost of expanded liability. Under these circumstances, auto no-fault seemed almost like a new welfare program—precisely the sort of thing that was anathema to the dominant ideology of the 1980s.

Although no-fault was in one sense just the opposite of strict liability— its major feature was, after all, that it was at least in part a *no-liability* system—in another sense strict liability and no-fault have an important characteristic in common. Like strict enterprise liability, auto no-fault rejected negligence as the basis of liability for accidental personal injury. And like strict enterprise liability, no-fault's rejection of the negligence standard was motivated in heavy measure by a concern for ensuring compensation of victims that limiting liability to injuries caused by negligence ignores.

Yet despite this significant common feature of strict liability and auto no-fault, their political valence was very different. In contrast to the expansion of strict liability, which was of course supported by the plaintiffs' bar, auto no-fault was the bête noire of the plaintiffs' bar. Strict liability would have made it easier for plaintiffs to recover damages in tort, whereas auto no-fault made that more difficult. And with these differences came differences in the fees plaintiffs' lawyers could anticipate. As criticisms of negligence and support for strict liability began to recede around 1980, the plaintiffs' bar would have been swimming against the tide in promoting strict liability. But it was swimming with the tide in opposing auto no-fault. Therefore, in the states where the plaintiffs' bar and the other opponents of auto no-fault were able to prevent its adoption during the 1970s, within a few years both the legal climate and the politics of no-fault were transformed, and it had no chance of enactment, because the momentum for expanding rights of compensation generally had been halted in its tracks.[51]

The second factor that impeded the spread of no-fault was that, ironically, it was not a demonstrable cost saver. One of the arguments for no-fault had always been that it would be less expensive than tort because it would not involve the high administrative and legal costs of the negligence system. When it turned out that the new system was not substantially less expensive than the one it replaced, no-fault proponents faced a much harder road to enactment. This difficulty was a result of the central compromise that was necessary to no-fault's enactment. Because it preserved tort liability for the most serious injuries and for all property damage claims, no-fault required the purchase of both liability and no-fault coverage. It was not surprising, therefore, that the cost of both the liability insurance that was still necessary plus the no-fault insurance that now also had to be purchased was greater than the proponents of no-fault would have hoped. As a consequence, the net savings produced by eliminating the cost of liability insurance against the small claims that were now excluded from tort were not sufficient to make a strong case for no-fault. This experience counted heavily against no-fault in the second wave of states that were considering it.

A third factor was that as time went on, some studies suggested that the accident rate—especially the rate of fatal accidents—was greater in no-fault than in negligence states. This impact was marginal, and the studies were not definitive (some have showed that no-fault did not increase the accident rate), but the possibility that the enactment of no-fault actually had resulted in an increase in auto-related injuries also counted against it in the states that were still considering it.[52]

Finally, and ultimately I think most important, the core of the argument for reform of auto liability, from the time of the Columbia Plan on, had been that the negligence system resulted in gaps in the fabric of compensation for auto-related accidents. As I indicated earlier, developments over time within auto insurance itself had closed some of these gaps. Omnibus and DOC coverage had helped extend liability insurance to more drivers. Uninsured motorist coverage had provided policyholders with coverage of their losses in the event that their claims against third parties could not be satisfied. And medical payments coverage had provided drivers and their passengers with small amounts of what was essentially no-fault medical coverage. To the proponents of no-fault these devices still were inadequate. Some of the devices depended on the existence of negligence by a third party as a prerequisite to compensation and therefore tolerated the gaps inherent in that approach. Others (in the case of medical payments coverage) were incomplete in that they usually provided only small amounts of coverage, and applied only to medical expenses and not to lost income resulting from auto injury.

By the time no-fault was being most hotly debated in the mid-1970s, however, other important and substantial sources of insurance were increasingly available to compensate the victims of auto accidents for their medical expenses and lost wages. The percentage of the population covered by public or private forms of health insurance had by then risen to just over 80 percent; many workers had sick pay benefits that covered at least part of the wages they might lose as a result of suffering auto (or other) injuries that were not work related; a minority but more than a negligible portion of the middle- and upper-income population was covered by private long-term disability insurance; and the Social Security Disability insurance program provided most individuals with subsistence-level income replacement in the event of permanent total disability.

Thus, at the very time when auto no-fault might otherwise have had its greatest appeal, a major argument in its favor—that it would fill important gaps in the fabric of compensation—was losing a considerable amount of its strength for a significant portion of the population, because of the rise of non-auto-related sources of compensation. The typical middle-class driver who suffered an injury that left him hospitalized for a few days and out of work for as much as several weeks probably did not need no-fault auto insurance in order to have most of his medical expenses or a few days or even a few weeks of lost income reimbursed. His health insurance and accumulated sick days were now likely to take care of much of this loss. It was only the poor, who did not have the same access to health and disability insurance, that were likely to need auto no-fault, as the low amounts of coverage required by most of the no-fault statutes that were actually enacted implicitly acknowledged.

In short, with the declining appeal of the liberal, anti-negligence argument for no-fault, with the opposition of the plaintiffs' bar, and with the rise of other sources of compensation for the lion's share of many drivers' injuries, no-fault could succeed only by showing that it would produce significant cost savings over the negligence system. Try though its proponents did, however, they were never able to deal negligence a knockout blow on cost-saving grounds. In fact, an effort in the late 1990s to enact elective no-fault at the federal level was attacked by the consumer advocate Ralph Nader on the ground that auto insurance costs had proved to be the highest in states that had adopted no-fault.[53] The accuracy of that charge remains uncertain, but the very fact that it could not be definitively refuted reflects the difficulty that the remaining proponents of no-fault now faced.

In the end, for all practical purposes no-fault breathed its last breath outside the dozen states where it was already in place when the auto liability insurers who in theory still favored it finally gave up the cause. They saw little point in pushing a reform that was unlikely to be enacted, and that in any event would leave them in an prolonged state of uncertainty if it was enacted but then had its constitutionality challenged in extended, state-by-state litigation.

The Contemporary Situation

Although no-fault never succeeded in defeating negligence on cost-saving grounds, the cost of liability insurance has not disappeared as a political issue. On the contrary, the cost of auto insurance has been the principal issue associated with auto liability in the more than 30 years since the no-fault movement was halted in its tracks. For example, in a hotly contested election in California in 1988 over Proposition 103, the voters narrowly chose to roll back liability insurance rates to a level that was at least 20 percent lower than a year earlier, rather than adopt no-fault.[54] In Arizona in 1990, no-fault was on the ballot and was rejected by 85 percent of those voting. California voters again rejected a no-fault measure in 1996. And in a number of New Jersey gubernatorial races during this period the cost of auto insurance was a major issue.

Despite its economic significance, however, auto liability has managed largely to stay out of the spotlight of the tort reform debate. One reason is that, almost as a side effect of the tort reform efforts of repeat-player defendants from other fields, auto liability has also seen reform. In the mid-1980s, for example, in the wake of the liability insurance "crisis" affecting business insurance, which I will discuss in later chapters, several dozen states enacted tort reform statutes. The most common reform was the placement of dollar caps on pain and suffering and punitive damages.[55] Although the enactment of these reforms was prompted by developments outside of auto liability, the reforms usually were contained in statutes of general application. Auto liability was therefore made subject to reforms that applied to tort liability across the board.

A second reason for auto liability's low profile is that although the average amount paid in auto bodily injury claims more than doubled between 1980 and 1993,[56] in the following 10 years this figure increased only slightly more than 10 percent.[57] The increase in the national average cost of auto liability insurance during this decade was correspondingly modest.[58] The comparatively small increases in claim severity during this period, when national health expenditures more than doubled, may seem to be an embarrassment for my theory that health-care cost increases can have a multiplier effect on settlements in routine tort claims. But almost uniquely, auto claims are subject to a natural ceiling that is set by each state's compulsory insurance requirements. Typically this is between $10,000 and $25,000 for a single claimant, and most states have not increased their mandatory minimums in years.[59] Most drivers can only pay a claim out of their auto liability insurance, and most drivers only purchase the minimum required amount of coverage. Many claims simply bump up against this natural ceiling on available dollars. When the effective amount of insurance available in most claims stays constant and comparatively low, average claims costs can be expected to increase only marginally even when actual losses are increasing. And that, in my opinion, is exactly what has happened. The available amount of liability insurance places a practical limit on the damages that are available in an auto liability claim, and the amount of insurance available in most instances has not risen.

A third reason that auto liability has stayed largely out of the spotlight is that the politics of auto liability do not align neatly into proreform and antireform interest groups. In such fields as products and medical malpractice liability, potential defendants know who they are, and know that they face the risk of very substantial liability. In auto liability, however, with the exception of the occasional business with a large fleet of vehicles, there are no auto liability defendants who systematically face the risk of catastrophic liability. Further, most potential auto liability defendants are also potential plaintiffs. At least in part for this reason, consumer advocates representing the interest of ordinary drivers have been split about whether such reforms as no-fault are desirable. The other common advocates for the ordinary driver, plaintiffs' lawyers, of course see ordinary victims, not ordinary defendants, as their potential clients. And auto liability insurers tend, at most, to be only lukewarm proponents of tort reform. As a consequence, among potential defendants in auto cases there has been no natural constituency favoring tort reform.

Finally, having an auto accident has become an unfortunate yet unsurprising occurrence in the lives of ordinary people, a bit like having a tree fall on one's roof, or needing knee surgery. And like both of these events, insurance turns many accidents that would have been a major financial misfortune into mere personal inconveniences. For most people, paying sizable sums for auto insurance has simply become a part of the background cost of living. The whole insurance and liability system for dealing with auto accidents has become so embedded in our lives that it is almost transparent. Auto liability is a prime example of how the routinization and bureaucratization in a field of liability tends to move it from the foreground to the background of public concern, despite the very substantial amount of money that is sometimes involved.

At present, the comparatively low amounts of liability insurance that drivers in most states are required to purchase is keeping the pressure off auto liability insurance rates. But over time these minimum amounts of coverage will be increased. When this occurs, premiums also will rise, not only because more coverage costs more but also because there will be more money available to pay claims. Average settlements will therefore increase disproportionately, as the availability of insurance drives up claim valuations. At this point the cost of auto liability insurance will again become a significant issue, as it already is in urbanized states where rates have increased because of increased claim frequency.

Thus, the auto insurance settlement process, ever-increasing health insurance costs, tort law's measure of damages, and the interaction among these phenomena are structural features of the system that from time to time will inevitably create upward pressure on the magnitude of tort settlements and awards. The system also provides an attractive opportunity for fraud or at least the padding of medical claims for soft tissue injury that produces a multiplier effect on pain and suffering damages.[60] As long as these structural features of the system are in place, doctrinal reforms of tort law are unlikely to have a significant impact on auto insurance costs or on the way the system operates.

Yet auto no-fault, the one truly significant auto liability reform of the last 50 years, has no prospect of spreading beyond the handful of states where it is now in force, and even there it is essentially a hybrid of tort and no-fault. The no-fault experience should be a sobering prospect for those who favor fundamental reform, not only in the auto liability field but elsewhere in the tort system as well. Not all the factors that prevented the spread of auto no-fault are present in fields such as medical malpractice and products liability. But as we will see in the next two chapters, the posture into which the interaction of liability and insurance has placed these two fields also affects both the way they operate and their prospects for reform.

—4—

The Physicians' Dilemma:
Medical Malpractice Liability
and the Health Insurance System

We saw in the last chapter that auto liability has considerable economic importance, but low political visibility. In contrast, medical malpractice liability occupies a place in contemporary policy debates far out of proportion to its seemingly minor economic importance. We spend a tiny percentage of the health-care dollar on medical malpractice insurance. Nonetheless, three times since the 1970s we have experienced "crises" that have affected the availability and cost of medical malpractice insurance in the short run and led to legislative tort reform in the longer run. The third crisis elevated the issue to prominence in the 2004 Presidential campaign and produced significant proposals for federal legislative reform of medical malpractice law.

Yet for all the heat there is about malpractice liability and malpractice insurance, there is comparatively little light. We have no definitive or even terribly persuasive empirical evidence of the effect of malpractice liability on physician behavior, whether positive or negative. For example, the studies are unable to distinguish the separate effects of health insurance, defensive medicine that is an overreaction to the threat of liability, and cost-effective increases in the quality of care resulting from the same threat. Similarly, data on the relation between the occurrence of malpractice and the filing of lawsuits shows that there is a substantial amount of malpractice that does not result in lawsuits, but that in at least some suits claiming malpractice, there was none. In short, we do not have a precise understanding of the impact of tort liability or insurance on the provision of health care. And the data we have on the impact of malpractice on the incidence of liability for malpractice does not suggest that there is necessarily a close connection between the two.[1]

Nevertheless, virtually all of the medical malpractice reforms enacted and proposed over the past 30 or more years have been designed to reduce the scope of liability or damages payable for medical malpractice, and thereby to reduce medical malpractice liability insurance premiums. The often unstated but rarely hidden premise behind these reforms has been that nothing sufficiently important will be lost, and something important will be gained, by their enactment. The fact that many of these reforms have been enacted without any sense of what their actual impact might be on physicians or patients testifies to the centrality of insurance to this whole field. The mere potential for certain reforms to contain or reduce malpractice insurance premiums has been enough to give them credibility, and sometimes enough to get them enacted into law. But whatever the effect of these reforms may have been on physicians and patients—and even after three decades that also is not entirely unclear—over the long term, in many states malpractice insurance premiums have continued to rise, those who pay malpractice premiums have continued to protest that the premiums are too high, and demands for further reform have persisted.

In the United States we now spend nearly $2 trillion each year on health care. Yet medical malpractice liability insurance premiums for physicians total at most about $16 billion each year—less 1 percent of all health-care spending. Even adding hospitals' malpractice liability insurance premiums raises the total to about 2.5 percent of total health-care expenditures, at most. How can so comparatively minor an economic feature of our health-care system generate so much continuing, seemingly permanent, controversy?

The answer lies in the combined impact on individual physicians of medical malpractice litigation and the history and structure of health-care delivery. The formal rules governing liability for medical malpractice are strongly prodefendant. On paper physicians are given much more protection against liability than defendants in ordinary tort cases. But because of the nature of American medicine and the way medical malpractice rules are applied in practice, the law has never provided physicians with the level of protection against liability for malpractice that they have desired. Before 1960, only one out of every seven physicians experienced a malpractice claim in an entire career. Today, on average one out of every twenty physicians experiences a claim each year. Medical malpractice is a powerful example of how the underlying structure of a field can be a more important determinant of its character than the legal doctrines that purport to govern it.

It is true that malpractice insurance premiums are only a small percentage of total health-care spending. But premium levels are volatile, and they are to a large extent a charge against the income of about 1 million individual physicians, who receive only about 15 percent of all health-care revenues. So $16 billion per year in premiums has a much more significant impact than it would have if it were charged directly to 300 million patients, or were passed through to them the instant each physician received an increased insurance bill.

Ironically, however, physicians have come to occupy their vulnerable position at least in part because of their longstanding resistance to developments that could have led to a transformation in the way health care is delivered in this country—a transformation that could thereby have generated much more protection against liability than physicians now have. Instead, as we will see in this chapter, for many decades organized medicine insisted that health insurance be provided on a fee-for-service basis and that physicians' professional and economic autonomy be maintained.

This stance placed the profession in the liability setting it now occupies. By fighting to preserve its autonomy in the face of a threat from the Left in the form of possible national health insurance, and a threat from the Right by the corporate health-care business, the profession has left itself exposed to malpractice liability straight up the middle. As long as most physicians continue to operate essentially individually or in small, independent group practices in a setting otherwise dominated by governments and large business enterprises, individual medical practitioners are likely to be stuck with the liability disadvantages that naturally accompany their position.

The Rise of Modern Malpractice Liability

Anyone who looks even quickly at the history of medical malpractice liability in this country is struck by a single recurring theme: physicians complaining about the increasing incidence of malpractice suits. From before the Civil War and virtually without interruption until the present, physicians have thought that they faced crises in the number of lawsuits against them. Worthington Hooker, a Connecticut doctor, wrote as early as 1849 that "the professional reputation of medical men seems to be considered by common consent as fair game for the shafts of all, whether high or low." Although accusing a physician of malpractice was a serious charge, in Hooker's view it was nevertheless "exceedingly common to hear this charge put forth without any hesitation."[2] After a brief respite during and after the Civil War, litigation commenced again in the 1870s and continued to increase. From our standpoint today the number of suits that were brought would not appear high. But professional pride has always made physicians highly sensitive about being sued.

During much of the nineteenth century, American medicine was a heterogeneous combination of educated and uneducated physicians, homeopathic practitioners, followers of other distinct schools of thought, and quacks. Competition between these groups was reflected in malpractice suits, in which practitioners from one group rather freely testified as expert witnesses against members of the others. It was not until the last quarter of the nineteenth century that modern medical schools were founded, state licensure requirements were solidified, and college-educated, medical school–trained M.D.s began to be produced. The social status of physicians then rose, and they began to zealously guard their professional status.

The Expert Testimony Issue

At this point two factors combined to affect the scope and application of medical malpractice law. Each limited physicians' exposure to liability. First, as conventional M.D.s came to dominate the health-care scene, competition among them tended to decline, or at least to become more genteel. As a consequence, physicians' willingness to testify against each other in malpractice suits declined. Second, as a clearly discernible, discrete medical profession composed of M.D.s emerged, the courts developed more concrete rules about who was qualified to testify as an expert.

The dominant rule came to be that only a licensed practitioner from the defendant's own locality could testify as an expert in a malpractice case, because the question to which expert testimony had to be directed was whether the defendant had complied with the standards of the profession in that area. This "strict locality" rule, as it became known, constituted a serious obstacle for potential plaintiffs. A case could not go to the jury without an expert testifying for the plaintiff, and that expert had to be one of the defendant's local fellow practitioners. As the profession become more homogeneous and developed greater solidarity, securing such testimony became correspondingly more difficult. The profession was controlling not only entry into it but also legal attacks on it. To paraphrase Ben Franklin, if local physicians hung together, they would not hang separately.

Nonetheless, some malpractice suits continued to be brought, and physicians needed legal representation. Around the turn of the century liability insurers began selling insurance against the cost of defending against malpractice suits, and some medical societies provided a free defense to their members.[3] But this approach afforded no protection to the physician who settled or lost a suit and had to pay a judgment. Apparently some insurance that paid both indemnity and defense also became available shortly after the turn of the century, but it was not the dominant form of coverage for at least another decade.[4] By the 1920s, however, conventional malpractice liability insurance was not only affording the insured physician a defense against claims but also providing indemnity against liability. Because this gave conventional liability insurance a distinct advantage over mere defense insurance, purchasing liability insurance became increasingly attractive for physicians.

The spread of malpractice insurance would prove to be a singular event in this field. Widespread awareness that physicians were insured against liability eventually bolstered patients' willingness to sue and jurors' willingness to impose liability on physicians. Indeed, tort law was so concerned about this effect that the mere mention of the fact that the defendant has liability insurance has long been a ground for a mistrial in most jurisdictions. In addition, once physicians began to rely on malpractice liability insurance, as inevitably they had to, their professional well-being was placed in the hands of a market controlled by insurance companies. The volatility of that market became a major contributor to the sense of crisis that would continually affect the field beginning in the 1970s.

By the middle decades of the twentieth century, malpractice actions had become routine. Indeed, the words of the commentators of this period sound remarkably familiar to anyone who listens to contemporary complaints from physicians. A 1940 Note in the *Virginia Law Review* opened with the observation: "Actions for negligence against members of the medical profession have become increasingly frequent in recent years."[5] In 1957 a similar piece in the *Stanford Law Review* began: "Reports of meetings with prominent medical groups reflect prevalent concern among physicians over the danger to the practice of medicine posed by excessive malpractice suits."[6] Six years later the *Harvard Law Review* repeated this message in the opening sentence of its analysis: "In recent years actions and judgments for malpractice have increased startlingly."[7]

There was a countervailing reaction, however, from those who were concerned that there were too many restrictions on malpractice liability. The obstacles the law placed in the path of plaintiffs were receiving increased scrutiny. The difficulty of securing expert witnesses to testify had become a focus of criticism by plaintiffs' attorneys, who called the reluctance of physicians to testify against a colleague the "conspiracy of silence." The problem was so well known that it was observed by appellate courts. A 1951 dissent in the Supreme Court of California asserted, for example: "It is a matter of common knowledge that members of any county medical society are extremely loath to testify against each other in a malpractice case . . . physicians who are members of medical societies flock to the defense of their fellow member charged with malpractice and the plaintiff is relegated, for his expert testimony, to the occasional lone wolf or heroic soul, who for the sake of truth and justice has the courage to run the risk of ostracism by his fellow practitioners and the cancellation of his public liability insurance policy."[8] There was even some fear, whether well founded is not clear, that a physician who testified for a plaintiff would have his malpractice insurance canceled, or be expelled from membership in the local medical society, and thereby risked losing hospital admitting privileges.[9]

Doctrinal Change

Three legal developments originating in this period addressed difficulties that potential plaintiffs faced. The first was the increasing willingness of the courts to permit a plaintiff's case to go to the jury without expert testimony. This was accomplished through the doctrine res ipsa loquitur ("the thing speaks for itself"), which provides that a case can go to the jury even without any proof of a specific act of negligence, if the harm in question ordinarily occurs only because there was negligence of some sort by the defendant. In malpractice the doctrine was first applied in the most obvious of cases, where even laypeople could understand that malpractice had occurred, such as leaving a sponge in the patient's abdomen after surgery.[10] And in the precedent-setting Ybarra case in California, the doctrine also was applied to hold a group of physicians and nurses liable when the unconscious patient could not identify the particular individual whose malpractice had caused his injury.[11]

The second legal development that facilitated suits for malpractice was the abolition of charitable immunity. At common law, charities, including nonprofit hospitals, were immune from tort liability. Beginning in the 1940s and continuing for several decades, however, the courts and legislatures of dozens of states limited or wholly abolished charitable immunity.[12] This made it possible to hold hospitals liable for negligence in their own right, and to hold them vicariously liable for the negligence or malpractice of their employees. Moreover, once charitable immunity was abolished, new doctrines imposing vicarious liability on hospitals for malpractice committed by nonemployees, based on apparent and ostensible authority, developed.[13]

The demise of charitable immunity made it easier for patients to sue hospitals for malpractice. Ironically, in certain cases the new liability of nonprofit hospitals probably exposed physicians to greater liability. When hospitals could not be named as defendants, physicians' attorneys could point to the "empty chair" at the defense table and argue that the hospital, not the physician, had been responsible for the patient's injury. Once both physicians and hospitals were defendants in the same suit, however, the empty-chair argument was unavailable; yet mutual finger-pointing was likely to be counterproductive. So the presence of a hospital as a defendant in a case had at least the potential to make it more likely that the physician would be found liable along with the hospital.

The last development that facilitated malpractice suits was the erosion, and ultimately the demise, of the strict locality rule. This began with the courts' recognition that medical standards were no longer entirely local (if they ever were), and that requiring testimony from a local expert was not necessary. Some courts held that experts who had familiarized themselves with the local standard could testify. Others held that the appropriate test for liability was the standard followed by practitioners not only in the same locality as the defendant but, alternatively, in similar localities. This enabled experts from other localities to testify. Once one or the other of these approaches was adopted the logjam was broken. Eventually the courts held that medical standards were not local but national, and permitted any qualified expert to testify. The courts' recognition of national medical standards did in a sense reinforce the professional status that physicians had been seeking all along to protect. But this recognition was a sword in the hands of plaintiffs' lawyers, since now they could look nationwide for expert witnesses to testify for the clients. Indeed, it was not long before expert witnesses who no longer practiced medicine and were in the business of testifying were placing advertisements in trial lawyers' magazines.

A Mixed Picture by the 1960s

Relaxation of the restrictions on expert testimony did not, of course, mean automatic success for plaintiffs. Physicians had both formal and informal protections that remained. The most distinctive formal protection afforded to physicians was the "respectable minority," or "school-of-thought," rule. The rule provided that a physician who complied with the standard followed by a respectable minority of practitioners had not committed malpractice. This was in theory considerable legal protection—far more protection than was or is now accorded nonprofessionals, who may be found to have been negligent even if they complied with a universally followed custom within their industry.

The trouble for physicians was that the respectable minority rule had to be applied to the facts of each case, and often that required a jury. For example, suppose that the plaintiff contended through expert testimony that the treatment provided by the defendant was not reflected in the standards of a respectable school of thought. Even if the defendant's expert testified that the defendant had followed a respectable minority (or perhaps even the majority) approach, the jury still had to decide which expert to believe. There was a "battle of experts." In addition, like legal standards, medical standards tend not to come all the way down to the ground on their own, but require application to a particular set of facts. Often there was medical judgment involved in applying the relevant standard; in effect the battling experts offered conflicting testimony about the appropriate application of the same standard to the situation the defendant had faced. The experts in this situation did not necessarily invoke different standards, but instead disagreed about the appropriate application of the same standard. This kind of conflict could only be resolved by the jury.

Finally, even if both sides agreed on the applicable standard and on its proper application, there might be a question of fact whether the defendant had followed that standard or whether his failure to follow the standard had caused the plaintiff's harm. These issues also had to be resolved by the jury. In all these instances, rules that were intended to provide physicians in malpractice cases with greater protection than was provided to ordinary, nonprofessional defendants were transformed into mere jury instructions that the jury that might or might not understand, and might or might not apply accurately. A physician therefore could be held liable notwithstanding the formal legal protections the law purported to provide him.

Nonetheless, physicians had informal protections against malpractice suits that might also protect them. The potentially strongest of these was their relationship with their patients. In its most idealized version, the image of the benevolent and self-sacrificing family doctor who made a house call to see a sick child on a stormy night conjured up someone patients were not inclined to sue. For many decades, however, each generation of patients seemed to believe that this ideal type of physician had once been the norm and had only just recently disappeared. As long ago as 1940 a commentator decried "the gradual disappearance of the family doctor," who "enjoyed a comparative immunity from legal action as a result of personal relationship." This had been replaced by "impersonal efficiency," which had "forced the physician's efforts to stand alone in the light of scientific merit, unprotected by the armor of friendship."[14]

In retrospect this complaint seems almost quaint. In recent decades the rise of professional specialization, the growth of medical technology, and the advent of managed health care have driven a wedge between physicians and patients that would have been unimaginable 70 years ago. But the commentator from the 1940s was prescient in his concern. Changes in the health-care environment during the ensuing decades have heavily influenced the context in which malpractice suits arise.

By the 1960s the new legal rules, modern patient attitudes, and an increasingly able plaintiffs' bar (whose rise I described in Chapter 3) were all in place. The stage was set for an escalation in the number of malpractice suits and for increases in the size of settlements and verdicts. Physicians would of course have to rely heavily on malpractice insurance to cushion the shock that changes in their liability exposure would bring. They would soon find, however, that the volatility of the market for malpractice insurance would prove to be perhaps the most troubling feature of the new malpractice world in which they practiced medicine. Without any institutional home or corporate umbrella to shield individual physicians from this volatility, their small businesses would be periodically disrupted by unexpected and difficult-to-distribute insurance costs, at the same time that their professional independence was being challenged. How they came to be in this predicament is the next part of the story.

Health Insurance and the Structure of American Medicine

For much of the twentieth century, organized medicine—in particular the American Medical Association (AMA)—fought against what it considered to be two significant threats to its members. The first threat was that national health insurance would be mandated and perhaps financed by the federal government. The second threat was that instead some form of private, prepaid health-care insurance would develop that would pay physicians only on a per-patient basis, rather than permitting them to charge their own individual fees for each medical service they provided to a patient. In each case the AMA's goals were essentially the same: to maintain physicians' right to set their own charges for their services and to preserve professional autonomy against the possibility that outside entities would influence or control how physicians practiced medicine.

The physicians' strongly held view was that their own professional medical expertise, not economic considerations or government (through what they called "socialized medicine") should determine what was best for patients. In combination with other forces, for many decades physicians were largely successful in their opposition to both national health insurance and prepaid health care. Their slogan was "no third party," by which they meant that they opposed any third party, such as government or a health insurer, who would stand between the physician and patient, controlling what care was provided or what the physician charged for that care.[15]

By the 1920s physicians had succeeded in placing themselves at the core of American medicine. Professional autonomy helped fuel their incomes by severely limiting outside control of what treatment they provided and what prices they charged, and it enhanced their social stature. They had carved out a highly favorable place for themselves in the health-care structure. Further, physicians bore no responsibility for financing the hospitals where so much of their services were provided and their patient revenue was earned. Instead, individual communities provided and financed hospitals in which physicians could practice. For decades physicians had maintained and solidified their status as independent contractors, only loosely controlled by hospitals but with the privilege of admitting their patients to hospitals. It was as if airplane pilots were independent contractors, permitted to charge passengers a separate fee for flying on airplanes that were supplied free of charge to the pilots. One of the costs individual physicians paid for this kind of independence, however, was their continued personal exposure to liability for medical malpractice. But in the era before the series of malpractice crises that first occurred in the mid-1970s, malpractice liability was considered a minor threat compared to national health insurance and prepaid care.

During the same decades the employment-based system of health insurance began to develop. In the 1930s group hospital insurance was offered to employers by the incipient, not-for-profit Blue Cross organizations that were developed with the support of the American Hospital Association.

The Blue Cross hospital insurance approach, however, had an Achilles' heel that would eventually lead to the commercialization of health insurance and the consequent decline of medical autonomy. Blue Cross used what it called "community rating" to set premiums. The price of Blue Cross insurance did not vary with the degree of risk posed by insured individuals or groups. The entire "community" was charged the same rates (actually one rate for individuals and one for families), since Blue Cross had been founded with the goal of providing a service to the community.[16]

When medical insurance covering physicians' (as distinguished from hospital) charges began to spread soon thereafter, a physician-sponsored nonprofit insurer called Blue Shield also employed community rating. At an abstract level the substantial socialization of risk entailed in community rating was objectionable to organized medicine, but the approach was tolerated because the Blues provided fee-for-service coverage only. Under a fee-for-service arrangement, the physician decides what care to provide, and the insurer pays for the care on a service-by-service basis, exercising little or no supervision over the physician's treatment decisions. Because the Blues provided fee-for-service coverage, they never threatened organized medicine with the prospect of offering prepaid health care.

The nonprofit Blues' use of community rating created an opportunity for commercial insurers, which also began to offer hospital and medical insurance in the late 1930s. During World War II demand for both forms of health insurance increased, as employers increasingly offered coverage in order to attract and retain employees, whom they could not provide with wage increases because of inflation controls. The commercial insurers were not burdened by the Blues' ethos and therefore felt no need to charge community rates. As a result, the commercial insurers could charge lower premiums to groups comprised largely of low-risk individuals, such as young workers. Eventually the Blues would find it impossible to compete with the commercial insurers, who could "skim" the good risks from the pool of potential customers and leave the Blues with the community-rated, higher-risk individuals and groups.

Naturally, the resulting cycle of adverse selection kept raising the Blues' community rates. By the 1950s community rating therefore had to be left behind. Like the commercial insurers, the Blues began to charge the highest risks the highest rates. It was of course the elderly who fell disproportionately into this category. Some new method of subsidizing these highest risks would be necessary, or many of them would be left without affordable coverage. Once the subsidy that community rating had provided to the elderly was withdrawn, the enactment of some other type of health insurance program for this group was in a sense inevitable. The solution ultimately adopted was Medicare, a social security–based federal health insurance program, which since 1965 has covered nearly the entire population of people over the age of 65.

With the most significant group of high risks removed from the private insurance pool, and with the American economy expanding, the private health insurance system grew substantially during the next decade. By the 1970s the combined private and public systems of health insurance had grown to a point where over 80 percent of the U.S. population had health insurance of some sort. There was coverage for a very substantial majority of the population, and on a fee-for-service basis.

This system was a bonanza for the medical profession. The Hill-Burton Act, enacted after World War II, financed hospital construction; the National Institutes of Health financed biomedical research; medical schools graduated M.D.s who were eager to train as residents in an increasing array of medical specialties. And as the availability of hospital and medical insurance increased, so did the demand for health care. The fee-for-service basis of this insurance enabled physicians to determine with comparative independence what tests to order, what treatment to provide, and what to charge. Only a loose "ordinary and necessary charges" standard placed a limit on what health insurers would pay for physicians' services; and the more physicians charged for any given service, the higher the average "ordinary" charge became. Nor did patients have much incentive to optimize the amount of care they consumed, for they paid only nominal deductibles for outpatient services. Eventually the inflationary effect of this "third-party payor" problem, as it was called at the time, would culminate in the rise of managed care and the restructuring of the health insurance system. But it took several decades before the system had to fall under its own weight.

A Changing Malpractice Environment

Between 1960 and 1980, national personal medical expenditures increased from $21 billion to $204 billion—an increase of 360 percent, adjusted for inflation.[17] The massive increases in the amount of health care that was being provided and in the technologies that were employed for diagnosis and treatment both raised patients' expectations and created more opportunities for unsuccessful treatment and patient disappointment. When a particular disease or condition cannot be effectively treated or cured, patient expectations are low. After effective treatment is introduced and cure is possible, however, treatment can be poorly provided, and even properly provided treatment can fail to produce results that satisfy patient expectations. Paradoxically, then, the greater the potential effectiveness of medicine, the greater the potential for malpractice and for malpractice claims.

More Suits and More Expensive Insurance

The natural result was a long-term increase in the incidence of malpractice suits. One survey of claims closed in 1970 showed that there had been a 76 percent increase in claim frequency between 1960 and 1968. The leading malpractice insurer during this period, St. Paul Fire & Marine Insurance Company, found that it had one claim pending for every 23 physicians it insured in 1970, but that by 1975 it had one claim pending for every 8 insured physicians.[18] And the increases continued. From 1980 to 1984, national claim frequency increased 56 percent. In that year St. Paul experienced 16.5 claims for every 100 insured physicians.[19] Not only claim frequency but also claim severity (the amount paid for a claim) increased. The average amount paid for a claim in New York increased from $46,000 in 1980 to $104,000 in 1984, and the countrywide increase was similar.[20]

The rising cost of malpractice insurance tracked these increases in both claim frequency and severity. From 1960 to 1980, for example, total premiums paid for medical malpractice insurance increased from $56 million to $1.2 billion.[21] The postwar health-care boom thus had a darker side for physicians. Clearly, the increasing cost of malpractice liability was tracking the increasing cost and consumption of health care.

In Chapter 3 I discussed the effect of rising health-care costs on auto liability settlements. Because settlement offers in routine tort cases typically are calculated by multiplying medical expenses by a factor of three or four, an increase in claimants' average medical expenses tends to increase settlements by a multiple of that increase. But most medical malpractice cases are not routine. They must involve sizable potential damages in order to justify an attorney's investment in them. Today, for example, the rule of thumb is that a case must be worth at least $50,000 for a malpractice attorney to take it. Even 40 years ago there were few "nuisance" malpractice cases. Consequently, the multiplier effect probably had much less influence on malpractice settlements, few of which involved routine claims, than it had on auto settlements. Nonetheless, the impact of this effect on rising malpractice costs during the 1970s and 1980s should not be entirely discounted. Increases in medical costs and in the amount of medical care consumed probably had at least something of a multiplier effect on the amounts paid for malpractice settlements during this period.

Further, although the aggregate increase in the cost of malpractice insurance during this 20-year period was staggering, physicians were not all affected in the same way. Those who practiced in urban areas and heavily populated states tended to be charged higher premiums, because rates of suit were higher in these places. And physicians who practiced in what had turned out to be high-risk specialties paid substantially more than those who were in low-risk fields. Most malpractice insurers divided policyholders into five premium classes on this basis. Surgical specialties were in the high-risk classes, and nonsurgical specialties in the lower-risk classes. Obstetricians and neurosurgeons, for example, tended to pay the highest premiums, and internists and pediatricians the lowest. It is true that there was a rough correspondence between a specialty's income level and the size of its malpractice premiums, but only that. An obstetrician with an inner-city practice who treated a large number of charity patients could find that her malpractice premiums were a substantial percentage of her total income.

Moreover, there was very little experience-rating on top of these classifications. Whatever a policyholder's risk class, even after he or she had been subjected to a claim, next year's premium was often no higher, or only modestly higher, than it would have been had the claim not been made. There were, it was thought, too many unjustified claims to warrant experience-rating. In addition, because only a handful of claims were likely be made against any given physician during an entire career, the fact that a claim had been made against a particular physician was only modest evidence of the increased probability that claims would be made against him in the future at a rate that was above average. Experience-rating, therefore, could reliably play only a minor role in the premium structure. It was primarily a physician's specialty and the place where he or she practiced that determined premium levels.

As a consequence, when physicians who had been sued for malpractice received premium increases in the 1970s, they felt aggrieved by what they regarded as the failure of their malpractice insurers to treat them as individuals. But physicians reserved even greater hostility for the legal system.

They blamed tort law and the judicial system for their increasing exposure to malpractice liability, and eventually sought the enactment of tort reforms that they thought would reduce liability and therefore contain their malpractice premiums.

Caught between Two Worlds

Whether physicians were correct to blame the legal system for their troubles is open to debate. On the one hand, physicians were not incorrect to hold the legal system responsible for the increasingly litigious malpractice climate that emerged during this period. The legal doctrines and practices that made these changes possible were put in place and applied by the legal system, and until the mid-1970s tort reforms were not even seriously proposed. The legal system had changed in a way that facilitated malpractice litigation, and those changes were in place when the other forces that caused an increase in litigation took hold.

On the other hand, it was too easy for physicians to ignore the context in which all this took place. Placing exclusive blame on the legal system for physicians' increased exposure to the threat of malpractice liability that emerged during this period ignored the economic and institutional influences for which the medical profession itself was heavily responsible. After all, the forces that were ultimately responsible for the increases originated as much outside the legal system as within it. Just as a legal system with different features might have prevented a series of malpractice "crises" from arising, a different health-care or health insurance system might have done so as well.

Indeed, if the health-care system that physicians had worked so hard to preserve had developed differently, then malpractice liability might have assumed a far more benevolent character for physicians. A different health-care system might well have provided physicians with the protections against liability that they lacked when the increase in malpractice litigation occurred during the 1960s and 1970s. It seems quite plausible that malpractice liability would have played a far less important role in a system of national health insurance than it played in the system that existed at that time.

For example, if by 1970 there had been guaranteed health care through national health insurance, surrendering or limiting the right to sue for malpractice might well have been regarded as a fair price for patients to pay in return for this social welfare benefit. Correspondingly, physicians had long been so opposed to what they called "socialized medicine" that it seems highly likely that they would have received some kind of quid pro quo for either acquiescing in national health care or having it crammed down their throats. Reduced liability for malpractice certainly might have been part of the overall package. Even apart from the practical politics that would have been involved, the principles that support imposing tort liability within an essentially private system of health care would not necessarily have transposed directly onto a system of universal government-provided or guaranteed health insurance. With medical expenses resulting from the adverse effects of treatment automatically covered for all, it seems doubtful that the compensatory aim of malpractice liability would have been given the same priority it now enjoys. One of the costs physicians may have paid to repeatedly defeat efforts to create a national health insurance system, therefore, may well have been the preservation of their liability for malpractice.

Similarly, the ethos surrounding a system of privately financed prepaid health care of the sort that physicians also long opposed might well have led to a much milder malpractice liability climate, at least for individual physicians. Such a system might have led much earlier to the institutionalization of health-care delivery that is now a fixture of the health-care scene. But if that institutionalization had been accomplished before the explosion of malpractice liability that began in the late 1960s, there probably would been have a shift in the focus of malpractice liability as well. If physicians' professional autonomy had diminished once there was widespread prepaid health care, as they feared it would, then the focus of malpractice liability also would likely have migrated from the individual physician to the organizations that controlled the delivery of health care—hospitals, health insurers, and what we would now call managed care organizations. Channeling the cost of malpractice liability through these organizations rather than through individual physicians would have merged the cost of liability into the web of contractual arrangements that physicians would have had with these organizations, as well as making it more feasible for the organizations to control the factors that give rise to malpractice and malpractice suits.

What happened instead was that physicians succeeded in preserving their autonomy and authority during the period of great expansions in the health-care system and in the incidence of health insurance. The very expansions that so benefited physicians then led to reforms that restricted their autonomy through attempts to control escalating costs. But while physicians' autonomy was being restricted in the service of cost control, little was done to curb their exposure to liability.

From 1965 to 1985, for example, national health-care expenditures rose from $42 billion to $419 billion per year, and from 6.1 percent of gross domestic product to 10.4 percent.[22] Under the fee-for-service health insurance that financed so much of this expansion, the medical treatment and financing functions had been separate and independent of each other. Physicians decided what treatment was appropriate, and after treatment had been provided, health insurers decided whether to pay for it—and normally they did pay. By the late 1980s expansion of the amount of medical treatment that was provided and paid for by insurers as a matter of course had led to such severe inflation of health-care costs that managed care emerged in a major way. Under managed care, the treatment and financing decisions were increasingly made, or at least much more heavily influenced than in the past, by the same entity—a managed-care organization that was normally nothing more or less than a health insurer.

By the mid-1990s, when this evolution was in full force, physicians were complaining bitterly about managed care: it restricted their autonomy and limited the availability of what they considered proper care for their patients. Increasingly, medical decisions were influenced or controlled by health insurers and other managed-care organizations, rather than exclusively by treating physicians. The changes in the institutional structure and financing of health care that organized medicine had successfully opposed for many years were now coming to pass despite their opposition. What amounted to prepaid health care was being adopted for the vast majority of their patients, and they could do little to prevent it. But the individual treating physician remained the focal point of liability for providing substandard care—that is, the focal point of liability for malpractice.

In short, at the same time that the health care system was expanding from roughly 1965 to 1990, the forces that affected malpractice liability were left free to operate essentially without the limitations that might have operated in a different health insurance context. As a consequence, liability expanded dramatically. When managed care was eventually introduced, the malpractice liability genie had long before been let out of the bottle. A robust system of liability for malpractice had by then been operating for several decades, and it was far more difficult to shrink the scope of liability than it would have been to prevent the expansion of liability in the first place. Physicians thus got what was for them the worst of both worlds: the restrictions on their autonomy that came with managed care, and the continued exposure to liability for malpractice that had been part of the price they had paid for preserving their autonomy.

In fact, physicians were hit with triple trouble. The problem for them under the malpractice system was not only the loss of their autonomy or the threat of liability but also the volatility and potential unreliability of malpractice insurance. The relation between malpractice liability and insurance against that liability had become complex. The price of insurance was unstable, and physicians could not always count on its availability. The controversy over malpractice liability that emerged in the 1970s and continues to this day has therefore focused not only on the substance of liability rules but also on the role played by insurance against that liability.

The Insurance Cycle and the Continuing Problem of Volatility

Certain forms of liability insurance are highly cyclical. They are subject to periodic swings in the price and availability of coverage. During the "soft" part of the cycle, premiums are comparatively low, policy terms are expansive, and coverage is readily available. In contrast, during the "hard" part of the cycle, premiums rise quickly and steeply, policy terms are sometimes less favorable, and coverage is harder to obtain.

The medical malpractice liability insurance market is especially cyclical in these respects. Three times since 1970 this market has experienced a prolonged soft period followed by a sudden shift to a hard market. The first such shift occurred around 1975, the second around 1985, and the third in 2001 and 2002. Each was characterized at the time as a "crisis." The second "crisis," which was the most severe of the three, affected not only malpractice insurance but a number of other forms of liability insurance as well, most notably the Commercial General Liability insurance (CGL) coverage sold to all American businesses. The effects of each crisis reverberated through the tort and insurance systems for years after the immediate disruptions they caused had quieted down.

Confronting the Cycle

Two factors make the insurance cycle especially disruptive for physicians. First, physicians are predominantly sole practitioners or members of relatively small practice groups. They engage in little capital reserving and they are not capable of, or at least do not practice, the kind of long-term financial planning that larger businesses characteristically can do. Sudden increases in malpractice premiums therefore create cash-flow shocks for physicians.

Second, with the rise of public and private health insurance, over time physicians have come increasingly to rely on these sources of reimbursement for payment of their fees. These sources, however, do not easily or quickly react to steep increases in physicians' charges. Consequently, when the insurance cycle turns hard and premiums for medical malpractice insurance skyrocket, at least over the short term physicians cannot pass these costs through to health insurers and must pay increased insurance costs out of their current income. In extreme cases the amount of these increases has been $100,000 or more in a single year—a sizable new expense to take out of the income of even the highly paid surgeons who have experienced increases of this magnitude.

These kinds of cash-flow disruptions could be somewhat ameliorated if physicians were able to plan for occasionally large premium increases and set aside reserves in anticipation of them. But of course part of what characterizes the insurance cycle is the inability of insurers themselves to do this kind of planning. Predicting the increases in premiums that occur during the hard part of the cycle is what insurers themselves seem unable to do with any reliability. It is therefore difficult to blame physicians for failing to reserve funds in anticipation of this eventuality.

To understand the insurance cycle, it is critically important to recognize the difference between the short-term and the long-term causes of changes in the price of malpractice insurance. Over the long term, the most significant influence on the cost of malpractice insurance, overwhelmingly, is the cost of defending against and paying malpractice claims. Like most markets, the market for malpractice insurance has flaws, but the effects of these flaws tend to be felt largely over the short term. Over the long term, fundamental forces are dominant. Simply put, the more the underlying cost of malpractice liability increases, the more the cost of malpractice liability insurance will increase.

The short-term problem is that increases in insurance premiums are not smooth and steady, but lumpy. Like the movements of the earth's tectonic plates that cause earthquakes, cost pressure seems to build up without any detectable price manifestation, until that pressure is sufficient to cause a major change in premium levels. Then premiums leap upward in a short period of time. A "crisis" is declared to exist, and a search for its cause, or causes, is launched.

There is a long-running debate in the economic and legal literature about the identity and nature of the causes of the short-term volatility that the insurance cycle reflects. (Much of the debate focuses on technical considerations that are not necessary to explore here. I discuss some of these considerations in the next chapter, in which the crisis of the mid-1980s that affected not only medical malpractice but also products liability figures prominently.) In medical malpractice, several factors seem most significant.[23] First, malpractice liability insurance is a "long tail" line of coverage. That is, claims are not paid until a comparatively long time after coverage is sold. Injuries may not be discovered immediately, and in any event malpractice cases are often complex and take a longer time to develop and resolve than simple auto accidents or slip-and-fall claims. The average claim is not paid or resolved for seven or more years after a policy is sold.

Consequently, in setting premiums, insurers must make predictions about how each of the factors that is a component of the ultimate costs they expect to incur will develop over the period during which claims against a given policy or set of policies are made and paid. One set of components involves claim costs and expenses. Since these all involve the future, it is no surprise that in setting premiums insurers sometimes underestimate, and sometimes overestimate, these future costs. In fact, during some years there have been sizable increases in claim frequency, followed by years with more normal increases, a change for which no one has provided an entirely satisfactory explanation.

If these errors in prediction were randomly distributed, we would see fluctuation, but not systemic cyclicality, in the market. We would expect a normal distribution of years showing a profit and years showing a loss, with corresponding premium increases and decreases adjusted to take account of claim and expense information as it accumulated. Consequently, mere difficulty in predicting the future incidence of claims cannot explain the cycle, though it probably contributes to it.

Another component of expected profit or loss from an insurer's operations, however, is investment income. Insurers hold premiums for a considerable period of time, earning investment income on these premiums while they hold them. Because insurers anticipate earning such income on invested premiums, and because they know that their competitors do the same, they take anticipated investment income into account in setting premiums. During periods when investment income is projected to be high, premiums can be correspondingly lower than they would be otherwise.

In contrast, when a bubble in a bull market for stocks bursts, or there is a long-term decline in investment returns, then anticipated investment income declines, and premiums must rise. There also appears to be a tendency for insurers to delay such increases as long as possible, in part out of pure concern for maintaining market share (no insurer wants to be the first to raise premiums) and in part because of tax considerations that make it attractive to retain capital and to finance the maintenance of market share out of capital surplus. But eventually there are substantial premium increases that mark the beginning of a hard market.

Despite the fact that the cycle has run its course three times in the last 40 years, each time the market turns hard there is surprise and outrage from the medical community. Instead of seeing the cycle as the inevitable byproduct of a very distinct and limited market, physicians seek to lay the blame for sharply increased premiums on the institutions that they believe could be brought under control if only we had the political will to do so. Some of the physicians' outrage is directed at the liability insurance industry, which is seen as profiteering at physicians' expense. But since so many of the malpractice insurers are state-based mutual companies owned by physicians themselves (more on this below), this attack tends to be muted and unpersuasive. Moreover, if so much profit was available from selling malpractice insurance, it is difficult to see why St. Paul, the industry leader in the field of malpractice insurance for so many years, withdrew from the market entirely just a few years ago. The one thing we can be sure that a company earning supercompetitive profits does not do is refuse to sell its product.

The remainder of physicians' outrage about the steep premium increases they face every decade or so is therefore directed at the tort system. As a result it is during the periods of "crisis" following the turn from a soft to a hard market that reform occurs. There have been three rounds of tort and insurance reform following the insurance cycles of the last three decades. They are instructive not only for what they have accomplished but also for what they have not been able to accomplish. The reforms have to some extent moderated increases in the frequency and severity of malpractice claims, but they have not eliminated premium increases, and they have done little to influence the insurance cycle.

Round One: The Crisis of the Mid-1970s

Medical malpractice claims increased throughout the 1960s, and they continued to do so during the first few years of the 1970s. The initial malpractice crisis of the modern era occurred during the mid-1970s, when premiums skyrocketed and significant proposals for reform began to appear. This was not simply the first modern malpractice crisis. It also marked the first time that sustained attention was devoted to fashioning legislative reform that modified tort doctrine but preserved the basic contours of liability.

INSURANCE REFORM.   The first adjustment malpractice insurers made at this time was a concession to the reality that they were no longer able to predict the frequency and severity of medical malpractice claims with sufficient reliability. In response to this concern, insurers altered what their policies covered so as to make prediction more feasible. But in doing this the insurers shifted the risk of an uncertain claim future back to their policyholders. They solved their own problem by making it the physician's problem.

Until the mid-1970s, insurers had sold "occurrence-based" malpractice policies, which covered all liability arising out of an injury that occurred during the policy year, regardless of when a suit alleging that the policyholder was liable for causing that injury was instituted. An injury that occurred today but was not discovered for decades could in theory result in a malpractice claim 30 years from now. But that claim would be covered under the malpractice policy issued this year. Pricing such occurrence policies, which in theory provide coverage until the end of time, can be a speculative enterprise, especially in a time of legal or economic transition.

Occurrence policies nevertheless function well enough, even in the face of this potential unpredictability, when they cover ordinary tort claims such as auto accidents, which must be brought within a specified number of years after injury. Only the near future need be predicted in order to set premiums for such policies, and unless the legal and claim environment is changing very rapidly, predicting the next few years' environment usually is feasible.

But by the 1970s, two factors undermined insurers' confidence in their ability to predict the future in a way that made pricing occurrence policies feasible. First, state statutes of limitations for bringing malpractice claims have long been interpreted to contain an exception for undiscovered injury. And medical treatment is more likely than most other forms of activity to result in injury that is not immediately discovered, or not immediately discovered to be the result of malpractice. In addition, well into the 1970s, statutes of limitations for bringing a malpractice action typically did not apply to children until they reached the age of majority. So suits by those allegedly injured by malpractice when they were children could be brought many years after the policy covering liability for that injury was sold. When there were few such suits, this uncertainty was manageable. But as the frequency of suits increased, the threat of such suits became more problematic.

Second, in the early 1970s there were unexpected increases in malpractice claims brought on, among other things, by the spread of health insurance, the rise of the consumer movement, and the growing expertise of the plaintiffs' bar. By this time, therefore, the frequency at which malpractice claims were being brought, and the amounts that had to be paid in settlement or judgment for those claims, had been increasing at rates that insurers had not predicted and were increasingly less confident that they could predict.

Insurers therefore introduced a new product that was designed to mitigate their prediction problems. They shifted from occurrence policies to a new form of coverage they called "claims-made" insurance. The new claims-made policies covered all liability arising out of claims made this year, but this year only. To set a price for a claims-made policy, an insurer therefore needed to predict only the incidence and ultimate severity of claims that would be made against the policyholder during the next policy year. Since what happened last year is a much better predictor of what will happen next year than of what will happen seven, or ten, or more years from now, the claims-made policy made the insurer's premium-setting task much easier.

But the very uncertainty that the shift to claims-made coverage reduced for malpractice insurers it transferred to their physician-policyholders. Under occurrence coverage the insurer bears the lion's share of the risk of an uncertain claims future. The insurer bears the risk that there will be changes in liability rules or economic conditions that intervene between the time it sets a price for coverage of liability arising out of injury during this year's policy period and the time that liability for that injury is imposed, no matter how many years later. In contrast, under claims-made coverage the insurer bears only the risk that such changes will influence claims made against the policyholder during the policy year. The impact of developments that would not have been predicted today, but that would nevertheless have been covered by this year's occurrence policy for a fixed premium, instead find their way into future, potentially much greater, claims-made premiums. In short, claims-made coverage provides less actual insurance than occurrence coverage. Yet the coverage provided by claims-made policies is all many physicians were able to obtain from the mid-1970s onward.

After the crisis struck, insurance commissioners in some states, at the behest of physicians, refused to approve steeply increased premium rates for occurrence policies. Others refused to approve requests by malpractice insurers to shift from selling occurrence-based to claims-made policies. This was in a sense the insurance commissioners' effort to see whether the insurers were bluffing, or at least to show physicians that they were calling the insurers' bluff. The response in at least some states showed that the insurers were not bluffing. They simply refused to sell any form of malpractice coverage in those states. Physicians then faced the possibility of being unable to obtain coverage at all. A reform that was to have an important impact reacted to these withdrawals by authorizing the establishment of physician-owned mutual insurance companies. These companies—"bedpan mutuals," as they were often nicknamed—stepped into the vacuum and began to write coverage. The conduct and profitability of these companies would later serve as a kind of control group when accusations of price-gouging were leveled at the commercial carriers who remained in or returned to the market. If the bedpan mutuals were selling only claims-made coverage and charging premiums that were just as high as the premiums the commercial carriers charged, it was more difficult to credibly accuse the latter of price-gouging and other anticompetitive behavior.

It turned out, however, that the issue was a bit more complicated than this. Many of the bedpan mutuals were so new and had such limited assets that they could not prudently bear all the liability risk they had covered. These companies therefore were forced to reinsure portions of this risk. In fixing their premiums, they anticipated their reinsurance costs, which were set by commercial reinsurers. And the prices for commercial reinsurance were set with a view to the same kinds of uncertainty about the future that had caused primary malpractice insurers to withdraw from the market when they were not permitted to raise premiums or shift to claims-made. So the premiums charged by the bedpan mutuals probably were not as neutral a measure of what constituted a fair premium as might have been supposed at the time.

In any event, the shift from occurrence to claims-made coverage never enhanced predictability to as great an extent as its proponents may have hoped. At any given point in the years after a policy has been sold, at most only 20 percent more losses have been incurred under claims-made than under occurrence policies. And after more than about six years after sale, the difference shrinks to about 10 percent.[24] As a consequence, even after malpractice insurers shifted to claims-made policies, prediction problems continued to plague them. And from time to time there would still be steep increases in claims-made premiums, as the market moved from the soft to the hard portion of the insurance cycle.

TORT REFORM.   The premium increases and shift to claims-made coverage that occurred in the mid-1970s led local medical societies and the insurance industry to descend on state legislatures and lobby for reform as they never had before. In response, nearly every state had enacted malpractice reform legislation of some sort by 1980. Interestingly, few of these reforms affected the actual standards governing liability. One popular reform was the institution of nonbinding review by a screening panel, typically composed of a physician, an attorney, and a third party. The idea behind this approach was to give the parties a realistic sense of the merits of the case and thereby to encourage settlement.[25] But there is no evidence that screening panels ever had this effect.

The most prominent of the reforms instead modified the measure of damages available in a successful case. And of these, placing a ceiling on the amount of damages that could be awarded for pain and suffering—typically $250,000—was by far the most common reform. Over the years some additional states have enacted ceilings, and some courts have declared their state's ceiling unconstitutional.[26] The idea behind a ceiling is both that it will reduce the amounts awarded in serious injury cases and will make it less likely that certain marginal suits involving serious injuries will be brought at all. It might be worth it to a plaintiff's attorney to take a case with a 5 percent chance of recovering $2 million, but not a case worth a maximum of $250,000 for pain and suffering. So the idea was that, among other things, a ceiling would help to control malpractice insurance costs.

Although the impact of ceilings is difficult to measure reliably, studies modeling the effect of the reforms show that the enactment of ceilings on pain and suffering damages probably had the effect of depressing settlements and judgments to between 15 and 20 percent below the levels they would otherwise have reached.[27] Another common reform, reversing the collateral-source rule that permitted recovery of both tort damages and first-party insurance, seemed to have a similar, though probably lesser, impact. The other reforms that were enacted, such as the mandatory use of screening panels and efforts to control attorneys' contingent fees, had less effect or no effect at all.[28]

WHY DID INSURERS SUPPORT TORT REFORM?   Malpractice insurers supported tort reforms of all sorts, but they put the most muscle behind the enactment of ceilings on the recovery of damages, especially for pain and suffering. The insurers' motive in supporting such ceilings is worth exploring, because this position may seem contrary to their own interest. After all, limiting the amount of damages a plaintiff can recover in a lawsuit reduces demand for a liability insurer's product. Why then did insurers support reforms whose effect would be to reduce their revenue? There are a number of possible explanations.

First, commercial insurers may have felt politically compelled to support reforms that their customers supported, especially because the insurers were themselves the subject of criticism at the time. Supporting tort reform, and especially ceilings on damages, helped to deflect this criticism away from the insurers and onto lawyers and the tort system. And the support of mutual insurers controlled by physicians was of course self-explanatory.

Second, one element of the unpredictability associated with malpractice liability is the amount of damages that are likely to be awarded. Pain and suffering awards exhibit considerably more variability than awards for out-of-pocket loss, which are more subject to objective proof. Liability insurers may have viewed the loss of revenue resulting from placing a ceiling on pain and suffering damages to be a price worth paying in order to enhance the predictability of their costs.

Third, as we saw in Chapter 3 in connection with proposals for mandatory auto liability insurance, insurers are always concerned about the prospect that their rates will be regulated in a manner that denies them what they regard as a fair profit. A damages ceiling that helped to limit increases in malpractice premiums could cost insurers revenue, but the enactment of a ceiling might also help them to moderate premium increases and thereby fend off efforts at more severe rate regulation than they were then facing.

Finally, ceilings would have reduced insurers' costs under already-sold policies. They might have thought that this saving would outweigh the loss of revenue they would experience in the sale of future policies. To the extent that management was more concerned with achieving short-term profit than building long-term revenue, the tradeoff would have been viewed even more favorably.

Whatever the reason, insurers, along with the physicians they insured, were able to secure at least some reform legislation in most states. But despite these reforms, it would be less than a decade before another crisis struck.

Round Two: The Crisis of the Mid-1980s

In the years after the crisis of the mid-1970s the hard cycle turned soft, perhaps a bit as a result of the tort reforms enacted during this period, but in all probability in large part because of the steep increases in interest rates that occurred during the oil crisis of the late 1970s. Interest rates stayed at nearly historic highs well into the mid-1980s, and insurers competed for premiums they could invest at double-digit rates of return. Because of this competition, premiums did not increase. General liability insurers were later accused of having engaged in what critics called "cash-flow underwriting"—clamoring to sell insurance to anyone who would buy it, regardless of the degree of risk the applicant posed, in order to get hold of premium dollars to invest. Some malpractice insurers probably had engaged in the same kind of conduct.

By the mid-1980s some of these chickens came home to roost. It turned out that the frequency and severity of malpractice suits had been increasing in at least some of the years following the last crisis, but that premiums had not kept pace with these increases. Extraordinarily high interest rates and the competition among insurers that resulted had been masking an increase in the underlying costs on which the long-term price of malpractice insurance depends. When interest rates finally began to fall, this effect was revealed.

In addition, tax reform was coming. For several years beginning around 1984, insurers had been expecting closure of the loophole in the Internal Revenue Code that permitted insurers to deduct reserves for unpaid claims without discounting them to present value. During the several-year run-up to this tax reform, many insurers seem to have "discovered" that their reserves had been inadequate, and they strengthened (i.e., increased) them, just coincidentally obtaining the tax advantage that they were about to lose if they did not use it then.[29] The loophole was finally closed by what became the Tax Reform Act of 1986.

The special reserve-strengthening in which insurers engaged prior to 1986 had the effect of reducing the amount of capital that was available to stand behind insurers' obligations going forward. Since capital is the raw material of insurance, the result was a shrinkage in the supply of coverage. Moreover, for insurers who sold more than malpractice insurance, their portfolio of risks had become less diversified, since malpractice reserves, having perhaps the longest tail on claim development of any line of insurance, had been strengthened disproportionately to other forms of coverage. Selling malpractice insurance had therefore become less attractive as compared to other forms of insurance.[30]

The impact of these developments on the supply side of the malpractice insurance market was twofold. First, because there was less malpractice insurance available to be sold, it became more difficult to obtain malpractice insurance. In some places for a period of time the highest-risk specialists, especially obstetricians, could not obtain coverage at any price. Second, the price of the coverage that was available skyrocketed. In 1985 and 1986, premiums increased as much as several hundred percent from one policy year to the next.

In contrast to the crisis of the mid-1970s, this time malpractice was not the only line of insurance affected. General liability insurance sold to businesses of all sorts experienced the same capacity shortages and premium increases, and for roughly the same reasons. Many municipalities, daycare centers, and product manufactures found that for a time that they could not obtain any liability insurance, or could obtain it only at a steeply increased price. There was prolonged national concern about liability insurance for the first time in history. *Time* magazine ran a cover story on the problem. As a consequence, there was a much more broad-based movement for tort reform than in the 1970s; there was clamor not just for the protection of physicians, but for wholesale change.

Nonetheless, ultimately the major impact of the crisis was the enactment of more reform of tort doctrine. Over 40 states enacted tort reform statutes of general application for the first time in their history. Among others, physicians were the beneficiaries of this legislation. Once again, however, the major reforms affected the measure of damages that were recoverable in tort suits rather liability standards. And once again the most prominent such reform was the enactment of a ceiling on pain and suffering damages. By 1988, 33 states had adopted damages ceilings of some sort.

It would take some time before these reforms could exercise influence and their impact could be assessed. Eventually the data would show that, again with the exception of ceilings on pain and suffering damages and reform of the collateral source rule, which had substantial impacts, each individual reform had only a minor influence on malpractice payouts and premium levels.[31] Of course, in states such as California, which has had the same dollar ceiling ($250,000), unindexed for inflation, for more than 30 years, the ceiling has had an increasingly powerful effect as the years have gone on. But maintaining a long-term ceiling without adjusting it for inflation is like enacting a new, lower ceiling each year. Moreover, a ceiling functions mainly like a one-time ratchet. It depresses costs on enactment, but if there are other factors creating an upward cost push, costs will begin to rise again. Finally, there is at least some evidence that juries adjust to ceilings on pain and suffering damages by awarding more damages for out-of-pocket losses than they would award if they were not constrained by such ceilings.[32]

In contrast to the crisis of a decade earlier, in the wake of this crisis two far more radical reforms also received attention, though none has ever been enacted.

ENTERPRISE MEDICAL LIABILITY.   The first reform, enterprise medical liability, would have relieved individual physicians of liability for malpractice altogether, and rendered such medical enterprises as hospitals and health maintenance organizations vicariously liable for malpractice. This proposal was made in a major report by the American Law Institute that was published in 1991.[33] The idea was then briefly floated by the Clinton Health Care Task Force in the spring of 1993, but the AMA, the American Hospital Association, and a group of liability insurers strenuously opposed the proposal. The physicians were afraid that enterprise medical liability would result in greater control over their professional behavior by hospitals and health maintenance organizations (HMOs). Their opposition was based on the same concern for professional autonomy that had motivated the AMA's opposition to socialized medicine decades earlier. The hospitals did not want the additional liability the proposals would entail for them. And the liability insurers seem to have been concerned that they would lose more business from physicians than they would gain from hospitals, which could more easily self-insure all or part of their liability.

Thus, as critical as each of these groups was of the existing malpractice liability regime, none was willing to support a reform that would have relieved the principal targets of liability of their exposure to claims. For all their opposition to malpractice suits, physicians in particular did not want their liability taken away from them if, in return, they had to risk sacrificing their professional autonomy to the newly liable enterprises who would seek to control them. The Clinton Health Care Task Force therefore dropped its proposal for enterprise liability, and physicians retained their liability. But ironically, physicians soon saw their autonomy begin to diminish anyway, as managed care came to dominate the health-care market within the next few years.

MEDICAL NO-FAULT.   The second far-reaching reform that received extended consideration after the crisis of the mid-1980s was medical no-fault. The no-fault idea had been on the policy back burner since the 1970s, but it was revived after a Harvard Medical Practice Study Group published the results of one of the largest empirical studies of medical malpractice ever undertaken. In a massive study of medical treatment in New York hospitals, the Harvard group found that 3.7 percent of all hospitalized patients suffered an adverse event related to treatment, but that only 27 percent of these events were caused by negligence. Thus a significant number of patients were suffering iatrogenic injury even apart from malpractice.

Yet most often, those who did suffer malpractice did not make a claim. For every seven patients who suffered a negligently caused adverse event, only one ever made a malpractice claim. Even for the more serious of these injuries, the ratio of injuries to claims was five to two.[34] Moreover, there was a very substantial mismatch between those who were injured by malpractice and those who made claims. Of the 47 claims made for malpractice in the Harvard sample, only 8 claims were brought by any of the 280 patients that the study determined had suffered an injury caused by malpractice. Thus, 39 of the 47 claims that were filed involved injuries that Study experts found were not caused by malpractice.[35] The latter finding has been questioned;[36] but the overall message of the Harvard Study remains: there is a considerable mismatch between those who are injured by malpractice and those who sue for it.

For a solution, the Harvard Study turned to the nearly century-old model of workers' compensation. The Study proposed a third-party strict liability system that it referred to as medical no-fault. Health-care providers would be liable for patient injuries without regard to malpractice, and would pay out-of-pocket losses, but no damages for pain and suffering, to those with long-term injuries. This approach would (in the Study group's view) more effectively provide compensation to those in need, avoid prolonged and expensive litigation, and promote injury prevention more effectively than the malpractice system.[37] Thus, many of the same considerations that had been relevant to workers' compensation 80 years earlier—ensuring compensation, promoting deterrence, and reducing administrative costs—were invoked in support of the Harvard group's proposal.

The great challenge for the Harvard proposal, however, as it has always been for medical no-fault, was how to define a simple, easily applicable compensable event. In workers' compensation and auto no-fault, that task had been simple. If a worker arrives at work healthy and leaves injured, he has almost always suffered an injury "arising out of and in the course of" employment. If a driver or passenger gets into a car healthy and emerges injured, he has almost always suffered an injury "arising out of and in the course of" the operation of a motor vehicle. There will always be borderline cases and potential fraud, but these are likely to be minimal. In these systems the basic question of whether an injury has been caused by work or by driving ordinarily is easy, and inexpensive, to answer.

In contrast, a medical no-fault system whose compensable event is an injury "arising out of and in the course of" medical treatment would face formidable problems of causal attribution. People often seek medical treatment when they are already sick or injured. Undesirable outcomes therefore do not always result from treatment; sometimes they result from the patient's underlying condition. Merely because a person emerges from medical treatment in an unhealthy or injured condition does not mean that she has suffered a loss caused by treatment.

In addition, any medical no-fault plan faces the need to place some limit on the scope of coverage for the consequences of the failure to properly diagnose a patient's condition. Otherwise the plan risks bringing the fault-based considerations that the system seeks to eliminate back into operation through the back door. A no-fault plan can hardly provide compensation for losses resulting from all undiagnosed ailments; to do so would very nearly provide broad-based health insurance. Yet it is unclear how to determine which losses resulting from the failure to diagnose should receive no-fault compensation without relying on some normative criterion that is likely to resemble a malpractice standard. For example, an eligibility standard that hinges on whether the physician should have diagnosed the patient's condition, or whether most physicians would have diagnosed the condition, arguably is merely a malpractice standard in disguise.

Nor has approaching the issue by designating a set of specifically compensable events (e.g., wound infection within three days of elective surgery) yet proved to be feasible. One obstacle is determining whether claims that would not qualify for no-fault compensation would still be actionable in tort or instead would be wholly foreclosed. If such claims remained actionable, they would generate an additional cost—determining which claims did and which did not fall within the coverage of the no-fault system. Some claimants—those with weak malpractice claims—would argue that their claims fell within the system. Others—those with strong malpractice claims—would argue that their claims fell outside no-fault.

Thus, for all these reasons, a medical no-fault system could not be administered with anything like the simplicity and low expense of workers' compensation and auto no-fault. The no-fault idea, attractive though it may have been to at least some people and groups, has never garnered enough support to be adopted in any state.

Round Three: The First Crisis of the Twenty-First Century

Just as happened in the 1970s, before the full impact of the reforms of the mid-1980s could be felt directly, the hard market turned soft. In an era of low inflation and a bull market for stocks, the malpractice insurance market stayed soft for an unusually long period, lasting from the late 1980s until the late 1990s. There were no widespread, substantial premium increases for medical malpractice insurance during this entire period. Looking at the average rate of change over a period of a decade or more presents a fairly stable picture. A Texas study found, for example, that adjusting for population growth and the number of physicians, between 1988 and 2002 there was little or no increase in the number of malpractice claims.[38] And professor Tom Baker has shown that over the period from 1980 to 2002, national predicted losses increased at a rate lower than medical inflation for much of the period.[39]

But long-term averages are little consolation to those who are affected by occasional, rapid change. The quiet climate of the early and mid-1990s gave way to exactly this kind of change late in the decade. Beginning around 1998, malpractice claim severity rose. From 1988 to 1997, the average annual increase in paid losses in a sample of states taken by the General Accounting Office was 3 percent, adjusted for inflation. From 1998 to 2001, however, paid losses in the sample states increased an average of 8.2 percent annually.[40] A more recent study has found that claim severity increased about 9 percent per year between 1990 and 2001.[41] Payouts made by the leading insurer during this period (before it withdrew completely from the market), St. Paul, rose from under $400 million in 1996 to nearly $1.4 billion in 2001.[42]

These increases would themselves have supported predictions about future claim frequency and severity warranting substantial increases in premiums. In addition, the stock market bubble burst early in 2001, and then several months later the insurance industry as a whole experienced a sudden enormous call on its capital because of claims arising out of 9/11. Finally, St. Paul concluded that it had overreserved for its losses until the early 1990s, and therefore adjusted its rates accordingly in the following decade. A number of other insurers, mainly small medical mutual insurers, apparently had not overreserved but nonetheless previously had adjusted their rates downward to follow St. Paul. After 9/11 these insurers raised their rates in an attempt to recoup losses they were now suffering under previously sold, underpriced policies.[43] Not surprisingly, this provoked new entrants into the market.[44] Nonetheless, at this point in some states the hard market for medical malpractice insurance intensified.

But there was considerable variation among the states. From 1998 to 2001, Mississippi's paid losses increased 142 percent, Pennsylvania's 70 percent, and California's 38 percent. Yet Minnesota's paid losses increased only 8 percent. It is no surprise, therefore, that rate increases varied from state to state, and even within states and between medical specialties within the same state.[45] There was something of a "crisis" in some states, but not in others. For example, the largest malpractice insurer in Pennsylvania increased its base rates for certain surgical specialties in the Harrisburg area by about 150 percent during the period 1999 to 2002. In contrast, in California and Minnesota, rates for these specialists rose by only 5 and 21 percent, respectively, and actually declined in certain areas.[46] The ferment for reform therefore varied a great deal from state to state.

In subsequent years rate increases again leveled off as the cycle progressed. The whole issue reappeared, however, when it became an issue in the 2004 Presidential campaign and was placed on President Bush's legislative agenda beginning in 2005. The President proposed federal legislation placing a ceiling of $250,000 on pain and suffering damages in medical malpractice suits.[47] But that legislation was defeated in 2006, and there is little prospect of its enactment. In any event, given past experience and the fact that many states already have such ceilings, it appears unlikely that the President's proposed ceiling would have had a significant impact on the cycle of premium and loss payout increases that have troubled the malpractice insurance market for nearly half a century now. The imposition of a federal ceiling on pain and suffering damages would ratchet down premiums by about 15 to 20 percent over time in the states that do not already have a ceiling. But a federal ceiling would do nothing to arrest the cycle and little to prevent the long-term but volatile increase of premiums from the new, lower baseline.

Rather, the existing relationship between malpractice insurance, malpractice liability, and the structure of the health-care delivery system seems likely to continue to produce a situation in which tort reforms have only a modest impact, the price of insurance is volatile, and physicians remain dissatisfied. Only fundamental change has the prospect of producing a more satisfactory situation. Yet, as we have seen, medical no-fault is at present technically infeasible, and probably politically infeasible as well. Shifting wholesale from individual to institutional responsibility for medical error probably is also politically infeasible. Nonetheless, incremental movement in the latter direction is more feasible. Holding hospitals, HMOs, and other managed-care organizations financially responsible for medical error could more fully enlist these enterprises in preventing malpractice. That responsibility could be direct, by refashioning liability rules, or indirect, by requiring health-care institutions to supply individual physicians with insurance or at least to be more responsible for system failures.[48] As health care is increasingly delivered through these institutions and within systems of treatment, a system-wide approach to optimizing patient safety is emerging anyway. The individual physician is not sensibly the exclusive focus of liability in this kind of setting, any more than the pilot of a commercial airliner should be the focus of liability when airplanes crash.

In addition, health-care institutions have greater ability to engage in financial planning and risk diversification than individual physicians and small practice groups. Most important, health-care institutions can more quickly pass on the cost of increased liability insurance to the consuming public or their shareholders. Greater institutional liability for medical error could therefore dampen the volatile effects of the insurance cycle on individual physicians.

Both the health-care market and the legal system are already moving, in a series of individually small steps, in this direction. Health-care institutions increasingly help to finance the malpractice insurance of physicians who are closely affiliated with them. University medical centers frequently purchase insurance for in-house personnel; HMOs tend to buy insurance for physicians whom they actually employ. And these institutions are increasingly held vicariously liable for malpractice committed by closely affiliated physicians. A conception of liability that focuses on the actions of individual physicians, however, remains the organizing legal paradigm.

As long as this individual malpractice paradigm is dominant and health-care institutions are not understood to be both the principal health-care actors and the appropriate focus of legal and financial responsibility, individual physicians will continue to be at the dramatic and legal center of lawsuits. Yet the malpractice paradigm will not be transformed until these institutions have the necessary means of influencing the factors that affect medical error. This of course includes influencing the behavior of individual physicians.

And there is the rub. On the one hand, physicians can fight to retain their remaining professional autonomy. But with that autonomy they will continue to face individual exposure to liability for malpractice. On the other hand, physicians can surrender more and more of their autonomy and slowly be relieved of their liability exposure. But ultimately physicians are not going to be able to have it both ways. The one combination physicians will be unable to achieve, but persist in seeking, is full professional autonomy and simultaneous freedom from significant exposure to liability for malpractice. That is an arrangement that the modern relationship between health care insurance and medical malpractice liability is not going to provide them.

—5—

Products Liability,
Environmental Liability,
and the Long Tail

In an important sense the history of products and environmental liability consists of a series of interactions between tort and insurance. The search for categories of defendants that could spread losses broadly, either by insuring or by passing liability costs through to a large customer base, was highly influential in the development of modern products liability doctrine. And environmental liability, which burst on the scene in a significant way only in the late 1970s, almost immediately set in motion changes in the liability insurance market whose effects are still felt today. One of the principal problems posed by both of these forms of liability is that they often seek to provide redress for injury or damage that is not manifested until decades after the defendant's liability-producing conduct occurred. This "long tail" on claims makes liability for these long-latency harms difficult to insure, because of the difficulties of prediction they pose.

At the same time, the deterrent effect of threatening enterprises with liability for long-latency harms is also uncertain. The long tail on claims makes it attractive for enterprises to discount the potential long-term cost of their risky conduct, while capturing the short-term benefits of that conduct. And the pricing of liability insurance does not neutralize this incentive. Premiums tend not to depend closely on the long-term riskiness of an enterprise's conduct, precisely because of the difficulty insurers face in predicting long tail claims. As a consequence, often the main advantage of imposing long-tail liability is not that it discourages risky conduct, but that it provides a source of compensation for victims whom that conduct ultimately has harmed.

At a time when little compensation for personal injuries was available from other sources, importing the insurance function into the liability system in this way may have seemed to make sense. But as we have seen in earlier chapters, in the second half of the twentieth century, first-party insurance, and especially health insurance, became far more widespread than it had been in the past. As a result, one of the effects of importing the insurance function into civil liability has been to create a liability-based compensation mechanism that is more expensive to operate than, but heavily duplicates the various forms of first-party insurance that are now available to personal injury victims.

Products and environmental liability reached their maturity at different times and in different ways. The doctrinal history of products liability is the story of the continuing dissolution of restrictions on the scope of manufacturer liability, through the progressive addition of new causes of action and the eventual relaxation of defenses. First, restrictions on manufacturers' liability for negligence were removed. By the 1930s, enterprise liability scholars were developing the insurance rationale for manufacturers' strict liability. In the 1940s the first judicial references to this rationale appeared. And in the 1960s the law changed rapidly, on the basis of this rationale in heavy measure. Then, in keeping with the enterprise liability philosophy and just as the development of product liability doctrine was finally reaching a plateau, the scope of liability for environmental harm expanded radically, largely through the enactment of a single federal statute, the Comprehensive Environmental Response, Compensation and Liability Act of 1980 (CERCLA).

Shortly thereafter, however, the modern law of products and environmental liability began to have a major, negative influence on the liability insurance system. The consequence of this influence has been a slow but steady erosion of both the attractiveness and the availability of products and environmental liability insurance. Ironically, in fields whose reason for being was in part that defendants had greater access to insurance than did plaintiffs, plaintiffs may now have greater access to insurance than defendants. It would be an exaggeration to say that these are now fields in search of a valid purpose. The threat of short-tail liability undoubtedly still has a deterrent effect that makes liability at some level worth preserving, and it may be that the threat of long-tail liability also has some deterrent effect, however uncertain its magnitude may be. But in view of the access of potential plaintiffs to insurance, one of the foundational rationales for the imposition of liability in these fields, based on insurance, risk-spreading, and compensation, has become far less persuasive than it was in the past.

The Path to Modern Products Liability Doctrine

In the nineteenth century there was no separate law of products liability. Rather, liability was governed by contract, under the privity doctrine established by the English decision of *Winterbottom v. Wright*.[1] Under this doctrine, being in a contract relationship (in "privity") with the defendant was a necessary condition of liability. The purchaser's only rights were against the party who sold him the product.

Today the privity rule seems arbitrary and formalistic. But in fact the rule had a substantive rationale. A manufacturer undertook to do what its contract of sale required of it. If a third party nevertheless had the right to sue the manufacturer, then the manufacturer could be held liable even if it had complied with all the terms of its contract of sale with a wholesaler or retailer. That contract could be "ripped open" by a tort action, as the court in *Winterbottom* had put it. Under such a threat, the manufacturer would have to either raise the price of the product, or make the product safer than the contract for its sale otherwise would have required the product to be. The private contract between two consenting parties would in effect have been altered by the law of torts, in order to protect individuals who were strangers to the contract.

Today this result seems unremarkable. A private contract for the sale of goods should not be inviolate if the terms of the contract threaten to cause harm to the public. In the nineteenth century, however, craftsmen tended to make and sell their products directly to those who would use them. Contract could at least in theory thoroughly order their legal relationship. In contrast, with the rise of mass-produced goods, the privity rule stood reality on its head. The very people who were most likely to be affected by a defective product were not the middlemen who purchased it directly from the manufacturer, but consumers who purchased it from a retailer, or innocent bystanders who were not in the chain of distribution at all.

MacPherson and Manufacturers' Liability for Negligence

It is no surprise, then, that the privity rule eventually had to give way. A new rule was born in the decision of the Court of Appeals of New York in *MacPherson v. Buick Motor Company,* a case decided in 1916.[2] In an opinion written by Judge Benjamin Cardozo, the court held that any product that was likely to cause injury if negligently made would subject its manufacturer to liability, if the manufacturer understood that it would be used by someone other than the party to whom the manufacturer sold it. The source of the manufacturer's liability was not "contract and nothing else," as Cardozo put it, but "the law," by which he meant the law of torts. The values of tort law would supercede the limitations written into, or implicit in, private contracts.

This was a definite victory for plaintiffs, but it was no panacea. Proving the manufacturer's negligence often was no easy task. As a practical matter, the product may have been damaged or destroyed in the accident that produced the injury in question, thus making it difficult to determine what had gone wrong. And even if there was no question about what had gone wrong, the plaintiff was required to prove that the manufacturer's negligence was responsible. In products liability cases the injury to the plaintiff takes place after the product has left the possession of the manufacturer, and sometimes many months or even years after. Whether the manufacturer was responsible for the defect in the product that caused the plaintiff's injury, because the defect was present when the product left the assembly line, or instead the flaw had been introduced during the product's use, after the manufacturer had transferred control over it, was often a potential issue. *MacPherson* itself, for example, involved a wooden wheel on a car that had been driven for a year on rough country roads before it splintered. Whether there was a defect in the wheel when it left the assembly line or the wheel broke because of wear and tear was uncertain.[3]

These were not the only problems for plaintiffs. Even if the factual issues associated with proving what was wrong with the product and when any defect was introduced were resolved, there remained the difficulty of determining what it meant for the manufacturer to have been negligent. Suppose, for example, that it was proved that the defect in question had been introduced on the assembly line. There was still the question of how much care in quality control was a "reasonable" amount. How much inspection was necessary? What percentage of defective units could an inspection miss and still be considered "reasonable"? And if the problem was not a manufacturing defect in a single unit, but something related to the design of every unit, how safe did a product's design have to be in order to be "reasonably" safe? These kinds of questions had to be addressed on a case-by-case basis, and the evidence that was a predicate for answering them had to come from the plaintiff. In short, the right to sue a manufacturer for negligence did not solve plaintiffs' problems; it created them.

Around the same time, however, another basis for imposing liability began to develop. The courts were holding that in the sale of goods, the direct seller impliedly promised the purchaser, or "warranted," that the goods were merchantable. Among other things, this was a warranty that the goods were minimally safe. When it breached that warranty, the seller could be held liable for resulting harm, including personal injury. This amounted to liability without fault, for it required no showing that the seller had failed to exercise reasonable care to comply with the warranty. If the warranty was breached, the seller was strictly liable for the consequences. The law of implied warranty thus helped plaintiffs avoid some of the difficulties that were entailed in proving negligence. But because implied warranty applied only where there was privity, it was not available in suits by consumers against product manufacturers.

The next step in the development of the implied warranty was small for practical purposes, but was actually an enormous conceptual leap. An exception to the privity limitation on implied warranty was created for cases involving impure food. The consumer injured by impure food could sue the manufacturer for breach of implied warranty, even in the absence of any direct contract between them.[4] This difference between liability for breach of an implied warranty by the immediate seller and liability for breach of an implied warranty by the manufacturer was the difference between contract and tort. It was the difference between *Winterbottom* and *MacPherson,* but on a strict liability rather than a negligence scale. In truth, this warranty was implied by law rather than in fact. It was the name given to a legal obligation that arose because the law imposed it, not because the law was recognizing what the parties had already agreed.

As fundamental a conceptual leap as creation of the manufacturer's implied warranty that food was merchantable was, however, it was limited in practical importance. Some courts applied it not only to food but also to products intended for intimate bodily use such as perfume. But there the expansion stopped. For several decades more, the privity limitation still applied to suits for breach of warranty in the sale of all other kinds of products. The manufacturer of such products was liable for negligence, but only for negligence, from the time of *MacPherson* through the late 1950s.

Enterprise-Based Strict Liability

During the same period the theory of enterprise liability that had been born out of workers' compensation had continued to develop and find its way into the legal literature. Academics such as Douglas, James, Kessler, and Prosser argued to varying degrees that tort law should require business enterprises to bear the costs of all accidents associated with their activities, and spread these costs among the public that benefited from those activities.[5] And it was during this period that the seminal judicial statement of the case for imposing strict liability in tort on the manufacturers of all kinds of products, based on the enterprise liability rationale, was published.

In *Escola v. Coca Cola Bottling Company of Fresno,* a waitress had been injured when a bottle of Coca Cola exploded in her hands. She sued the manufacturer for negligence.[6] Like so many plaintiffs who found it difficult to take advantage of *MacPherson,* she had no direct evidence that the manufacturer was negligent. She could not reconstruct what had happened on the assembly line, and the explosion of the bottle also destroyed any evidence there might have been that the bottle had been defectively manufactured or improperly filled with soda. The plaintiff argued that she was nonetheless entitled to rely on the doctrine *res ipsa loquitur* (the thing speaks for itself) to supply the inference that the manufacturer had been negligent in overcharging the pressure in the bottle. Both the trial court and the Supreme Court of California agreed.

In his 1944 opinion concurring with the result, Justice Roger Traynor argued that plaintiffs in cases involving defective products should not be required to prove negligence. The time had come, in his view, to impose strict liability (he called it "absolute" liability) on a manufacturer for product defects that caused personal injury. He offered three reasons for his proposed approach. The first was that strict liability would help to reduce injury. Responsibility should be fixed "wherever it will most effectively reduce the hazards to life and health inherent in defective products that reach the market." The manufacturer could best "anticipate some hazards and guard against the occurrence of others, as the public cannot."

The second reason for imposing strict liability was that manufacturers could best insure against liability for injury that did occur, even when the manufacturer could not prevent it. The cost of injury could be "insured by the manufacturer and distributed among the public as a cost of doing business." The risk of injury required "constant protection and the manufacturer is best situated to provide such protection."

Finally, even if the manufacturer was negligent, it was sometimes difficult for the plaintiff to prove negligence. Evidence of negligence often could not be obtained. The *res ipsa loquitur* doctrine was not always available to fill this gap, and even then the manufacturer was permitted to offer evidence that it was not negligent. The plaintiff was "not ordinarily in a position to refute such evidence or identify the cause of the defect." Strict liability in tort was the proper solution, rather than reliance on negligence or on warranty law.

Traynor's concurrence in *Escola* had no status as precedent. But it soon became influential anyway. By the mid-1950s tort theorists in law schools were turning their attention to products liability, and considering whether the enterprise liability ideas that had produced workers' compensation and were by then in general circulation could be applied specifically to this field.[7] They found ready support in *Escola*.

And by the early 1960s, as Prosser would put it, the citadel fell.[8] The Supreme Court of California, in a 1963 opinion in *Greenman v. Yuba Power Products, Inc.,* written by Traynor, now chief justice, held that manufacturers (and other sellers) faced strict liability in tort for injuries caused by defects in their products.[9] What Traynor had proposed two decades earlier in *Escola* he was now able to make law in *Greenman*. Then, in one of the quickest transformations in the history of tort law, strict products liability swept the country. In 1965, in its influential *Restatement (Second) of Torts,* the American Law Institute (ALI) squeezed a hastily created strict products liability provision, section 402A, in between the already prepared sections 402 and 403. The courts of dozens of states then followed California and the *Restatement,* which had described the law as providing strict products liability for injuries caused by products that were in a "defective condition unreasonably dangerous" to the user or consumer.

An incipient change during this period in the flavor of tort law scholarship also would contribute to the expansion of products liability. The early enterprise liability theorists, including Traynor, had tended to emphasize the loss-spreading benefits of expanded liability. Corporate defendants, in their view, were in a better position than consumers to bear the costs of accidents, to insure against them, or to pass them on to the consuming public. Although the possibility that the threat of increased liability would reduce the occurrence of accidents was also sometimes mentioned, accident reduction had taken a decidedly secondary place in enterprise liability theory prior to the 1960s. For example, Fleming James, a leading proponent of enterprise liability, was extremely skeptical about the accident-reduction potential of tort liability, saying of tort law that "it is doubtful whether it contributes very much to accident prevention."[10]

By the 1960s, in contrast, the economic analysis of law was coming into its own in the elite law schools, and its proponents began to focus on the deterrent effect of tort liability. Guido Calabresi of Yale argued in a series of important articles that strict liability was superior to negligence in this respect.[11] His book further developing these ideas, *The Costs of Accidents,* was published in 1970. At the same time, a body of work directed at the deterrence issue, most prominently that of Richard Posner, was emerging from the University of Chicago.[12] By the 1970s, if academic writing had not entirely promoted deterrence and demoted loss spreading and compensation as the primary goal of products liability, the former had certainly become the equal of the latter. The idea that threatening more liability could prevent accidents, and thereby reduce the amount of liability that actually needed to be imposed, became a standard feature of tort theory. When Prosser and his colleagues put together section 402A, therefore, they were drawing not only on recent case law but also an evolving intellectual background supporting the expansion of liability.

Design and Warning Defects

Exactly what kinds of product defects the courts and the ALI had in mind for strict liability, however, was not immediately clear. The paradigm case seemed to involve manufacturing defects—products with a feature that departed from the manufacturer's intended design and caused the plaintiff's injury. These were the exceptional, poorly produced units of a product rather than the normal, properly made units that came off the assembly line. They were unintentional mistakes in manufacture, fabrication, or construction.

During the 1970s it became clear that there were two other kinds of defects that posed greater conceptual difficulties than manufacturing defects. One involved defects of design. Unlike a product with a manufacturing defect, a product with a design defect is not exceptional. A design defect affects every unit of the product that comes off the assembly line. The same is true of the other form of defect that emerged in litigation during the 1970s: inadequate warnings or instructions that accompanied the product.

Products with design or warning defects have much greater potential to cause mass injuries than products with manufacturing defects, because the former two categories are present in every unit of the product that is sold. And in the 1970s the first mass product liability tort cases alleging design and warning defects were filed. The first involved asbestos; but suits quickly followed involving the Dalkon Shield, diethystilbestrol (DES), breast implants, and Bendectin, to name just a few.[13]

At the same time that design and warning litigation emerged as distinct categories and the early mass tort cases were filed, the jurisprudence of defenses to products liability claims was crystalizing in a manner that also facilitated recovery by plaintiffs. In particular, the increasing tendency of the courts to treat the assumption of risk defense narrowly, and the enactment of comparative negligence statutes in virtually every state, made it more likely than ever before that products liability claims would succeed.

Finally, the latent nature of the harms involved in many of the mass products and tortious exposure cases posed causal uncertainties with which tort doctrine had to deal. Liability was sometimes imposed on the basis of market share or some other proxy rather than requiring conventional proof of causation.[14]

By the mid-1980s these doctrinal expansions of product liability ceased, but that expansion had already proceeded pretty far. Products liability doctrine had at that point reached the plateau on which it has stood for nearly 25 years now. With only very minor exceptions, the rules governing products liability have neither expanded nor contracted the scope of liability during the ensuing quarter of a century. In fact, in the early 1990s the ALI took a look at this mature body of doctrine and concluded that most of products liability had never actually become strict liability. There was true strict liability for manufacturing defects. But whether a product was defective in design had turned out ordinarily to be a question of weighing the costs and benefits of that design and any reasonable alternatives to it. And there was liability for failure to warn only if there was "inadequate" disclosure of the risks posed and those risks could have been reduced by "reasonable" warnings or instructions.[15] These were essentially negligence questions, although, like strict liability, they focused on the nature of the product at issue rather than on the behavior of the manufacturer. There simply was no meaningful way to impose liability for injury caused by a defectively designed product, for example, without hinging liability in some way on a substandard feature of the product. Otherwise there could be liability for all product-related injury—falls from safe ladders, cuts from properly sharpened knives, and so on—that would have been imposed even if the product had no defect.

Thus, the steep trajectory of doctrinal expansion that products liability experienced beginning around 1960 became flat around 1985.[16] What had seemed just a few years before to be an inevitable move to full strict products liability, and perhaps to enterprise strict liability generally, turned out, at least on paper, to be a more modest set of doctrinal changes. The big changes were not in the law, but in the increased frequency of suit and in the amounts recovered.

Nonetheless, in actual practice products liability litigation in the last 25 years can be understood to have extended liability further than the law on the books suggests. There were and still are many cases in which a product design is defective or an adequate warning was not given. But there have also been cases that pay only lip service to these negligence-based standards when, in fact, loss-spreading or the insurance rationale appears to be the true basis for imposing liability.[17] For example, an automobile frame might be found defective because it permitted deformation of the vehicle in a crash. A different frame might be found defective in another case, however, precisely because it did not permit deformation. In such a setting the manufacturer is in effect providing insurance against the risk of suffering design-related injury, whether a design is defective or not. As one respected federal judge put it in just such a case, "under these circumstances, the law imposes on the industry the responsibility of insuring [a] vast number of persons in automobile accidents."[18]

Similarly, the effect of imposing liability in certain failure-to-warn cases seems to have been to insure against the unfortunate effects of product use, rather than to hold the manufacturer liable for any real deficiencies in the warning the product carried. For example, juries have been permitted to find seemingly suitable warnings of potential side effects to have been inadequate;[19] and in some vaccine cases plaintiffs have not been required to prove that they would have heeded the warning at issue and declined vaccination if a more detailed or explicit warning had been given.[20] These cases seem to be directed mainly at ensuring that the cost of compensating the unlucky victims of drug side-effects is included in the price of the product, rather than affecting consumers' actual knowledge of product risks or their behavior in response to this knowledge. Often, for practical purposes, there was little if anything the maker of such a drug could do to eliminate the risk of liability, or reduce it to a comfortable level, other than ceasing to make the product. For some drugs, especially childhood vaccines, the latter actually occurred.

*   *   *

In short, the modern law of products liability on the books purports to limit liability based on defective design or inadequate warning to cases in which there has been what amounts to negligence on the part of the manufacturer. But there is a distinct subset of these cases in which, in practice, strict liability is imposed. In this subset of cases the main effect of imposing liability is to provide insurance to the victims of the losses that are associated with these products, regardless of whether the products are in fact nondefective or carry adequate warnings.

CERCLA and the Environmental Liability Revolution

Modern, statutory-based environmental liability developed later than products liability, and largely in response to the inadequacies of the traditional common law rules. In theory the law of nuisance had long been available to deal with pollution that resulted in property damage and, in most jurisdictions, personal injury as well. But nuisance law imposes liability only after pollution is occurring. And nuisance, like all causes of action in tort, requires proof of a causal connection between the defendant's conduct and the harm of which the plaintiff complains. When that harm is immediate and visible, nuisance law may be able to function effectively.[21] Because exposure to pollutants may cause illness only over a long period of time, however, that the defendant's past action caused the plaintiff's present harm may be difficult to prove. The consequence is that the threat of common law liability for pollution did not result in the reduction of pollution to optimal levels, especially as industrial pollution increased in the period following World War II.

In the 1960s, popular concern about environmental protection accelerated, in part because the law of nuisance was not up to the task of protecting the environment. Rachel Carson's seminal 1962 book *Silent Spring* dramatized the dangers posed by pesticides; a major oil spill off the coast of southern California late in the decade galvanized the environmental movement; and the first Earth Day, held in April 1970, made the environment a focus of national politics. Later that year President Nixon established the Environmental Protection Agency (EPA); and during the first five years of the 1970s the U.S. Congress enacted a series of important command-and-control environmental regulation programs, including the Clean Air and Clean Water acts. All this both reflected and heightened the public's environmental consciousness. But this legislation did nothing directly to expand civil liability for environmental pollution or for personal injuries associated with pollution.

Then, in 1978, it was discovered that some of the residents at the Love Canal housing development near Niagara Falls, New York, had been mysteriously contracting diseases for a number of years. It turned out that, decades earlier, the Hooker Chemical Company had used the site as a waste depository. Hazardous waste had been leaking into the basements of the residents and contaminating their property. As a consequence, the homes at Love Canal had to be boarded up and abandoned. Over $200 million was spent on cleanup of the hazardous waste at the site, but only after prolonged recrimination and uncertainty about the scope of the state and federal governments' authority to undertake or order cleanup, and about Hooker's responsibility for what had happened.

Love Canal became a symbol of corporate irresponsibility in the handling of hazardous waste, although in the course of the controversy it was learned that Hooker had warned municipal authorities of the presence of waste on the site before being pressured to transfer ownership to the municipality.[22] Further investigation revealed that there were thousands of hazardous waste deposit sites around the country. Yet, despite the cascade of federal environmental legislation that had been enacted since 1970, none directly addressed this problem or gave the federal or state governments authority to address it effectively.

As a result, in 1980 Congress enacted CERCLA.[23] Nicknamed the "Superfund" Act because of the fund it created to finance government action taken to prevent or remedy environmental harm, CERCLA was a great deal more than a pot of money. In effect, it created a statutory form of tort liability for the cost of cleaning up hazardous waste deposit sites.

But this was liability with a vengeance. Although the components of the regime each had precedents in existing tort law, never before had they all been combined into so far-reaching a liability scheme. The Act imposed retroactive, strict, and joint and several liability for the cost of cleaning up any hazardous waste deposit site (indeed, any site, although virtually all involved waste) that posed a threat to health or the environment. Liability for the entire cost of cleanup at a site could be imposed regardless of whether disposal had been lawful and nontortious at the time it occurred; regardless of whether the defendant had been negligent; and regardless of whether other parties had contributed to the problem. And this retroactive, strict, and joint and several liability could be imposed on virtually anyone who had any connection with a dangerous site. These "responsible parties" included any past or present owner or operator of the site; anyone who had ever transported material to the site; and anyone who had ever generated waste that was later deposited at the site.[24]

The Act set up a $1.6 billion fund the EPA could use to fund cleanup; the fund would be replenished by EPA cost-recovery lawsuits imposing CERCLA liability on responsible parties. In addition, the EPA could issue administrative orders directing responsible parties to undertake cleanup themselves, and could seek injunctions from the federal courts directing them to do so. The potential penalties for noncompliance with these administrative orders and injunctions were severe. Filling out the program, many states enacted mini-Superfund acts whose provisions paralleled the federal regime but addressed the cleanup of smaller or less dangerous sites that fell below the federal program's radar screen.

After a few years of operation, two things became clear. First, the national cost of cleanup would be far greater than was originally anticipated—it would amount to as much as $500 billion, according to some of the estimates. Second, more was being spent on litigation over cleanup liability than on cleanup itself. In 1986 the Congress therefore amended CERCLA to specify in greater detail how its liability scheme would work. The acronym for these amendments was SARA—"Superfund Act Reauthorization Amendments." But some wits in Washington quipped that a more acccurate biblical acronym would have been RACHEL—"Reauthorization Amendments Clarifying How Everyone Is Liable."

Under the CERCLA regime as it matured, the federal and state governments now identified dangerous sites and ordered responsible parties to undertake cleanup, or funded a cleanup out of the Superfund and then sued responsible parties for reimbursement. Because the scheme permitted the imposition of the entire cost of cleanup on one responsible party, leaving that party to seek contribution from other parties after the fact if they were still in existence and solvent, the government had enormous leverage when it focused its attention on a particular site. And because government took the lead in identifying sites and determining the dangers they posed, private parties living in the vicinity of these sites were often able to piggyback, as it were, by bringing private tort suits against responsible parties for personal injury and property damage in the wake of CERCLA cleanup actions.

Not only were CERCLA liabilities Procrustean; they could be enormous. The principal danger posed by leaking hazardous waste is to groundwater—that is, underground water that directly or indirectly serves as a municipal or individual drinking water supply. The cost of remedying contamination to groundwater is very high, because it is not easily accessible. It is often necessary to employ multidecade "pump and treat" remedies in which billions of gallons of groundwater are slowly pumped out of an aquifer, treated to remove contamination, and then pumped back into the ground. The capital and operating costs of securing a site, removing above-ground waste, decontaminating soil, and treating groundwater sometimes ran into hundreds of millions of dollars at major sites, where hazardous waste had migrated offsite and contaminated groundwater for miles around.

The CERCLA regime transformed the landscape of environmental liability. In addition to the actual liabilities the federal CERCLA program and its state-based imitators imposed, every major industrial company in the United States preemptively addressed its potential liabilities, often investing millions of dollars in voluntary cleanup, or agreed in advance to a binding settlement with the authorities in order to avoid government-initiated administrative proceedings and outright litigation.

Liability Insurance and the Problem of the Long Tail

One of the greatest challenges to liability insurance, as we saw in Chapter 4 in connection with medical malpractice liability, is predicting the scope of long-term liability. Ordinary tort liability tends to involve accidents that occur abruptly and in the physical presence or vicinity of the defendant. Lawsuits ensue in due course, and insurers who contemplate issuing or renewing liability insurance policies can predict the scope of their exposure to this kind of liability on the basis of (among other things) the applicant's recent liability experience. Products and environmental liability, however, are different in this respect. These fields often involve injury or damage that occurs gradually, out of sight, and away from the defendant. This produces what has come to be called the "long tail" on claims and generates the problems of prediction that have challenged liability insurers for decades.

The Rise of Products Liability Insurance

As we saw in Chapter 1, the liability insurance policies that developed after workers' compensation was enacted were known as "public liability" insurance policies. These policies provided what soon came to be called "premises and operations" coverage. That is, the policies insured against liability for injury or damage occurring on or near the policyholder's place of business—the "premises" described in the policy—and during "operations" that took place elsewhere.[25] These policies did not cover liability for product-related injuries that occurred away from the insured's place of business, and they did not cover liability for injuries resulting from the insured's offsite operations after these operations had been completed.

The rationale that is sometimes given for these limitations on the scope of coverage is that the insurance that was excluded was not needed. Early on, product manufacturers had no liability in negligence because of the privity requirement, and even later there was little such liability because of the difficulty of proving negligence. As to completed operations, the received wisdom is that it was difficult for a plaintiff to prove negligence and causation arising out of an operation on which the insured was no longer working, such as a building construction or repair job that has been completed.[26]

I am a bit skeptical of these explanations. If risks arising out of products liability and completed operations had not existed at all, then there would of course have been no reason to insure against them. But as time went on, the risk that these forms of liability would be incurred did exist, and increased. Retail sellers of products began fairly early in the twentieth century to face liability for injury or damage resulting from breach of the implied warranty of merchantability, as did the manufacturers of food. These risks may have been so small that the administrative costs entailed in selling coverage would have required premiums too high for coverage to have been an attractive purchase for policyholders, and perhaps that is part of the explanation for the early absence of products liability insurance.

I think that a more complete explanation, however, lies in the problem of adverse selection and the difficulty of premium setting that it generated. Policyholders would naturally be exposed to different levels of products and completed-operations risk. Some would face little or no such risk, some would face moderate levels, and others might face significant exposure. If products and completed-operations liability had been automatically covered by public liability policies, then in order to avoid adverse selection, insurers would have needed to calibrate all premiums to the degree of risk posed by each of their policyholders. The cost of doing this for every policyholder could easily have outweighed the profits that could have been earned from those few policyholders who actually faced substantial products and completed-operations liability risk and therefore could have been charged substantially higher-than-average premiums.

In addition, public liability policies were written on what we would now call an "occurrence" basis. That is, they covered liability for bodily injury or property damage that occurred during the policy period, regardless of when a lawsuit alleging liability for that injury or damage was instituted. As a consequence, the risk posed by premises/operations and products/completed-operations liability could be very different. The former had a comparatively short tail, and the latter a comparatively long one. Injury or damage arising out of the use of business premises and ongoing operations is likely to be brought immediately to the attention of the policyholder. When there is a slip and fall in a store or a bystander is injured by a board that falls onto a sidewalk from the second floor of a construction site, for example, the policyholder or its agents tend to be present or nearby. Even if the defendant is not present, the incident is likely to be quickly reported, and the making of a claim is in any event subject to a statute of limitations that begins to run at the time of injury. Moreover, the risks posed at the policyholder's premises or at sites where it is conducting operations can be specifically assessed by the insurer and figured into the premiums charged for premises and operations coverage.

In contrast, assessing the risk of liability arising out of products that have left the manufacturer's hands, and completed operations at locations that have been returned to the possession of third parties, requires a very different kind of calculation. Injury or damage resulting from these risks is less likely to be reported immediately to the policyholder and then to its insurer. A policy year might therefore end without the insurer having a basis for determining the total level of harm that had materialized from the insured's products or completed operations during that year. Only after the applicable statute of limitations extinguished an injured person's right to bring suit would the possibility of covered claims being made under past policies be fully eliminated. An insurer seeking to set a premium for next year's products and completed operations coverage is therefore likely to have less reliable data about the policyholder's recent loss experience than it has regarding premises and operations-loss experience.

For all these reasons, instead of providing all policyholders with products and completed operations coverage, a more cost-effective approach was to exclude coverage from the standard policy and then to sell it as an add-on to those few policyholders who signaled that they had a need for it. The risk posed by this comparatively small number of policyholders could be more cost-effectively evaluated. That is what occurred, at first piecemeal, but eventually through the development of standard-form coverage. In 1940, the property/casualty insurers who sold public liability insurance got together and promulgated the first modern business liability insurance policy, which they called the Comprehensive General Liability (CGL) insurance policy. The contemporary CGL policy (renamed the "Commercial General Liability" policy in 1986) still provides separate coverage of premises/operations and products/completed-operations liability, though many policyholders buy both. Freestanding products liability insurance is a much less frequently purchased, but also available, form of coverage.

The lesson of this brief history is that by the time of *Escola,* the products liability insurance Justice Traynor envisioned did exist; it could be purchased as an add-on to CGL policies. But it was a comparatively difficult form of coverage for insurers to price, because there was a longer tail on products and completed operations claims than on premises and operations claims. The long tail on claims would prove to be a major factor in the controversies over products liability and insurance during the last several decades of the twentieth century, after the courts followed Traynor's advice and substantially expanded the scope of products liability.

Insuring the Tail

Liability insurers' exposure to long-tail liability results from an insurance concept known as the "trigger" of coverage, which we have already seen function in the medical malpractice context. Occurrence-based CGL insurance policies are triggered, or activated, by the occurrence of bodily injury or property damage during the policy period, regardless of the year when liability arising out of that injury or damage actually is imposed. The length of the tail on claims, of course, depends on the applicable statute of limitations specifying the period during which suit might be brought. Typically a tort statute of limitations provides that the right to sue terminates a particular number of years after injury, usually somewhere between two and six years, depending on the statute. But over time exceptions to this firm limitation have been engrafted onto the statutes, by both judicial decision and legislative modification. The two most significant exceptions for my purposes are for minors and for subsequently discovered injuries.

The exception for minors is self-explanatory, but enormously important.

In many states the period during which a tort claim can be made does not begin to run until a minor reaches the age of majority. A products liability insurer therefore could not be assured that all potential claims by those injured when they were minors had been lodged against the policyholder until more than 21 years after a product was marketed. Similarly, whether the injured party was a minor or not, many courts have held, and some legislatures have provided, that the period for bringing suit does not begin to run until the injured party has discovered, or in the exercise of reasonable care should have discovered, that he has suffered an injury caused by the product in question.[27] In most cases this exception poses no problem for insurers, because the typical product-related injury is an abrupt and violent or at least forceful event that the injured party cannot fail to notice. The statute of limitations begins to run immediately.

Exposure to drugs and chemicals, however, can cause disease rather than injury. An individual suffering a disease may not be able to ascribe that disease to exposure to a particular drug or chemical until epidemiological or other studies identify a causal link between exposure and disease. Some courts hold that the period of limitations does not begin to run until the plaintiff knew or should have known of this causal link. Moreover, some diseases are subject to a latency period of many years. Bodily harm occurs silently but sometimes does not manifest itself until decades after disease first begins to cause physical harm. Examples include the thickening of the pleural lining of the lungs caused by exposure to asbestosis, and vaginal adenocarcinoma caused by exposure to DES in utero. When the applicable period of limitations for bringing suit against the maker of a disease-causing product does not begin to run until manifestation of the disease, insurers can find themselves subject to coverage responsibility under policies that they had sold decades earlier. The policies cover liability for bodily injury that occurred during the policy period, but a suit alleging liability for that injury might not be brought until decades after the injury turns out to have occurred.

By the 1950s, some suits alleging that exposure to a dangerous product or substance caused disease rather than abrupt injury were being brought, and policyholders in turn began to claim coverage of the liability imposed in these suits. Insurers then sought a way to avoid covering this long-tail liability under previously issued policies. The defense that insurers attempted to erect was based on language in the CGL policy insuring against liability for injury or damage "caused by accident." The insurers argued that the term "accident" meant an event that was short in duration. Therefore, they contended, injury caused by long-term exposure to a drug or chemical was not "caused by accident" even if the resulting disease was accidentally incurred.

The case law that developed during the 1950s on this issue was divided, although policyholders seemed to be getting the best of it.[28] Toward the end of the decade, however, the London insurance market saw an opportunity for itself in this controversy and took action that soon rendered the meaning of the term "accident" moot. The London insurers began offering to sell CGL policies to U.S. policyholders containing an endorsement that not only provided coverage of liability for injury caused by accident but also for injury caused by what they called an "occurrence." And they defined an occurrence as "an accident, *including injurious exposure to conditions.*" The London policies thus even more clearly gave policyholders the coverage of liability for long-term events that policyholders thought—or at least hoped—they had been getting all along from U.S. insurers.

The attractiveness of the London CGL policies prompted many U.S. insurers to offer occurrence endorsements to their own policies. This competition then culminated in the revision of the standard-form CGL policy in 1966 to incorporate coverage of liability for injury caused by an "occurrence" into the body of the policy itself. Ever since, the policy has been referred to as the "occurrence" CGL policy. In this respect the major contribution of the 1966 modification was of course to confirm that the policy provided broad coverage against long-tail liability. That was the whole point of the move from accident-based to occurrence-based coverage.

Within just a few years of the introduction of the new CGL occurrence policy, however, CGL insurers found that it was becoming increasingly difficult to set a reliable price for coverage, because of new, increased difficulties in predicting economic and legal change.[29] The economic forces that affect civil liability became less stable; the law of torts and of environmental liability changed rapidly; the courts seemed to be interpreting apparently restrictive insurance policy language more aggressively than they had in the past; and the economy experienced sharp swings that heightened insurers' investment risk. For these reasons, as I will explain below, in a sense the 1966 policy revision making it clear that there was coverage of long-tail liability began to blow up in the insurers' faces.

EXOGENOUS ECONOMIC CHANGE.   One dimension of change during the period following the 1966 CGL revision involved economic developments that affected the level and magnitude of tort claims. Increasingly, new products were being introduced. The number of pharmaceuticals especially, but of consumer products in general, increased. This made injury costs more difficult to predict because the nature, frequency, and severity of the injuries that might be caused by these new products were not fully known.

Developments in health care also accelerated. As I indicated in earlier chapters, more people had private health insurance than ever before; Medicare and Medicaid were making public coverage available to more of the elderly and poor; and health-care technologies that made the provision of care more effective but often much more expensive were being introduced. Because health-care costs are a substantial component of any tort award, CGL insurers could reasonably anticipate that this feature of their policyholders' liability, and therefore the insurers' exposure, would grow. But by how much was difficult to predict.

LIABILITY CHANGE.   A second dimension of change took place within the civil liability system. Both the changes in products liability rules that were generated by Section 402A of the 1965 torts Restatement and in the rules governing recoverable damages and class action procedures posed prediction challenges. For example, lawsuits involving small or modest injuries suffered by a large number of individuals that might not have been worth instituting in the past were becoming more feasible once class action and other aggregative procedures started to develop. The federal class action rules, for example, were liberalized in 1966. And the willingness of injured parties to bring suit also seemed to be changing.[30]

Consequently, products liability litigation heated up in the decade of the 1970s. There has never been very reliable data on the extent of products-liability litigation in the states. Data on federal cases, however, is more systematic. Product-liability filings in the federal courts increased fourfold in the period from 1976 to 1986. A major portion of these filings involved asbestos, which by 1986 comprised 44 percent of the entire federal products liability caseload. There was also a large number of filings against pharmaceutical and health-care product defendants, especially those involving Dalkon Shield and Bendectin.

Although it was the initial avalanche of claims in the late 1970s and early 1980s that was most destabilizing, filings have continued to fluctuate and therefore to confound insurers' attempts at predicting losses. Between 1986 and 1988, federal filings increased another 28 percent, although all of this growth was attributable to asbestos. In 1989 the jurisdictional amount, or floor, for a federal suit increased from $10,000 to $50,000, and federal filings decreased. But federal products liability filings in subsequent years varied. Nonasbestos filings reached a high of nearly 25,000 in 1997, dropped to their lowest level since 1992 in 2001 (under 7,000), but then skyrocketed to over 19,000 in 2003. These fluctuations are probably the result of the coming and going of major mass tort cases, involving products such as diet and antiinflammatory drugs and breast implants. Asbestos filings continued to comprise a substantial percentage of the filings, though they have varied from year to year.[31]

There has been a long-running dispute in the literature about whether there was a litigation "explosion" at some point during the last three decades, or merely an avalanche of asbestos claims and modest increases in other classes of claims.[32] Without reliable state-based data it is not possible to resolve this dispute definitively. Looking at the federal filings alone, there can be no doubt that asbestos has been the dominant form of products liability. The critics of the litigation explosion thesis also seem to be correct in suggesting that standard, sporadic product-injury cases have increased only modestly. But it is the occasional, hard-to-anticipate mass products cases or cases involving hundreds, thousands, or even more claimants that continue to be destabilizing. There is every indication that such mass tort cases will continue to arise. So even if it were a bit misleading to say that there has been a general litigation explosion, it would also be misleading to suggest that nothing out of the ordinary has been happening for the last 30 years. The unusual but catastrophic mass tort suit has become something every business and every insurer must anticipate.

In addition to these changes in the scope of products liability beginning in the 1970s, insurers began to experience the changes in environmental liability I have already canvassed. The impact of these changes was in certain respects even more striking. Insurers at least had already understood that their policyholders faced the risk of products liability under the occurrence policies they issued, even if the scope of this form of liability turned out to be greater than the insurers had predicted. But the enactment of CERCLA in 1980 abruptly introduced a form of liability that was unheard-of at common law. Insurers now had to predict the scope of future CERCLA liability under the policies they sold after its enactment—a task that was in many ways more speculative than actuarial. In addition, the insurers soon found that, because CERCLA liability was retroactive, they faced liability under policies they had sold long before CERCLA was enacted. Depending on the age of the policies, the premiums charged often had not reflected any significant risk of the policyholder incurring environmental liability.

INSURANCE LAW CHANGE.   At the same time, CGL insurers also confronted the increased risk of change along a third dimension. As the 1970s turned into the 1980s, insurers encountered a greater tendency on the part of the courts to interpret CGL insurance policies in favor of coverage. The most prominent example of this phenomenon was especially disconcerting for the insurers because it involved a quintessential long-tail issue: interpretation of the "pollution exclusion" in CGL insurance policies.

The 1966 shift to occurrence coverage had made it clear that liability for injury of damage caused by pollution fell within the insuring clause of CGL policies. Pollution was a prime example of the "injurious exposure to conditions" that was now clearly covered by the definition of an "occurrence." Within a few years, however, the modern environmental movement had been born, a series of environmental disasters had occurred, and the U.S. Congress had begun to enact pollution control legislation. Insurers could see that private lawsuits alleging liability for harm caused by pollution threatened to skyrocket, and that the insurers could find themselves the target of claims for coverage of this liability under CGL insurance policies.

To address this threat, the 1973 revision of the CGL policy incorporated an exclusion that precluded coverage of liability for injury or damage caused by pollution unless the discharge of pollutants was "sudden and accidental." This qualified pollution exclusion was, in effect, an effort to retreat from occurrence-based coverage and to return at least in part, to the accident-based coverage that it had replaced just a few years earlier. Insurers thought the requirement that a discharge be "sudden" precluded coverage of liability for gradually occurring pollution. But by the early 1980s some courts were ruling that the term "sudden" was ambiguous, because it could mean either "abrupt" or "unexpected," and that the term therefore should be interpreted against its drafter, the insurer.[33]

This ambiguity doctrine, or *contra proferentem* ("against the drafter"), proved to be a major policyholder weapon in the battle for insurance coverage. Partly because CGL insurance policy language was essentially standard and nonnegotiable, if a policy provision was reasonably subject to two interpretations, then under the ambiguity doctrine the courts were to adopt the interpretation that favored coverage. In addition, some courts took a different route to the same result, invoking a kind of "regulatory estoppel" that denied insurers the right to assert the "sudden and accidental" discharge requirement, because the insurers had submitted a letter to state Insurance Commissioners when the pollution exclusion was first approved, reassuring them that the exclusion did not significantly limit coverage beyond the limitations already embodied in the standard-form occurrence policy.[34] Of course, the whole point of the exclusion had been to limit coverage.

The pollution exclusion decisions undermined insurers' confidence in their ability to craft policy provisions that would reliably limit coverage obligations under CGL policies. In effect, many courts were holding that the term "sudden" in the exclusion could be interpreted to mean "gradual." And the insurers' concern was multiplied because of the threat they faced for coverage of liability under CERCLA. It soon became apparent that the cost of CERCLA cleanups could be several hundred billion dollars. CGL insurance policies sold between 1941 and 1980 potentially covered CERCLA cleanup liability, because the pollution damage in question had sometimes occurred during the periods these policies covered. The insurance industry could therefore be on the hook for a major share of this total cleanup cost. And since most of the leakage at CERCLA sites involved the gradual discharge of pollutants, the possible inapplicability of the pollution exclusion to claims for coverage of CERCLA liability was a matter of tremendous concern to CGL insurers.

Judicial decisions in the 1980s took a broad view of insurers' coverage obligations in other respects as well. Although the insurers won some coverage victories, on the whole they did not fare well in the courts.[35] Courts held, for example, that every CGL policy that was in effect during multiyear periods of bodily injury or property damage was triggered and potentially covered the policyholders' liability for that harm. And it turned out that there were many more instances of possible multiyear injury or damage than might have been supposed. In perhaps the most important application of this notion, asbestos was held to result in injury beginning with the year of a tort claimant's first exposure to asbestos fibers, but not only that year. A substantial number of courts held that there was bodily injury during each subsequent year even after exposure had ceased, until the year when the asbestos-related disease was manifested, because the presence of asbestos fibers in the plaintiff's lungs continued to cause injury even after he had ceased to breathe in additional fibers.[36]

The import of the multiyear trigger decisions was that every CGL policy in effect during the several decades after the tort plaintiff had been exposed to asbestos therefore potentially provided coverage of this liability. What might have been relatively limited coverage under CGL policies could thereby be transformed into hundreds of millions of dollars' worth of insurance for any given policyholder. More important, what might have been limited liability for the insurance industry as a whole turned out to be potentially catastrophic liability. It is quite possible that the insurance industry's payouts for asbestos claims alone—payouts that continue to be made today, more than 30 years after the first asbestos cases were filed—will eventually exceed $200 billion, a vast multiple of the premiums paid for all CGL insurance policies sold during any recent year.[37]

The advent of CERCLA, asbestos, and other mass tort liabilities was a watershed event for the CGL insurers. They had predicted little of this liability, and they believed that their policies excluded, limited, or simply did not afford coverage of at least a sizable portion of it. The liability the insurers faced was not only a serious financial blow to the industry. In addition, they lost a substantial amount of confidence in their ability to predict what other civil liability developments might occur in the future, and how the courts would interpret CGL policy provisions designed by the insurers to limit the scope of coverage for such developments under these policies.

INVESTMENT RISK CHANGE.   The final factor that confronted the insurers came from the economy at large. The double-digit inflation resulting from, among other things, the oil crisis of the late 1970s and early 1980s presented insurers with a far more volatile financial situation than they had faced in the past. In any long-tail line of coverage, income from invested premiums is a major factor, because premiums are held for a considerable period of time before payout for claims and litigation expenses. Inflation was brought under control in the early 1980s, but the experience of the previous years had made it clear to insurers that their premium calculations would have to take account of an investment future that was far less certain than it had been, or at least had seemed to be, in the past.

For all these reasons, it is no surprise that over time, product liability insurance premiums rates rose substantially. The advisory products liability rates of the Insurance Services Office (ISO), the statistical and policy preparation arm of the property/casualty insurance industry, increased significantly during this period, at least in part in reaction to these different forms of unpredictability. These rates increased 195 percent from 1974 through 1976, were comparatively stable from 1976 to 1983, increased 105 percent from 1983 to 1988, and then receded by 27 percent between 1988 and 1990. Not only insurers' claims future, but also their investment future, was far less certain than it had been in the more stable past.

The Crisis of the Mid-1980s and the Shortened Tail

At least partly in reaction to the challenges CGL insurers began to face, as well as to those that it feared would soon be upon the insurance industry, in the early 1980s the Insurance Services Office (ISO), the organization through which the drafting of most standardized property and casualty insurance policies took place, began the process of revising the 1973 standard-form CGL policy. What happened during this process eventually became the subject of litigation that made its way to the Supreme Court of the United States in *Hartford Fire v. California*, in which 19 states charged a group of insurers with unlawfully attempting to manipulate the ISO drafting process.[38] The Supreme Court sent the case back for trial and it was then settled, but the allegations recounted in the Court's opinion, together with what we know for certain about the behavior of the insurance market during this period, can provide us with a glimpse of what was probably happening behind the scenes.

In the early 1980s the market for CGL coverage was soft. Insurers were clamoring for premium dollars to invest at double-digit interest rates, in what some called "cash-flow underwriting." The implications for insurers of the enactment of CERCLA and of the mass tort liabilities that were just beginning to work their way into the courts had not yet been fully appreciated, at least not by all the players in the market. However, one group of insurers within ISO, apparently concerned with the scope of their exposure to liability for long-tail claims under CGL policies, sought to have the CGL policy revised in a manner that would limit this exposure. Among other things these insurers proposed that the revised policy shorten the tail on covered claims by shifting from occurrence to claims-made CGL coverage, and eliminating all pollution coverage from CGL policies.

Recall that under occurrence coverage a policy is triggered, or activated, during the year when injury occurs regardless of how many years later a suit alleging liability for that injury is instituted. A policy therefore potentially provides coverage until the end of time, limited only by the restrictions applied by a statute of limitations for bringing suit against the policyholder. In contrast, as I described in Chapter 4, under a different form of policy affording "claims-made" coverage, a policy is triggered only by a claim made against the policyholder during the policy period. Claims-made policies therefore shift the risk of an uncertain claims future arising out of long-tail liability from the insurer to the policyholder. Similarly, since liability for gradual, unseen pollution (for example, leaking waste deposit sites) was a prime example of long-tail liability, a truly absolute pollution exclusion would eliminate coverage of this risk from CGL policies.

Ultimately the insurance industry, acting through ISO, was willing only to make one of these proposed changes, by including what has sometimes been called an "absolute" pollution exclusion in the 1986 CGL policy revision. ISO did not substitute a claims-made policy for its occurrence policy, though it did begin to make available an alternative claims-made policy. Commercial policyholders were not enormously receptive to the new claims-made approach, but it has not been uncommon in subsequent years to see claims-made CGL policies.

An equally important development occurring at virtually the same time, however, was the insurance "crisis" of the mid-1980s. During a period of months during 1985 and 1986, at just about the time that the new CGL policy was introduced, premiums for many forms of CGL insurance (and others, such as medical malpractice) skyrocketed, sometimes more than doubling. For some policyholders for a limited time, CGL coverage was not available at any price. The causes of this crisis were complex. Because interest rates had declined precipitously from their historic highs in the beginning of the 1980s, smaller amounts of investment income were available to offset underwriting losses; insurers recognized more clearly that both the frequency and severity of mass tort and product liability claims had been increasing over the past several years; and the impending enactment of the Tax Reform Act of 1986 caused them to strengthen their reserves in a manner that limited the amount of coverage they could sell during the ensuing few months.[39] This accounting change temporarily limited supply and therefore correspondingly increased the price of coverage.

Just as the medical malpractice crisis of the mid-1970s generated tort reforms, this crisis did as well. As in the earlier crisis, with one exception, the principal reforms that were enacted addressed the level of damages that were awardable rather than liability itself. Ceilings on the recovery of pain and suffering were enacted in nearly half the states, and a smaller number reversed the collateral source rule, which permits a plaintiff to recover damages from a defendant that have already been paid by a first-party insurer. As I indicated in Chapter 4, these two reforms have had a moderate but noticeable impact on tort recoveries—roughly 15 percent. But they have had little effect on the long-term trajectory of tort claims or liability insurance premiums.

Another type of reform enacted in the wake of the crisis more specifically addressed the long-tail issue. About half the states now have in force "statutes of repose" applicable to products liability. These statutes extinguish the right to bring a products liability suit, regardless of any exception to the statute of limitation, in one of two ways. Time-certain statutes extinguish the right to sue a specified number of years after the sale of a product—typically 15 to 20 years. Useful-life statutes extinguish the right to sue only after the useful life of the product has ended—a product-specific determination in each case.[40] Exactly what impact these statutes have had or will have is uncertain, although there is as yet no evidence that they have had any significant impact on the frequency of suit.

Even apart from tort reform, from the vantage point of nearly a quarter century later it is clear that the crisis marked a moment of great importance in the history of policyholder–insurer relations. The crisis of the mid-1970s that I discussed in Chapter 4 had been limited to medical malpractice insurance. This crisis was far broader, and had an impact on most commercial policyholders. *Time* magazine's cover story for March 24, 1986, "Sorry, America, Your Insurance Has Been Cancelled," could not escape the attention of the business community. In the CGL insurance market prior to this time, the norm was that there would be a continuing relationship between the corporate policyholder and its primary CGL insurer. Policies were renewed for manageable premium increases each year. Without question, this paradigm was not as firmly entrenched by the 1980s as it had been in past, but the crisis shattered it. Often what had been a multiyear, mutually accommodating business relationship turned adversarial, as policies were not renewed or were renewed only for unprecedented premium increases. This world had probably been poised on the brink of change already, since claims for coverage of CERCLA and mass tort liabilities were about to drive a wedge between policyholders and their insurers. The crisis ushered out that old world in spectacular fashion.

The New Era of Distrust and the Implied "Big-Claim" Exclusion

Although the crisis abated within a couple of years and CGL insurance premiums leveled off or even declined, the business insurance climate would never be the same again. No longer would corporate purchasers trust that in the future their insurance could be easily obtained for predictable premium increases. The result was that in the years to come, policyholders did two things that had important ripple effects throughout the liability insurance system. First, over time policyholders increased the amount of the Self-Insured Retentions (SIRs), or deductibles, to which their CGL policies were subject. In 1973, roughly 6 percent of commercial liability losses were self-insured. By 2003 that figure had risen to an estimated 32 percent.[41] This action helped limit the size of premiums, especially since the policyholder typically defends claims that fall within an SIR at its own expense. Of course, policyholders now faced the increased cost of paying and defending claims falling within their larger SIRs, but they also were now less dependent on their insurers.

The second effect of the crisis of 1985 and 1986 was that with the regular-renewal paradigm shattered, policyholders' remaining loyalty to their own insurers dissipated, and they began to shop more aggressively for coverage. As the insurance cycle progressed at the end of the 1980s, policyholders' more aggressive shopping made the market even more competitive and helped usher in a prolonged soft period during which premiums did not increase substantially.

But the disappearance of loyalty on both sides had implications for much more than the likelihood of policy renewal. Once there was no longer a significant business relationship between a policyholder and its insurers to preserve, provoking antagonism was not a cost to either side. To a number of longtime observers, the disappearance of loyalty made insurers more likely to deny marginal claims, and policyholders more likely to sue for coverage. The insurance coverage environment has certainly been much more litigious in the period since the mid-1980s than it was previously. And because policyholders were purchasing coverage subject to ever-larger SIRs, when they did have a claim that was arguably covered by their policy, it was more likely than ever before to be a large claim worth fighting over.

Indeed, some policyholders' lawyers referred facetiously to the insurers' tendency to deny coverage of sizable losses as the "big-claim" exclusion. With premiums staying low and insurer–insured loyalty dissolved, a vicious cycle took over. Some insurers could not pay marginal claims and still make a satisfactory profit. Increasingly these insurers seemed to deny marginal claims, especially the large ones. Insurance therefore became less reliable, and policyholders valued it less. Whether to litigate a coverage claim was frequently determined by a cold risk–reward calculation rather than as part of an ongoing business relationship.

In the meantime, it became more and more difficult for insurers to provide reliability.[42] They had to meet the prices charged by their competitors in order to maintain market share, and once they met those prices the pressure to turn a profit made denying marginal claims increasingly attractive. A kind of reverse adverse selection problem arose, in which the price of coverage was kept lower than it would otherwise have been, because purchasers could not differentiate between high- and low-reliability insurers. Then, as a consequence, all insurers were forced to deny more claims than they would have otherwise, because they had charged low premiums for that coverage.

The difficulty of recovering big claims is most severe in relation to claims for coverage of long-tail liability, for obvious reasons. Long-tail claims trigger the coverage provided by a policy sold a decade or more before the claim is made. Insurers that sold policies more than a decade earlier were much less likely to still be selling coverage to the policyholder making a claim, and therefore had even less incentive to pay marginal claims. For an insurer receiving a long-tail claim against an old policy, dealing with the claim is like looking at light from a long-dead star. The light is real, but what it represents is not. Liability for a long-tail claim under an old CGL policy may be real, but that policy no longer represents a present relationship between the parties. So the parties are more than ready to fight over the millions of dollars that may be involved, depending on how the policy is interpreted.

Caught between Tort Suits and Insurance Claims

The relation between mass liability suits and claims for coverage of liability that may be imposed in these suits now often creates a catch-22 for policyholders. Major products liability, mass tort, and environmental liability litigation has become a multiparty affair, with the plaintiffs, the defendant, and the defendant's insurers all at war with each other. Insurers that sold policies covering a number of different years are likely to have potential coverage responsibility, because bodily injury or property damage occurring in multiple years will be alleged. Yet these insurers do not necessarily have the same interests, because their coverage defenses may vary. In addition to the underlying tort or environmental liability case against it, therefore, the policyholder and its insurers are caught up in a multisided coverage dispute that either is being litigated simultaneously with the underlying case or is hanging over their heads as the next step in the process.[43]

In the meantime the underlying products liability, mass tort, or environmental liability case proceeds, often with discovery that may affect not only the strength of the tort plaintiffs' case but also the insured defendant's coverage case. Most important, the tort plaintiffs will be looking to discover smoking-gun evidence of the defendant's awareness that its product or conduct was likely to cause harm to those who used or were affected by it. Proof that the defendant knew of this risk and consciously decided to expose people to it, rather than merely that it should have known of the risk, multiplies the value of the plaintiffs' claim. The defendant is more likely to be found liable in such a case, is likely to be found liable for more damages, and is exposed to potential liability for punitive damages if it knew that the risk it was taking was unreasonable.

The tort plaintiffs' search for smoking-gun evidence, however, drives a wedge between the interests of the policyholder-defendant and its insurers. It is in both the defendant's and its insurers' interest for the plaintiffs' case to fail completely. Yet CGL policies always contain an exclusion that denies the insured coverage of liability for bodily injury or property damage that the insured "expected or intended." So the insured's interest, if the plaintiffs' claim cannot be defeated, is to be found liable only for negligence. Such a finding will preserve the insured's claim for insurance coverage. In contrast, the insurers' interest is that the plaintiffs' claim either fail completely or succeed to such a degree that the insured is found liable for expecting or intending harm. The insured that declines to settle with the plaintiffs thus not only risks being held liable to them but also faces the possibility that a finding of liability, depending on what it is, will simultaneously deprive it of insurance coverage for that liability.[44]

For this reason, the policyholder's incentive to settle a mega-lawsuit is skewed, not only by the risk of suffering liability for large sums of money, including punitive damages (which typically are not insured at all), but also by the risk that an adverse jury verdict will deprive the policyholder of its liability insurance. Settlement is therefore all the more attractive. The insurers may be brought into the negotiations and encouraged to contribute to settlement. But even if they decline to do so, the policyholder has lived to fight another day; its claim for coverage of the settlement is still alive.

Nevertheless, an array of obstacles stand in the way of obtaining coverage. The insurers are free to raise any defenses to coverage that they have previously reserved, including defenses that depend on factual questions that may or may not have been adjudicated in the underlying tort suit against the policyholder. For example, even if the policyholder has been held liable only for negligence or strictly liable, the insurers, not being parties to the underlying suit, often are not bound by that finding, and may assert that the policyholder is not entitled to coverage because it "expected or intended" bodily injury or property damage to result from marketing its product or engaging in the activity that generated liability.

The expected or intended defense not only combats moral hazard but also is an indirect check on adverse selection in the very kinds of long-tail situations that are most difficult for insurers to handle. A policyholder that expected or intended harm at the time it took risky actions is more likely to have known of those risks at the time it applied for coverage. Yet avoiding coverage by proving that the policyholder misrepresented facts on an application for insurance may be more difficult than proving that the policyholder expected the harm it caused, especially in cases involving applications that are decades old. The long-tail character of the underlying liabilities that are the subject of products, mass tort, and environmental liability claims therefore makes the expected or intended issue all the more salient. As a consequence, the two sides of a coverage lawsuit sometimes look mismatched. The policyholder puts in evidence supporting its insurance claim, whereas the insurer attempts to prove what may amount to a products or environmental liability suit all over again, by showing that the policyholder expected harm.

In short, the expense and uncertainty of these megacoverage cases make them high-risk propositions for both sides, but especially for policyholders. The fact that often multiple insurers, who provided coverage in multiple years, may be responsible for coverage is a double-edged sword for policyholders. In theory all this coverage is at least potentially available to the policyholder. But the more insurers involved, the more multilateral and complex the coverage issues become, and the more difficult it is for the policyholder to pin down any individual insurer. And in such disputes the insurers can share at least some litigation costs; but the policyholder must fund the entire cost of its case, and under the American rule governing counsel fees, there is no prospect of recovering these fees even if the coverage case is successful and the insurers are held liable.

In the contemporary setting, therefore, no policyholder contemplating the purchase of CGL insurance can be anything but uncertain about the prospect of recovering insurance monies in the event that it is named as a defendant in a major products, mass tort, or environmental liability action. Liability insurance is sometimes a speculative investment; it may pay off a very significant return, but it cannot always be relied on to provide the policyholder with full financial security against catastrophic legal liability. In many instances a policyholder who buys insurance against several hundred million dollars of liability merely buys the right to claim coverage and to litigate future claims. Thus, Justice Traynor's *Escola* rationale for the expansion of products liability more than 60 years ago was only half right. Manufacturers can insure against liability. But whether they can recover that insurance when they are held liable is an open question in many major cases. A field of liability that was originally designed at least in part to take advantage of defendants' superior access to insurance now finds that one of its major reasons for being is in question.

—6—

Which Came First,
the Liability or the Insurance?

A century ago, negligence was the dominant basis of liability for accidental physical harm. It is true that there were small pockets of strict liability, and that workers' compensation, a quintessential strict liability system, would shortly be adopted across the nation. But within the tort system, the negligence standard was the lodestar.

Paradoxically, after a century of momentous change in the law of torts, the same description is still accurate. Strict liability may have expanded slightly, and a dozen states have created limited exceptions to the negligence standard through the enactment of auto no-fault. But negligence remains the basis for imposing liability in the overwhelming majority of cases involving accidental bodily injury or property damage.

The explanation for this paradox, of course, is that although the basis for imposing liability has not changed, the occasions for doing so have expanded. There has been a transformation in the scope of negligence liability far beyond what anyone living at the turn of the twentieth century could have predicted. Earlier chapters were devoted to some of these changes: the exponential growth of auto-related liability resulting from the spread of this now nearly universal means of transportation; manifold increases in medical malpractice suits; and the imposition of liability on manufacturers for defects in their products, as a consequence of the demise of the privity rule. Along with the increased frequency of these essentially negligence-based causes of action have come increases in severity—that is, in the magnitude of damages that tend to be awarded in negligence suits.

These developments in auto, medical, and products liability, however, are only part of the story. In addition to the increased frequency and severity of suits in these fields, it is notable that a century ago the law of negligence itself was very different from the law of negligence today. It is only a slight exaggeration to say that negligence law has evolved from providing for patches of liability for bodily injury and property damage against a backdrop of no-liability at the turn of the twentieth century, to providing for a baseline of liability subject to patches of no-liability at the turn of the twenty-first century.[1]

The *Restatement of Torts (Third)*, the influential recapitulation of tort law rules published periodically by the ALI, clearly states the twenty-first century state of the law on this point:

(a) An actor ordinarily has a duty to exercise reasonable care when the actor's conduct creates a risk of physical harm.
(b) In exceptional cases, when an articulated countervailing principle or policy warrants denying or limiting liability in a particular class of cases, a court may decide that the defendant has no duty or that the ordinary duty of reasonable care requires modification.[2]

Thus, there is now a general duty not to negligently risk causing physical harm, subject to some exceptional situations in which there is "no duty" not to be negligent—that is, in which there is no liability for physical harm caused by negligence.

In contrast, the law of negligence one hundred years ago was shot through with no-duty rules, to such an extent that it would have been misleading to call them exceptions to the norm. Rather, a fair-minded description would have been that in some situations there was liability for negligence, and in others there was no duty not to be negligent. Much of the history of twentieth century negligence law involves the progressive dissolution of many of these no-duty rules, and their replacement with a general duty of care of the sort the *Restatement* describes.

The great twentieth-century torts scholar William L. Prosser thought that insurance had exercised little influence on the development of tort liability, apparently including having little influence on the erosion or elimination of these no-duty rules. Purporting to put his words in the mouth of a "dispassionate observer," Prosser observed that "the impact of insurance on the law of torts has been slight" and that "it is in truth astonishing that a system by which defendants can and do obtain relief from all liability upon payment of a relatively small premium has received so little mention and visible recognition in the tort decisions."[3]

Prosser was entirely correct in suggesting that growth of the particular forms of negligence liability that I have examined in earlier chapters tended to precede the introduction of insurance against these forms of liability. As these chapters showed, the emergence of employers' liability generated the first liability insurance policies; the introduction of the automobile and the imposition of liability for negligent driving produced auto liability insurance; and the advent of products liability led to the development of products liability insurance. As I tried to show, once insurance against these forms of liability was available, it contributed to the willingness of injured parties to seek recovery, and helped to produce expansions in the scope of liability, once these forms of liability were established. But the cause-and-effect relationship between liability and insurance in these fields is clear in the first instance: tort liability came first, and insurance against these forms of liability followed thereafter.

This chapter examines a series of relationships between tort liability and insurance that operated in the opposite direction and that contradict Prosser's assessment. The prime examples are the no-duty limitations on liability for negligence that once obtained but that have now been relaxed to give negligence more nearly full reign. The forms of liability I will explore in this chapter appeared only after general-purpose liability insurance that would cover the new liabilities was already in existence. In fact, the courts only began seriously to consider abolition of the no-duty rules after a new form of "general" personal liability insurance was put in place after World War II. In these situations, I think, the unavailability of insurance had prevented legal change that might well otherwise have occurred earlier. Once personal liability insurance did become available, the forces that promoted the dissolution of the no-duty rules were free to operate. Thus, in these fields of liability the availability of insurance was a necessary condition for the expansion of liability, though not a sufficient condition.

The courts only occasionally acknowledged that the preexisting availability of insurance against the new forms of liability they were creating influenced their decisions. But as I will attempt to show, often the chronology of decision is strongly suggestive of this influence, and in a number of instances the limits the courts placed on the particular forms of liability that they created bear the imprint of the effort to match up the new liabilities with the scope of the insurance that was now available to cover them. Here, and in my view pretty clearly, the imposition of liability awaited the availability of an insured source of recovery.

The Development of General Personal Liability Insurance

General commercial liability insurance developed earlier than general personal liability insurance, and developments on the commercial side of the market set the stage for personal insurance. In the early years after introduction of the Employers Liability and then Public Liability insurance that I described in Chapter 1, commercial liability insurance was hazard specific. Some of the hazards insured were fairly broad, but others were very specific. A building contractor could buy Contractors' Public Liability insurance, for example, but a policyholder with elevators needed Elevator Liability insurance, a policyholder operating a theater needed Theater Liability insurance, and so forth. In certain respects even today some insurance is hazard specific—auto and products liability insurance are still separate forms of coverage, for example, because the hazards they insure are so distinctive. The disadvantages of the hazard-by-hazard approach eventually became obvious, however, and the property/casualty insurance industry, working through its rate organizations, developed the Comprehensive General Liability (CGL) policy, which combined coverage of liability for different hazards into a single instrument.

This was the standard-form CGL insurance policy that was first marketed to businesses in 1941, that figured so prominently in the preceding chapter, and that has figured since that time in products and environmental liability insurance coverage disputes. This policy provided "general" liability insurance in two senses. First, from that time on, the CGL policy has covered liability for bodily injury and property damage regardless of the hazard out of which liability arises. The policy has of course been subject to certain hazard-specific exclusions—it has never covered auto liability, for example.[4] But the coverage the policy affirmatively provided did not (and still does not) hinge on the particular hazard that gave rise to the policyholder's liability.

The coverage provided by the CGL policy was general in a second sense as well. Coverage did not depend on the particular legal doctrine or cause of action that was the basis for the imposition of liability on the policyholder. Rather, claims arising out of changes in the law that took place during the policy period were still covered if the other terms of the policy applied, because the policy covered "liability imposed by law," or the policyholder's "legal liability," or obliged the insurer to pay sums that the insured became "legally obligated to pay," in each instance "because of" or "on account of" or "by reason of" bodily injury or property damage.

For example, if a jurisdiction for the first time imposed strict liability for damage caused by blasting, preexisting CGL insurance policy language would cover this form of liability, even though there had not been strict liability for blasting at the time the policy was issued. As a consequence, there was no need continually to amend or change the terms of coverage to take account of legal change. For the same reason, there was no need to revise the insuring language of liability insurance policies to cover new liabilities as they were created; they tended to fall automatically within that insuring language. Amendment of policy language was necessary only if the insurer wanted to avoid covering a new form of liability; otherwise, coverage was, in effect, automatic. This approach worked well for commercial policyholders, who began to buy the CGL policy as a matter of course.

During the 1940s, however, personal insurance sold to individuals was general only in this second sense. The liability insurance provided by personal insurance policies did not depend on the particular legal doctrine under which the policyholder's liability arose, but was hazard specific. Insurance against liability arising out of the use of a residence was widely available, but it was limited to injuries associated with that particular piece of property. Liabilities arising out of other hazards had to be separately covered under independently purchased policies. Auto liability insurance, of course, had to be purchased separately. But so did sports liability insurance, for example, for those who wanted to be covered against liabilities arising out of playing baseball or golf. And precisely because this hazard-specific insurance had to be purchased separately, it was subject to substantial adverse selection. Those who decided to purchase these forms of specialized coverage tended to be at higher-than-average risk of suffering a loss that would be covered—otherwise, they would have had little reason to purchase it. The splintered, hazard-specific character of personal liability insurance, and the threat of adverse selection accompanying it, tended to inhibit the development of a more robust market for coverage against personal tort liability.

Moreover, because of regulatory restrictions, the insurance industry could not easily develop integrated, general, personal insurance. Most important, liability insurance could not be provided within the same policy as property insurance. This made little difference on the commercial side of the market, because most businesses would purchase both property and CGL insurance anyway. But on the personal, consumer side of the market, where few individuals wished to purchase much liability insurance, this regulatory obstacle to integration mattered.

For example, a homeowner could purchase fire insurance—or be required by the bank that held his mortgage to do so—without purchasing any liability insurance. The absence of any tie-in of liability insurance with fire insurance covering residential property meant that the purchase of personal liability insurance was wholly discretionary. Even those who would ordinarily purchase auto liability insurance had no need to purchase any other form of liability insurance. As a consequence, the sale of personal liability insurance, aside from auto liability coverage, was minimal. But there was a potentially massive market for personal liability insurance, consisting of the portion of the American population with assets worth protecting in the event that it incurred tort liability, if insurers could only capture that market.

To take advantage of this potential market, insurers needed to do two things. First, they had to develop general personal liability insurance coverage on the model of the CGL policies that commercial policyholders had been buying for almost a decade. Potential policyholders would then no longer be able to choose to purchase only the policy insuring against liability for the hazard to which they were particularly exposed. It would be necessary instead to purchase broad, general liability coverage. This approach would largely solve the adverse selection problem the insurers faced under hazard-specific policies.

This first step was taken in the mid-1940s, with the development and marketing of a Comprehensive Personal Liability (CPL) insurance policy that was directly analogous to the CGL policy sold to businesses.[5] This policy provided general coverage that was not hazard specific. But the combination of wartime preoccupation with other matters and the absence of any strong reason for most people to purchase the CPL policy at all meant that the integration of personal liability insurance into a single policy did not significantly increase the demand for this coverage.

The second thing insurers needed to do to take advantage of their potential market, therefore, was to find a way to make the purchase of CPL insurance much more nearly automatic for ordinary individuals and families than it was at that time. Of course, a substantial increase in the risk that an ordinary person would be named as the defendant in a nonautomobile tort suit would have created that demand. But there had been no such increase, and there was no apparent prospect of it. Rather, in the immediate postwar period, tort law was a stable field. Extraordinarily prudent, risk-averse people might want to buy CPL insurance, as would those few people who were actually at high risk of incurring liability in connection with a particular hazard, but most ordinary people would not want to buy nonauto liability insurance.

The moves that the insurers made to solve this problem and effectively to create demand for personal liability insurance were a master stroke. First, beginning in 1949 in New York, whose regulatory apparatus served as a model for other states, the insurers obtained repeal of the statutory and regulatory restrictions on multiline underwriting.[6] Liability and property insurance could thereafter be sold as part of one policy by a single insurer. This was a long-overdue change in its own right, since these restrictions were the anticompetitive residue of an earlier era when concern over the threat to insurers' solvency might have justified the restrictions.

With the restrictions on integrating different forms of coverage into a single policy repealed, the insurers then folded CPL coverage into residential property insurance policies, and sold the two forms of coverage in a single package. This was the industry's key move, because buying residential property insurance, and therefore the personal liability insurance that now came with it, was becoming effectively mandatory for an increasing portion of the population during this period. As veterans returned from the World War II and the postwar housing boom began, the demand for residential property insurance escalated. Mortgage loans backed by the Veterans Administration and the Federal Housing Administration required that homeowners purchase property insurance, as did the conventional noninsured mortgage loans that were being made by local savings and loan institutions. In 1950 there were 17 million mortgaged residences; by 1959 there were 46 million. All of these were likely purchasers of personal insurance that had a liability insurance component.[7] The housing lenders were perfectly happy with the tie-in of liability insurance and property insurance, because liability insurance protected their debtors' solvency and therefore their ability to pay the mortgage loans and avoid foreclosure if they were in debt because of tort liability.[8]

By providing the same liability insurance afforded by the previously optional CPL policies within the residential property insurance policies that homeowners were in effect required to purchase, the insurers could sell vastly greater amounts of personal liability insurance. They could sell this insurance to everyone, or to everyone who expressly chose not to opt out of the liability insurance, when opting out was permitted, as it was for a while in some states. And once people who did not need, or at least thought they did not need, personal liability insurance had to buy it anyway, any residue of adverse selection the insurers still faced in selling optional CPL policies disappeared. The way to avoid adverse selection is to eliminate any selection at all, by requiring the purchase of insurance. That is exactly what the insurers and the housing lenders, acting in tandem, accomplished.

Residential property insurance had already expanded to become "fire and extended" coverage, insuring such additional perils as windstorm, hail, and theft; soon it would become "all-risk" insurance, covering all perils except those that were excluded. With the addition of personal liability insurance to standard fire and extended coverage, everything was in place for the policy to become what it eventually was named: "homeowner's insurance." When the time came, and it would come soon, the liability component of homeowner's insurance would be available to cover the expansions of tort liability that would expose ordinary people to the risk of greater liability than they had faced in the past, because of changes in the no-duty rules.

Personal Liability Insurance and the Demise of the No-Duty Rules

One of the major developments in mid-twentieth-century negligence law that took place after the spread of homeowner's liability insurance was the erosion of a whole series of no-duty and immunity rules that had been in place prior to that time. Over time the deficiencies of many of these rules had been recognized. The courts sometimes acknowledged them, and the commentators often criticized them. But the rules persisted anyway.

A previously unrecognized part of the explanation for the persistence of these rules, in my view, is that there was an unstated precondition to the elimination or modification of a no-duty rule. If a no-duty rule was to be abolished or replaced by a rule that permitted liability under specified circumstances, the ordinary individuals on whom liability was imposed had to have access to insurance against the new liability. By the early decades of the twentieth century, typically businesses already had, or had access to, CGL insurance. But the very nature of most negligence rules is that they tend to threaten both businesses and individuals with liability, because such rules require the exercise of reasonable care generally.

Until homeowner policies containing personal liability insurance were developed, however, most ordinary people were unlikely to be covered by general liability insurance. Permitting the imposition of a liability that previously would have been precluded by a no-duty rule would have meant

subjecting a considerable number of ordinary people to the risk of catastrophic, or at least substantial, financial loss. The courts seem not to have
been ready to abolish no-duty rules until personal insurance against these
kinds of liabilities was introduced and became relatively widespread, or at
least readily available.

Moreover, many of the no-duty limits on liability for physical harm either were going to be preserved, or would, in effect, fall together. Although
these rules were doctrinally separate, they were similar in an important way.
Each rule ignored the reasonable foreseeability of harm in preserving the
no-duty approach; that is what it meant to say that there was no duty not to
be negligent with respect to a particular set of risks. And in one way or another each new approach would have to make foreseeability the basis of liability if a no-duty limit were removed. Courts that removed one no-duty
rule would be stepping onto a slippery conceptual slope, and would find it
difficult to stop at the abolition of any particular no-duty rule. It would be
difficult, for example, to abolish the no-duty protections accorded
landowners without also eventually removing, or at least modifying, the
no-duty limits on liability for negligently caused emotional distress, because the logic behind abolition of one protection would tend to apply to
the others as well. If the foreseeability of an unreasonable risk of harm
was the touchstone of liability for negligence, then only in exceptional cases
(as the third *Restatement* would eventually put it) would there be no duty
not to be negligent. It is true that the courts could simply have decided to be
inconsistent, or could have invoked special reasons for limiting liability
even in cases of foreseeable harm.[9] But to the extent that the foreseeability
of harm was seen as an appropriate basis for imposing liability, all the no-
duty rules had a similar flaw.

Yet until there was insurance against most of the liabilities that would be
threatened once the full logic of foreseeability was let loose, the courts appear to have been reluctant to begin. However comfortable the courts already may have been with the prospect of imposing new liabilities on
institutions and enterprises that had liability insurance, imposing substantial uninsured liabilities on ordinary individuals was another matter. And
removal of the no-duty limits would apply to both enterprises and individuals equally; there was no logical way to distinguish the two categories. The
spread of homeowner's insurance containing a personal liability insurance
component therefore filled the last major gap in the fabric of liability insurance and made it possible for the courts to dismantle many no-duty limita-

tions on liability in the next two decades. One of the background conditions within which tort liability would operate thereafter had changed.

There are any number of examples of this phenomenon. In the following section I discuss four: the liability of landowners; the special standard of care applicable to children; intrafamily and charitable immunities; and liability for "pure" emotional distress—that is, distress not caused by a physical injury to the plaintiff. The first three examples support my thesis in straightforward fashion. The old no-duty rules in these areas persisted as long as most ordinary individuals had no insurance against the liabilities that the rules precluded; once such insurance became available and widespread, the no-duty rules were substantially modified or abolished. The last· example, involving negligently inflicted emotional distress, is more complicated. The fact that there has been only limited movement away from the no-duty approach in this area might be taken to contradict my thesis. I will try to show, however, that the interaction of legal doctrine and liability insurance provides at least part of the explanation for the current state of the law in this area as well.

Premises Liability

A baroque set of distinctions developed in the nineteenth century to govern property owners' liability for injuries suffered by people on their premises. There was a tripartite categorization of entrants onto land: trespassers, licensees, and invitees. The owner of property owed progressively greater duties of care to each category. Trespassers could recover from the owner for bodily injury suffered while on the property only if the owner's conduct was in wanton and willful disregard of the trespasser's safety. The owner could not intentionally injure trespassers or set hidden traps for them. But there was no liability for failing to remedy or repair dangerous conditions that caused injury to trespassers.

In the licensee category were people invited onto property for their own purpose or benefit rather than for the economic benefit of the owner. The main group of people who fell into this category were social guests of the owner, but others included those with an actual "license" to be on the property, express or implied, such as people permitted to take a shortcut across the property. Licensees could recover from the owner only if the owner failed to disclose hidden dangerous characteristics of the property. In effect, the owner had a duty to make the premises as safe for licensees as he did for himself, but there was no duty to make the premises reasonably safe—that is, there was no liability to licensees for ordinary negligence.

Finally, invitees were either business visitors such as customers, or members of the public who were entitled to be on the property by general invitation, such as people watching a baseball game in a public park or waiting to pick someone up at a train station. The owner of property was liable to these invitees for bodily injury caused by his failure to keep the premises reasonably safe.

Thus, a property owner was liable to invitees for negligence, but had no duty to trespassers or licensees not to be negligent. The owner owed those in the latter two categories some care, but not reasonable care. Over time, however, two major exceptions developed. There was a duty to exercise reasonable care to trespassers whom the property owner discovered on the premises. And under the "attractive nuisance" doctrine, there was a duty to exercise reasonable care to actually foreseen, and in some states to foreseeable, child trespassers who were drawn to the property by a condition (the attraction) whose dangers the children could not appreciate. But aside from these exceptions, the formalistic distinctions among categories of entrants onto property were maintained far beyond the period of legal realism that began in the 1930s, and well into the period when the expansion of products liability, for example, had already occurred.

It is important to see that the principal effect of these no-duty and limited-duty rules regarding premises liability was to protect private individuals, not businesses. Although businesses might be just as likely to have people trespass on their property as private individuals, tort actions involving trespassers would have been rare no matter what rule applied. So the real action here involved the licensee–invitee distinction. And on this score there was a difference. Businesses do not have social guests; anyone on their property with permission is an invitee, to whom the business has a duty to exercise reasonable care. Conversely, private individuals have few business visitors in their homes. Most of their visitors are social guests. The licensee–invitee distinction therefore had no appreciable effect on the liability of businesses, while limiting the scope of individuals' premises liability.

In many instances it would in any event have been pointless for a social guest to sue a host for negligence, because the host would have had no means of paying a substantial judgment. So the pressure for a change in the rule regarding the licensee–invitee distinction would have been minimal. And in cases where the host did have some assets, subjecting the host to liability could have had the disruptive consequence of depriving families of their savings or even their homes. It is true that in the absence of the host's liability, social guests would have been left to bear the costs of their injuries themselves. But imposing liability would simply have shifted costs from one individual risk-bearer to another, without much prospect of reducing the incidence of accidents as a result.

In contrast, the law of negligence already imposed premises liability where property owners were, in fact, superior risk-bearers. Businesses had always been liable to customers and other invitees who were injured on their property. And as we saw in Chapter 1, these owners of business property had been able to buy insurance against this liability, first in the form of Public Liability and later in the form of CGL insurance policies, since the 1880s. By the early years of the twentieth century, then, in the case of people who were properly or at least understandably on someone's property, the premises-liability rules provided for a right to recover for negligence where there was some prospect that the property owner either would or could insure against liability, but these rules insulated owners from premises liability where the owner ordinarily would be a private individual without insurance.

The exceptions to the rules insulating landowners from liability probably had the same impact, leaving businesses exposed to liability and individuals protected from it. In theory private individuals might maintain conditions on their land that qualified as attractive nuisances. But the major cases applying this doctrine involved commercial defendants, and especially railroads. And most of the leading appellate cases involved businesses rather than individuals.[10] Thus, while requiring reasonable care toward discovered trespassers could have burdened private individuals as well as businesses, in practice that probably did not often occur.

In short, the premises liability rules survived as long as they did despite the fact that, by the 1930s and 1940s, abolishing them would have been otherwise unremarkable from a tort theory standpoint. Certainly the licensee category as it applied to social guests had little to recommend it from the standpoint of the legal realists who began to ascend to the bench during this period. For them the categories were the arbitrary residue of legal formalism. But few homeowners whom a new rule would have exposed to liability would have had insurance against that liability. Once insurance that would cover such liability became widespread, it was only a matter of time before the courts overcame their inertia and abolished the no-duty and limited-duty rules. In fact, Nancy Christian, the insured defendant in the landmark California case that abolished the categories of premises liability, was a defendant in name only. When professor Robert Rabin tracked her down more than 30 years later, she had no idea what had happened to the suit against her. She had given a pretrial deposition and then simply left her liability insurer to handle everything else.[11] The insurer was the real party in interest, having defended the case against her, unsuccessfully it turned out, all the way to the Supreme Court of California.

In Christian's case the Supreme Court of California became the first to abolish the categories.[12] About half the states have followed, though many have retained the separate rules governing liability to trespassers.[13] These distinctions were maintained as long as they were—and are still maintained in many states—for a number of cultural and philosophical reasons. The lesser duty to trespassers has moral staying power, for example. But it seems clear to me that one of the factors that helped to maintain the rigid distinctions for so long was that typical homeowners did not even begin to have insurance against liability to their social guests until the 1950s. Until such insurance was widely purchased, and until the courts understood that it was purchased, abolishing the distinction between invitees and licensees would have had implications that the availability of personal liability insurance eliminated. With this form of insurance likely to be available even in suits against ordinary individuals, the courts would have felt much less compunction about abolishing the old limited-duty rules than they had felt decades earlier. The availability of liability insurance liberated the courts to follow the jurisprudential inclinations and logic of liability that had probably been in place for some time.

The Child's Standard of Care

From the time that liability for negligence first emerged as a distinct cause of action, an objective standard of reasonable care has applied to adult defendants. They are liable if they fail to exercise the care that would have been exercised by a reasonable person under the circumstances in question. Under this standard the elderly, the infirm, the subpar, and the below average must measure up to the minimum required objective standard of care or they are held liable for negligence. Good faith is no defense, nor is the lack of sufficient intelligence, good sense, or experience necessary to enable the defendant to behave as carefully as the reasonable person would have behaved under the circumstances. In most jurisdictions even the insane were held liable for failing to comply with this objective standard.

The common law provided that children could be negligent. But what it meant for a child to be negligent was different from what that meant for an adult. Children under the age of about seven were considered incapable of negligence. And children over seven were held to what amounted to a semi-objective, child-oriented standard of care. A child defendant was required only to exercise the level of care that a child of like age, intelligence, and experience would have exercised. In effect, a child had to be as careful as he or she was capable of being, but that was all.

This children's standard of care applied regardless of whether a child defendant had been playing jacks, driving a car, or shooting a gun. If an eight-year-old managed to grab the key to his parents' car and drove as well as a child would be expected to drive, he was not negligent. If a nine-year-old started a fire in a neighbor's garage with a pack of matches he had found on the street, he was judged by reference to the degree of care that should be exercised by a nine-year-old with his intelligence and experience.

Even when a child had failed to comply with the applicable standard of care, however, it would rarely have made sense to bother suing a child for negligence. Few children had any assets, and parents were not (and in the absence of statute still are not) liable for the torts of their children. Parents were and are liable for their own negligence in supervising their children, but a child's injury-causing action often is not the result of a parent's negligent supervision. Children can be loose cannons, and parents cannot always prevent them from rolling into people.

Since few children had any assets, the special rule limiting childrens' liability for negligence usually made little difference in practice. Even if children had been held to an objective, adult standard of care, most plaintiffs would have been unable to collect the judgments they could have obtained against child defendants, and therefore most potential plaintiffs probably would not have bothered to bring suit against children. The objective adult standard demanded more care from some adults than they were capable of exercising, and avoided what would have been a costly inquiry into each individual defendant's capabilities. The result was that adults, who more often had assets than did children, were more exposed to liability for negligence than were children—although, as we have seen, many adults tended to be without insurance and could not otherwise pay judgments either.

By the 1950s, however, a fundamental change in this state of affairs was in process. As we saw in Chapter 3, auto liability insurance covering the owner of a vehicle and the residents of his or her household had spread. The majority of the driving population now had this coverage, and it would begin to be compulsory in many states in the 1960s. In addition, as we have just seen, homeowner's insurance providing general personal liability insurance was spreading at precisely the same time. Everyone in a family that bought a house and financed it with a mortgage, including children, was likely to be covered by this insurance.

When the courts subsequently came to consider the applicability of the child standard of care, therefore, circumstances had changed. Which standard applied to children actually would now make a difference, because most children were no longer automatically judgment proof. The approach that was adopted, beginning with the seminal decision in *Dellwo v. Pearson* in 1961, has been to apply an adult standard to children engaging in what the courts have called "adult activities."[14] Operating a car, boat, or plane falls into this category, while skiing and playing sand-lot sports ordinarily do not. The rule that a child under the age of about seven was incapable of being negligent still prevailed, but few such children ever engaged in adult activities. For children above that age, which standard applied now made a difference. The availability of insurance was not the factor that divided activities to which an adult or a child's standard of care applied, or virtually all activities would have been subject to the former standard. Indeed, homeowner's insurance was more likely to cover liability arising out of skiing or playing ball in the street than liability arising out of operating a power boat, which typically required the purchase of separate insurance. Rather, the spread of homeowner's insurance made it possible for the courts to consider the line they wished to draw between adult and children's activities, because it now mattered where the line was drawn. Liability insurance had made the question practical and meaningful.

Moreover, even in cases to which the courts continued to apply a child standard, the spread of homeowner's insurance could make a difference. The typical child who violated the child standard no longer was judgment proof; there was homeowner's insurance to cover his or her liability for violating the standard of care applicable to children's activities. And the same homeowner's insurance covered the parent who was held liable for negligently supervising a child who had nonnegligently but dangerously engaged in a child activity. Thus, the spread of auto liability and homeowner's insurance, but especially the latter, permitted meaningful reconfiguration of the whole environment of liability associated with child-related accidents. Today the courts may address the scope of children's liability, and that of their parents, knowing that personal liability insurance is likely to cover whatever level and form of liability the courts consider appropriate.

Dissolving Immunity

An analogous process led to the dissolution of certain common law immunities from liability, the most prominent of which was intrafamily immunity. In contrast to a no-duty rule, technically an immunity is an exemption from a liability that would exist but for an actor's status. But in practice an immunity from tort liability is the functional equivalent of a no-duty rule.

At common law there was both interspousal and parent-child immunity from tort liability. The bases for these immunities were both conceptual and practical. A blatantly sexist common law metaphysics precluded liability between husbands and wives because in many respects they were considered to have the same legal identity; they were "one." And in any event, the imposition of tort liability between spouses, or between parents and their children, usually would have involved a pointless transfer of funds within the same family or, if the suit was not pointless because individual assets were meaningfully segregated, a substantial interference with family tranquility.

By the 1950s the argument for blanket intrafamily immunity had holes in it. Spouses clearly were separate people, often with separate interests and assets. Family tranquility would not always be disrupted by litigation within the family. And insurance against intrafamily liability had become available. A few courts abolished these immunities before auto liability and homeowner's insurance were widespread, but abolition did not gain momentum until the 1950s, when these forms of personal liability insurance became common. Sometimes the abolitions came from courts, and on occasion from legislatures.[15] The availability of liability insurance meant that the imposition of liability would not produce a mere transfer of funds within the family; whether there was liability would now make a difference, since it was the family's liability insurer that would pay the judgment.

The proof of the pudding is that some of the abolitions at first applied only to automobile liability, where the presence of auto liability insurance protecting a family-member defendant was most likely. In this situation family harmony was least likely to be disrupted, and the transfer of funds would not be pointless, since it would provide real compensation for loss. Concerned about the possibility of fraudulent suits designed to achieve precisely this purpose, insurers sometimes opposed the abolition of intrafamily immunity. When the insurers' opposition failed, there were some attempts to include intrafamily exclusions in their liability insurance policies. Often, though not always, these were declared to be against public policy.[16]

Intrafamily immunities still exist in some states, and in others they are subject to significant exceptions. For example, it is common to see immunity preserved for injury that results from the exercise of ordinary parental discretion. But on the whole the immunities are well into the process of withering away, and the availability of insurance against liability within the family has been the catalyst making it possible for the courts to address the issue forthrightly.

The close connection between the relaxation or abolition of immunity and the availability of liability insurance is further illustrated by the experience of nonprofit organizations. Recall from my discussion of hospital liability in Chapter 4 that charities enjoyed immunity from tort liability until the middle of the twentieth century. The rationale for this immunity was that the assets of charities should be preserved for serving charitable purposes. But as charities became large enterprises themselves—for example, both the Red Cross and Harvard University were significant "charities" at the time—this rationale lost much of its force. At this point, by both judicial decision and statute, this immunity began to disappear, at least in part because of the increasing ability of charitable entities to purchase liability insurance.[17] The availability of this insurance often figured expressly in debates about the abolition of charitable immunity, and in fact sometimes immunity was abolished only to the extent that a charitable entity was protected by liability insurance. Although hospitals were originally the main object of the new liability rule, it applied to all nonprofit organizations.

Over time the threat of liability on the part of all sorts of nonprofits therefore made it increasingly prudent for these organizations to purchase liability insurance, and they often did so. The individuals who worked for nonprofits on a voluntary basis, however, were also potentially subject to liability for harm arising out of their conduct. The broader forms of homeowner's insurance covered nonprofit volunteers against nonautomobile liability arising out of their volunteer service, and their auto policies covered them against auto liability incurred in the course of their service, since neither policy contained a relevant exclusion. Nonetheless, those who volunteered for nonprofit organizations were often understandably concerned about whether they were insured against these and other forms of liability, and in any event were disinclined to risk steep increases in their own liability insurance premiums if they were sued for injury arising out of a volunteering-related accident. Perhaps just as important, neither a homeowner's nor an auto policy would cover a volunteer against liability for pure economic loss, for example, for breach of duty as the member of the board of directors of a nonprofit organization, as distinguished from liability for personal injury or property damage.

With the rise of lawsuits against the directors and officers of for-profit corporations in the 1980s, a new form of insurance covering that liability— directors and officers (D & O) liability insurance—was developed. The volunteer directors and officers of nonprofit organizations often had full-time jobs with for-profit businesses, and therefore were sophisticated about, and sensitive to, their potential exposure to liability for their volunteer work. They naturally wanted to ensure that they were protected against this exposure. And the nonprofits themselves wanted to protect their assets against the prospect that a director or officer would be held liable for actions within the scope of his office and seek indemnification from the organization. Nonprofits therefore began to purchase D & O insurance to cover both individual and indemnification risks.

Yet the cost of such insurance to nonprofit organizations, especially small ones like Little League baseball teams and community improvement associations, was often prohibitively high.[18] Even sizable nonprofit organizations were disadvantaged when they had to devote substantial sums to purchasing this insurance. And the price of D & O insurance was often highly variable from year to year, because it was subject to the same insurance underwriting cycle that I discussed in Chapters 4 and 5. For an organization attempting to do long-term financial planning, the threat of substantial, unexpected increases in D & O premiums was frustratingly disruptive.

In response, some states enacted statutes that either created immunity for nonprofit volunteers or lowered their required standard of care so that they were liable only for recklessness or intentional injury.[19] Then in 1997 the U.S. Congress enacted a volunteer protection statute that preserved nonprofit volunteers' auto liability, but otherwise permitted suit against a volunteer only for willful or gross negligence.[20] The influence of the cost and availability of liability insurance on the scope of volunteer liability is strikingly evident here. At least in part because of the potentially high cost of D & O insurance, partial immunity for the liabilities it otherwise covered was granted; but because auto insurance was readily available at a manageable price, auto liability was preserved.

In the nonprofit area, then, immunity from tort liability has risen and fallen not only with the literal availability of insurance but also with its cost. For some small nonprofit organizations to be able to function, it might not be enough that insurance against liability that might be incurred by their volunteers could in theory be purchased. If that insurance is not affordable given such organizations' budgets, then they apparently have enough political clout to secure at least partial immunity from tort liability for such volunteers. Whether or not this arrangement is sensible as a matter of public policy, it certainly demonstrates the strong connection between the practical availability of liability insurance and the scope of immunity from tort liability.

Liability for Negligently Inflicted Emotional Distress

My last example reflects a more complicated interaction between tort and insurance. Here liability came first, and for the most part, insurance did not follow. At least partly as a consequence, liability has never expanded to nearly the extent it might otherwise have been expected to.

Tort law has long awarded damages for what amounts to emotional distress or mental suffering, when that distress results from physical injury. Thus, general damages for "pain and suffering" are recoverable for experiencing physical pain, for anguish resulting from the death of a close relative, and for loss of life's enjoyments as a consequence of injury. In contrast, the right to recover for negligently inflicted emotional distress that is not a consequence of or, as is sometimes said, is not "parasitic" on physical injury, has always been extremely limited.

The traditional rule permitted such recovery only where there was mishandling of a corpse or an inaccurate report of a loved one's death. In other respects a no-duty rule applied. By the early decades of the twentieth century the courts were beginning to recognize an additional, general exception in cases in which there had been a physical impact with the plaintiff's person even in the absence of actual injury, and emotional distress resulted. This so-called "impact" rule persisted well into midcentury, despite its obvious arbitrariness. There was no recovery in cases involving close calls without impact, but recovery was not restricted as long as there had been some physical contact.[21] The courts justified this bright-line rule largely based on their concern that an open-ended rule permitting recovery for all emotional distress that was a foreseeable result of the defendant's negligence would open up the floodgates of litigation and risk drawing fraudulent claims into the tort system.

Interestingly, however, the line between recoverable and nonrecoverable damages that the impact rule drew dovetailed closely with the scope of liability insurance coverage that was available, and likely would be available, for such claims. The public liability, CGL, and auto liability insurance policies that provided the vast majority of liability insurance coverage during the first half of the twentieth century, when the impact rule was dominant, typically limited coverage to liability imposed "on account of" or "because of" bodily injury or property damage. And bodily injury was defined in physical, not mental or emotional terms. So liability for emotional distress resulting from impact that caused even minimal physical injury was covered, whereas liability for emotional distress without impact clearly would not have been covered.

Whether emotional distress resulting from a noninjurious physical impact was insured because it was "on account of" or "because of" bodily injury was never definitively resolved; but under the law of most states, liability for mental anguish alone clearly did not satisfy a liability insurance policy's bodily injury requirement.[22] Moreover, it would have been considerably more difficult for insurers to set a price for a policy that included coverage of liability for mental distress not caused by physical injury. The physical injury requirement made calculation of the prospect of liability, and therefore the scope of the insurer's potential coverage responsibility, more feasible.

In the next step in the evolution of tort liability for emotional distress, some courts held that the plaintiff could recover for emotional distress even in the absence of actual physical impact with the plaintiff, as long as the negligence of the defendant had placed her in a zone of physical danger and the emotional distress was caused by fear for her own safety.[23] And the last expansion of liability in this field goes a bit further, but has been undertaken only in a minority of states. These states have held that under limited circumstances a plaintiff may recover not only when she fears for her own safety as a result of the defendant's negligence but also under limited circumstances when she is outside the zone of physical danger to herself, but suffers emotional distress as a result of the defendant's actions. The limitations on this cause of action all tend to involve the requirements that (1) the plaintiff fear for the safety of another person, (2) the plaintiff be in close proximity to or actually witness the scene in which another person is placed at risk by the defendant's negligence, and (3) the person placed at risk be closely related to the plaintiff.[24]

Thus, this extension of liability does not involve the creation of a general cause of action for negligent infliction of emotional distress. Rather, like the zone-of-danger extension before it, the new cause of action requires that the defendant negligently risk causing physical harm. Under the zone-of-danger rule it had to be the plaintiff's own safety that was at risk; under the extension, the safety of a close relative must be placed at risk, and the plaintiff must be an eyewitness, or nearly that, to what happens. There have been a few cases that do not rest on the defendant's having negligently created a risk of physical harm to someone, but even they usually involve some kind of wrong to one person that results in emotional distress suffered by a different person.[25]

On the basis of the insuring language I quoted above, standard-form business and auto liability insurance policies would not in the past, and do not now, cover expansions of liability beyond the impact rule.[26] Therefore, I cannot claim that the zone-of-danger rule or the extension of the rule that has been adopted in a minority of states have been carefully fashioned to take advantage of available insurance. On the contrary, if the plaintiff is in the zone of danger but suffers no physical injury, liability for her emotional distress is not incurred "because of" bodily injury under standard liability insurance policies. Rather, this liability is incurred only because of the fear of bodily injury and would not be covered. The same would be true if the plaintiff witnessed her child being placed at risk and neither the child nor the plaintiff were physically injured. By an artifact of the standard coverage language, and somewhat peculiarly, I suppose, if the child were physically injured and the plaintiff suffered emotional distress as a result, I think that liability for the plaintiff's emotional distress would be covered. This is because, under the standard coverage language, liability for emotional distress arguably would be incurred at least in part "because of" bodily injury, albeit bodily injury to the child rather than to the plaintiff. But this is an abstruse point of which few people, and certainly few appellate judges, would be aware.

On the whole, then, the absence of liability insurance coverage for the recent expansions of liability for negligently inflicted emotional distress could be understood to provide a counterexample to my thesis. The modern premises, children's, and intrafamily liabilities were not created until *after* the spread of homeowner's liability insurance that would cover them. In contrast, the most recent expansions of liability for emotional distress were adopted before there was liability insurance available to cover them, and for the most part even after these expansions, liability insurance covering the new liabilities has not developed. As a matter of fact, certain deluxe liability insurance policies now cover liability for emotional distress, but most standard policies do not, and coverage under the deluxe policies was developed only after the new liabilities came into being. In a sense, therefore, the entire area of liability for emotional distress could be regarded as an embarrassment to my contention that the demise of the no-duty rules could only occur after there was liability insurance in place to cover the new duties.

But that is only one way of looking at it. In another sense, the very limited and incremental way in which this field has extended beyond the no-duty baseline at which it began confirms the importance of insurance to the relaxation of no-duty rules. When the other no-duty rules were modified, they were either abolished outright or abolished precisely and expressly to the extent that there was insurance against them, as in the case of charitable immunity. In contrast, the rule precluding recovery for negligently inflicted emotional distress has not been abolished outright. Rather, liability is carefully circumscribed, and except in very rare cases may be imposed only where the defendant negligently risks causing physical injury to one party and instead, or in addition, causes emotional distress to a close relative who is nearby. There is no general liability for negligently causing emotional distress in cases where there is no risk of physical harm. What does exist, in limited measure, is a species of liability for one of the additional foreseeable consequences of negligently risking physical harm. In short, the courts have been extremely reluctant to expand liability for emotional distress much beyond its traditional bounds.

There are many explanations for this reluctance, including the courts' concern, evident from the beginning, that unconstrained liability for emotional distress would promote large numbers of fraudulent claims.[27] But even though many courts have expressed frustration with the arbitrary limitations on the recovery of damages for emotional distress, they have not treated these limitations the same way they have treated the other new no-duty limits. Long after the other no-duty rules were essentially abolished, a much more measured approach to liability for emotional distress remains in place.

I want to suggest that, in addition to the other jurisprudential and policy factors contributing to this state of affairs, the unavailability of insurance against liability for emotional distress has been an indirect influence on the slow pace of change in this area. Had standard liability insurance policies already provided coverage against liability for emotional distress, the courts might well have been less reluctant to expand liability than they have proved to be. I do not mean that the courts have been consciously thinking, one way or the other, about whether liability insurance covers liability for emotional distress. But if standard liability insurance policies did cover emotional distress, then that message would not have been lost on the courts. Lawyers whom judges knew to be regularly hired by insurers would have appeared to defend cases seeking damages for emotional distress; and plaintiffs' lawyers would undoubtedly have found ways to bring the existence of defendants' insurance coverage to the attention of the courts. The courts would then have been aware that substantially expanding liability would not produce uninsured judgments against individual defendants. But none of this was brought to the attention of the courts, because it was not the case.

Furthermore, had insurance against liability for emotional distress been regularly available, there might well have been more suits seeking damages for this kind of loss against ordinary individuals. In the absence of such insurance, however, there was much less incentive to bring such suits, since most individual defendants would be effectively judgment proof. And the more suits that had been brought, the more opportunity the courts would have had to consider the wide variety of factual situations in which the traditional no-duty rules might have been modified.

In short, at least in these indirect ways, I think that the unavailability of insurance against liability for emotional distress has contributed to the slow pace of expansion in this area of tort liability. In this field, the absence of liability insurance has been like the dog that did not bark. The courts have paid no particular attention to that absence, but liability insurance might well have played a meaningful influence if it had been present.

The General Nature of the Influence

I have now provided several examples of the way the rise of personal liability insurance paved the way for changes in the liabilities to which no-duty rules had previously applied, and one example in which the absence of insurance probably helped to inhibit the pace of change. In this last section I will set out with a bit more precision what I contend about the way the availability of insurance influenced these legal changes, as well as what I do not contend.

My argument is that both the conceptual and practical reasons for modifying or abolishing the no-duty rules I have discussed had been accumulating for some time in the twentieth century. The distinction between licensees and invitees was seen as both formalistic and out of line with common moral sentiments; concern with the compensation of victims argued for at least some of the expansion of children's liability for negligence; and blanket intrafamily and charitable immunity no longer were considered necessary to promote tranquil family life or the purposes of charitable organizations. The impact that the expansion of liability in these fields would have had on uninsured individuals, however, was one of the potential negative side-effects that contributed to judicial inertia and the courts' consequent reluctance to overrule the no-duty rules in each field. Once this impediment to the expansion of liability was removed, however, the forces that promoted legal change were able to operate without this constraint. In short, I think that in these instances the availability of liability insurance has been a necessary condition of liability, not that it has been a sufficient condition.

Thus, I do not contend that, in these situations, the courts changed long-standing no-duty rules solely because liability insurance previously had not been, but recently had become, available. On the contrary, certain other no-duty rules have hardly been modified at all, even though there clearly would be coverage under existing insurance policies against the liabilities that would result if these no-duty rules were eliminated. The no-duty-to-rescue rule is an example. The mere fact that homeowner's and CGL policies would clearly cover liability for bodily injury resulting from the negligent breach of a duty to rescue, if that duty existed, has not prompted the courts to modify the traditional rule. Tort law principles and policies militating against a duty to rescue have been so influential that a strong no-duty rule remains in force, although very plausible arguments can be made for imposing a duty in this field as well.[28]

But I think that my analysis of the evolution of the four no-duty rules that have been modified demonstrates that the availability of insurance does influence the modification or abolition of such rules when the other conditions necessary for change are satisfied. The structure of influence in these situations contrasts with those I discussed in earlier chapters, in which a new form of liability was first created, and only then was insurance developed to cover the new liability. In their expansion of products liability, for example, the courts' assumption was that insurance against liability for injuries caused by defective products would develop further if such liability was imposed. Indeed, in the development of strict liability the prospect that such insurance would become available was an express reason for changing the law. Manufacturers' greater access to insurance counted in favor of making a legal change. The same had been true 50 years earlier, not for courts, but for legislatures, in connection with workers' compensation. As we saw in Chapter 2, for example, in 1910 New York's Wainright Commission had emphasized that workers did not, and practically could not, purchase insurance against the risk of suffering injury on the job. That employers were in a better position to purchase such insurance counted in favor of the adoption of workers' compensation. The legislatures were confident that if workers' compensation were enacted, insurance against the new liabilities it created would come into existence. And they were correct. In these fields, potential defendants' anticipated loss-spreading capacity was enlisted precisely in order to provide victims with access to a source of insurance. The new liabilities in these fields were created, at least in part, in order to transform tort into what amounted to a form of insurance for victims.

In contrast, the courts' objective in relaxing the no-duty and immunity rules was to impose liability in situations where what they considered to be the inner logic of the law of torts and previously articulated policy required it. The unavailability of insurance had simply been preventing that logic and policy from being fully developed and implemented. Here the courts did not modify the rules in the expectation that, once new liabilities were in place, insurance against these liabilities would develop. Rather, the prospect of burdensome or even crushing judgments against individuals had been a background condition that contributed to legal inertia. The introduction of insurance that would cover individuals against such judgments dissolved this inertia. Once most potential defendants had been able to acquire liability insurance, the courts were free to weigh the other factors bearing on the retention or modification of the rules without being affected by the obstacle that the absence of insurance covering the liability of ordinary individuals had previously presented.

Precisely what the courts were actually thinking about the availability of insurance in the situations I have surveyed is largely inaccessible to us now. The judges of the time were lawyers, however, and it would not be surprising if they had read the homeowner's policies that they had purchased. They would have known from such a reading that the policies would cover the liabilities that were being litigated. And even judges who had not read their homeowner's policies and did not otherwise know what they covered would likely have been able to say to themselves and their colleagues, "insurance will take care of this liability if we create it." Twenty years earlier that supposition would not have been accurate; by the 1950s, it was. The mere fact that the availability of insurance is not mentioned in the relevant judicial opinions, then, does not mean that it was not influential.

In connection with what Robert Rabin has creatively called "enabling torts" a variation of this process has occurred.[29] Liability has sometimes been imposed on might be called secondary wrongdoers at least in part because principal wrongdoers in certain settings are likely to be uninsured or underinsured. For example, an apartment owner may have negligently provided inadequate security that results in an assault on a tenant by an intruder;[30] or a psychiatrist may have failed to notify police that a third party is in danger of being harmed by his patient.[31] Relaxation of the no-duty rules in such situations holds a secondary wrongdoer such as the landlord or psychiatrist liable for the consequences of the principal wrongdoer's action. In many of these enabling torts the secondary wrongdoer is a socially and economically more responsible individual or enterprise that is far more likely to have liability insurance, and to be covered by that insurance because an intentional-injury exclusion in the policy is inapplicable to a claim for coverage of negligent enabling, than the principal wrongdoer. The expansion of liability for certain enabling torts therefore takes advantage of liability insurance covering categories of actors who previously were protected by a no-duty rule.

Interestingly, with only limited exceptions, the influence of the availability of insurance on the doctrinal movement away from the no-duty rules has been one-directional. The introduction of a new form of insurance may help to speed along the expansion of liability. But even if this insurance later becomes less available or significantly more expensive, the courts let the expanded liabilities remain in force. The expansion of liability has a genie-out-of-the-bottle quality that tends to make it irreversible, at least by common law decision. It takes legislation to produce a contraction of or limitation on liability. General statutorily set ceilings on the recovery of damages for pain and suffering and the legislative enactment of immunity for nonprofit volunteers are both examples of legislation that cuts back on expanded common law liabilities at least in part because of the way these liabilities have affected liability insurance. The increasing cost of insurance against these liabilities had no discernible impact on the scope of the existing common law rules governing them; only the imposition of legislative limits on liability could modify these rules once they were in force.

To summarize, then, I have tried to show that Prosser's contention that insurance has had virtually no influence on the development of tort liability is, in fact, highly questionable. Prosser was of course correct in that the courts rarely have cited the availability of insurance as a basis for the expansion of liability. On the occasions when the courts created a form of liability with the purpose of seeking out insurance against that liability, they were open about it, as Roger Traynor was in his concurrence in *Escola*.

What happened in the fields I have surveyed in this chapter was more subtle. An important background condition, the unavailability of liability insurance, had changed. A constraint that had prevented doctrinal logic and judicial policymaking from running their normal course was removed; these forces could now be deployed freely, without any need for judicial concern for or reference to insurance. The old world in which, aside from auto liability, it was either pointless or potentially disastrous to impose tort liability on ordinary individuals was transformed into a new world in which a liability insurer would likely shoulder the burden of most such liabilities. That is the world in which the law of negligence as we now know it has operated ever since.

—7—

Collateral Sources, Mega-Liability, and the Stresses of 9/11

The legal impact of the terrorist attacks of September 11, 2001, pales in comparison to their human and historical effects. Over two thousand people died; many more survivors have suffered physical or emotional injury, or both, as a result of the attacks; and in response to the attacks a continuing "war on terrorism" with far-reaching global effects was begun.

Nonetheless, as legal impacts go, the results of 9/11 were significant. In order to avoid multibillion-dollar tort suits against U.S. airlines, a federally financed fund for compensating the 9/11 victims and their families was established. This Victim Compensation Fund (VCF) attempted to provide compensation that, in rough measure, mirrored what plaintiffs could have recovered in tort suits against the airlines, if those suits were successful. But there was one exception. Life insurance was deducted from the payments the VCF made, and that is never done in tort. The result was a major controversy about what would constitute fair compensation and how to measure it.

In total, the VCF made payments of just over $7 billion to the survivors of 2,880 people killed in the attacks, and to 2,680 individuals who were injured in the attacks or in subsequent rescue actions.[1] At one level, the public debate that erupted as the process of providing VCF compensation evolved was about whether the victims of 9/11 should have received any compensation at all from the government's efforts. The victims of other terrorist attacks such as the 1995 Oklahoma City bombing, for example, had received no such compensation.

At another level, however, the debate was not about whether compensation should be paid at all, but about the appropriate measure of compensation for the victims and their families. And while the measure of compensation under the VCF was the immediate focus of this debate, the issues the debate raised had broader implications. What role should other sources of compensation available to victims play in a tort-like approach such as the VCF, or indeed in tort itself? Should life insurance benefits, which traditionally have been treated differently from all other sources, continue to receive special treatment, or should life insurance be treated the same way as health and disability insurance? The debate about the VCF put these issues on the table, but the issues have not disappeared merely because that particular debate has subsided. As the tort and insurance systems evolve, they will continually be faced with the need to fashion an appropriate relationship between the compensation paid in tort and the various sources of first-party insurance that also are available to tort claimants.

Mega-Liability and 9/11

Perhaps surprisingly, the situation the VCF addressed after 9/11 had a number of parallels with the problems that arise in mass tort and similar cases. As substantial as the sums paid by the VCF were, recoveries of this order of magnitude are not unprecedented. For example, payments of hundreds of millions of dollars to settle the kinds of mass tort, products, and environmental liability actions I discussed in Chapter 5 have frequently been made; it is not entirely uncommon for settlements in cases such as these to exceed the billion-dollar mark; and over $70 billion has thus far been paid to asbestos claimants in the years since that litigation began several decades ago.[2]

Beyond the fact that the total amount of compensation the VCF paid was within the bounds of what might be called "mega-tort normality," and despite its uniqueness, in obvious respects the 9/11 scenario resembled more conventional mega-tort cases in several other ways as well. First, deterrence has a limited or nonexistent role to play in both settings. Whatever other considerations arguably did affect or should have affected the terms of the VCF, deterrence of future terrorist attacks was not one of them. It would have strained credulity to the breaking point to imagine that either potential terrorists' future behavior, or the level of precautions taken in the future by the U.S. government, would be affected by the prospect that another VCF might be created in the event of another terrorist attack. Similarly, the deterrent effect of imposing certain mega-tort liabilities, if not nonexistent, is at least speculative. As I discussed in Chapter 5, because so many such liabilities involve long-latent harm, it is unclear how much incentive potential defendants have to compare the uncertain risk of incurring future liability for harm in the distant future with the more easily quantified benefits that can be gained in the present from taking action that is risky only in the long term.

Second, corrective justice and civil redress also are arguably of less significance in both of these settings, for virtually the same reason that deterrence concerns are minimal. In the VCF context there was not a defendant that was being forced to bear responsibility for correcting or redressing the wrong that it had done to the victims. The terrorists were not being sued; it was the U.S. government that would provide compensation. And any obligation that the citizens of the United States and their government had to these victims and their families did not rest on corrective justice or civil redress, but on a different set of political and moral values. By the same token, in at least the long-latency version of mega-tort cases, corrective justice and civil redress values are even more attenuated than in conventional tort cases and other, non-latent-injury mega-tort cases. The corporate defendants in long-latency cases tend to resemble the mythical ship of Theseus, which was slowly reconstructed plank by plank until it consisted only of new lumber, and its connection to the original ship became problematic. In extreme instances there may not be a single shareholder of a corporate defendant held liable for long-latent harm today who owned a share of the corporation decades ago, at the time of the corporation's tortious conduct. Whatever arguments there may be for imposing liability on the corporate defendant in this situation, including the notion that current shareholders have been unjustly enriched by the excess value of their shares, the argument for imposing liability on such a corporation is not that its current owners have wronged the plaintiffs.

Finally, precisely because neither deterrence nor corrective justice have as significant a role to play in the 9/11 and mega-tort settings as in conventional cases, the intersection of tort with other sources of insurance and compensation occupies a more important place in thinking about the proper method of handling the problems that such cases raise. The fewer implications a claim has for the incentives of future parties or for justice as between claimants and the defendant, the more consideration is naturally due to the best way to provide compensation to claimants. Inevitably, that kind of analysis will take into account other potential sources of compensation. In both the 9/11 and mega-tort settings, therefore, compensatory considerations often tend to be dominant. For this reason the role to be played by collateral sources is a necessary ingredient in thinking about the proper approach to take in these settings.

In the Introduction I briefly discussed the scope and availability of these nontort sources of compensation. It is time to turn to them again in this context, for it is here that the relationship of these sources to tort is drawn into sharpest relief. Indeed, it is in considering the role that collateral sources should play in tort that some of the deepest questions about the purposes of tort itself arise.

Another Tour of the Compensation Universe

In the United States we spend about $1.7 trillion per year on tort and workers' compensation, and on health, life, and disability insurance, in order to compensate the victims of injury, illness, and death. Tort liability's share of this expenditure is at most $175 billion, or about 10 percent of the total. Benefits paid to victims (as distinguished from total expenditures for benefits plus administrative costs) by all the above sources of compensation are approximately $1.1 trillion per year, with tort providing compensation to victims, net of their counsel fees, of at most $90 billion per year—about 8 percent of the total benefits paid for injury, illness, and death.[3] Each year all these dollar figures rise, but their proportions remain nearly the same.

Two important practical features of the system are often overlooked in thinking about the proper shape and scope of tort liability. These are the comparative administrative costs of distributing all this compensation, and the way the different sources of compensation are coordinated when more than one source is available.

Administrative Costs

It is obvious from the foregoing data that tort provides only a small percentage of all compensation for bodily injury, illness, and death. Moreover, tort is a comparatively inefficient method of providing the compensation it does provide. Net compensation paid to victims constitutes less than 50 percent of all tort's expenditures. The majority of these expenditures goes to plaintiffs' and defense counsel, insurance companies, and administrative expenses. In contrast, the other sources of compensation all pay a much higher percentage of their expenditures to beneficiaries, most of them more than 75 percent of total expenditures. To put the same point another way, it costs roughly twice as much to pay a dollar of tort compensation to a victim as it costs to pay a dollar of workers' compensation or first-party insurance benefits.

To say that tort law is inefficient in this sense, however, is not necessarily to criticize tort, all things considered. In contrast to the other forms of compensation, tort is more capable of rectifying or redressing wrongs, and more capable of promoting deterrence. Tort can achieve these goals only by carefully identifying the subset of all injury-producing events that warrants the imposition of liability. This process requires detailed pretrial preparation and discovery and, in some cases, formal adjudication of issues regarding fault, causation, and damages, by jury trial. These are far more expensive undertakings than the more nearly clerical administration that the other sources of compensation employ. Moreover, of the other forms of compensation, only workers' compensation even remotely resembles tort in its ability to pursue deterrence as a goal. But workers' compensation achieves deterrence by imposing virtually absolute liability on the employer for scheduled benefits that are less expensive to compute than tort damages. Workers' compensation thereby avoids a portion of tort's higher administrative costs.

Coordinating Compensation

Our "system" of compensation is extensive, but it is not systematic. Indeed, it has developed almost chaotically and through a number of different mechanisms. Historically, tort liability has largely been a product of the courts, although recently it has received an overlay of mainly state-based legislative modifications. Other sources of compensation, such as workers' compensation, Medicare, and Medicaid, have legislative origins. Still others, such as life, health, and disability insurance, are generated by market forces and implemented through private contract rather than by judicial decision or legislation.

Given their different methods of adoption, it is no surprise that these sources of compensation potentially overlap or duplicate each other. Two or more sources, for example, may be available to provide compensation for the same medical expenses, lost wages, or death. The methods by which these different sources of compensation are coordinated—or are not coordinated, as the case may be—can be enormously complex.[4]

For my purposes, however, the crucial issue involves one subcategory of these multiple relationships: how coordination occurs when tort overlaps with one of the other sources available to provide compensation for injury, illness, or death. How such coordination occurs both affects tort's achievement of its goals and reflects an important part of the deep structure of our compensation "system."

We can see this by taking a look at the ways tort can interact with other sources of insurance in a typical and comparatively simple accident that results in bodily injury. First, simply by virtue of the time it takes to make and resolve tort claims, nontort sources of compensation typically make payments to the victim before tort is meaningfully in the picture. For example, by the time a tort claim is made, the majority of a victim's medical expenses are likely already to have been paid by health insurance or, if the injury occurred on the job, by workers' compensation; lost wages may also have been reimbursed, at least in part, by disability insurance, workers' compensation, or employment-based sick leave. If the victim has died as a result of tortious conduct, life insurance and other death benefits will have been paid to survivors. Consequently, in the vast majority of cases, tort must have a rule dictating how to take account of payments already made, or that will be made, to those who also receive compensation in tort. This is typically referred to as a "collateral source" or "collateral benefits" rule. This rule specifies the role tort plays in the larger compensation universe of which it is a part.

TWO COLLATERAL SOURCE RULES.   Under the traditional, common law collateral source rule, evidence of payments made or that will be made to the plaintiff by collateral sources such as health and disability insurance is not admissible in a tort suit. As a result, the plaintiff can recover at least some losses twice—both from his or her own first-party insurance and also from the tort defendant. The traditional collateral source rule takes this approach in order to assure that the defendant pays, and that future defendants are threatened with, liability for all the losses the defendant's tortious conduct has caused. Otherwise defendants would not expect to bear liability for all the harm they cause, and would therefore underinvest in taking precautions against causing harm. But while that approach may more effectively encourage potential defendants to take optimal precautions, it risks overcompensating the victim.

An alternative approach that addresses this risk of overcompensation has been adopted by statute in a minority of states since the mid-1980s. This approach deducts from the compensation that the tort defendant would otherwise be required to pay the plaintiff the amount of any compensation the plaintiff has already received, or will receive in the future, from other sources. In contrast to the traditional collateral source rule, this minority approach precludes duplicate recovery of the same losses, but it entails a greater risk of underdeterring potential injurers, because their net expected liability is lower than what it would be under the traditional rule.

SUBROGATION.   This standard way of describing the difference between the two approaches to coordinating tort and collateral sources is accurate, but incomplete. Although the traditional approach may result in the first instance in duplicate compensation, ultimately that need not be the case. The insurance device of subrogation is available to help avoid the overcompensation that otherwise accompanies the traditional rule. Under the doctrine of subrogation, a party who has paid another party's loss acquires (is "subrogated to") the latter party's right to recover from the third party, if any, who caused the loss. For example, under the traditional rule, a health insurer is subrogated to its policyholder's rights against a tortfeasor who has caused the policyholder to incur medical expenses. Subrogation of this sort is provided for by contract provisions included in health and disability insurance policies, by statutes governing workers' compensation and Medicare, and sometimes by common law rule even in the absence of contract or statutory subrogation rights.

Instead of actually bringing suit against tortfeasors, however, typically the subrogation rights of these sources of compensation are implemented by requiring the policyholder to reimburse these sources out of any tort recovery the policyholder obtains, often with a deduction for the insurer's pro-rata share of the plaintiff's counsel fees. The result, to the extent that subrogation works out in practice as it is designed, is that (1) the tort defendant pays for all the loss it has caused, without any deduction for collateral source payments, thus avoiding any sacrifice of the deterrent effect of tort liability; (2) the plaintiff's net recovery after reimbursing collateral sources provides him no duplicate or overlapping compensation; and (3) first-party insurance costs are marginally reduced, because insurers can expect reimbursement out of tort recoveries for some fraction of the benefits they pay, and over the long run can take this anticipated reimbursement into account in fixing premiums.

Unfortunately, often subrogation doesn't work out this way. One reason is that actually securing reimbursement out of a tort recovery takes substantial effort by a first-party insurer or other source of compensation. A health or disability insurer must first identify which of its policyholders to whom it is paying benefits suffered an injury that may have been tortiously caused. Then the insurer must monitor the progress of any litigation the policyholder has instituted seeking recovery of tort damages for that injury. Both of these tasks require costly effort from the insurer. For example, in order to secure reimbursement at the end of such litigation, health insurers must first ask anyone claiming benefits how their injuries occurred, whether a third party was involved, and whether a tort claim has been made or lawsuit brought. The information the insurers receive must either be accepted on faith or verified, and then there must be continuing follow-up, often for several years or more, in situations where there is reason to think that reimbursement might ultimately be possible. In the end the insurer must either be involved at the moment of settlement or verdict or file a lien on recovery where statute permits doing so. Only cases in which the amount of the potential reimbursement warrants such considerable investment by the insurer are likely to be monitored in these ways. In cases that are not monitored, the victim may well be able to retain both insurance benefits and a tort recovery.

Subrogation is often problematic in an additional way, because most tort cases are settled. Settlements are almost by definition for less than the victim's full losses. If a victim's insurer is nonetheless entitled to full reimbursement out of a settlement, then the victim may be left with only partial compensation. Thus, automatic, full reimbursement of insurers out of tort settlements does not merely prevent overcompensation; it ensures undercompensation.

One alternative is to deny reimbursement unless the sum of insurance benefits paid plus the tort settlement exceeds the victim's losses, and then to permit reimbursement only to the extent necessary to prevent overcompensation. This is known as the "make-whole" rule.[5] Another alternative is the "pro-rata" rule: to permit the insurer a partial reimbursement when the victim has not been made whole, based on the proportion of the victim's total loss that the settlement represents.[6] Under this alternative, for example, a settlement for 60 percent of the victim's losses requires reimbursement of only 60 percent of the amount of benefits paid by collateral sources, net of their pro-rata share of the plaintiff's counsel fees necessary to obtain the settlement.

In theory either of these two alternatives would be more sensible than permitting insurers full reimbursement out of partial settlements. But in practice both the make-whole and pro-rata approaches are more difficult to apply than the full reimbursement approach. The reason is that neither of these approaches can be implemented without determining the total amount of the plaintiff's damages. The make-whole rule precludes reimbursement until the plaintiff has recovered, in total, more than his total damages; the pro-rata rule provides the insurer with reimbursement for a fraction of its expenditures in which the total amount of the plaintiff's damages is the denominator. Yet it is a necessary feature of settlement, as well as one of its principal advantages, that facts such as the total amount of the plaintiff's damages do not have to be determined. For the make-whole or pro-rata rule to be enforceable, therefore, some form of postsettlement adjudicatory proceeding is necessary. After the parties settle a case in order to avoid adjudicating the issues of liability and damages, under the make-whole and pro-rata approaches the damages issue still must be adjudicated in some way, albeit sometimes in a streamlined and summary proceeding.

To avoid this post settlement complication, the parties whose rights and liabilities ultimately are at stake in tort cases—plaintiffs and their first-party insurers, defendants and their liability insurers—have developed an informal, presettlement method of solving the reimbursement-out-of-settlement problem, in jurisdictions where the make-whole or pro-rata rule would apply after settlement. At least in cases involving substantial losses, the plaintiff's insurer or insurers often are given a seat at the table where settlement is negotiated. Instead of a postsettlement adjudicatory proceeding establishing the insurer's reimbursable share, that share is negotiated prior to settlement. A settlement does not take place until the issue is resolved, so that nothing remains to be decided after the plaintiff and defendant have settled. In some settings an informal "rule of thirds" has emerged, providing that where there are large losses, the plaintiff will get one-third of the settlement, the plaintiff's attorney will get one-third, and the plaintiff's insurer or insurers will get one-third.[7]

The result is that, as we saw in earlier chapters, in addition to the other reasons plaintiffs with comparatively large amounts of loss tend to recover a lower percentage of their losses than plaintiffs with small losses, subrogation-reimbursement further contributes to this disparity. In smaller cases the insurer may simply go unreimbursed, because it has not invested in monitoring the plaintiff's claim, and settlement therefore occurs without the insurer's knowledge. That may produce more nearly full compensation for those who settle comparatively small claims, but it does nothing for the large claimants who do have to reimburse their insurers out of their settlements.

A final reason that subrogation sometimes does not work in practice the way the theory behind it suggests involves situations where there is a tort settlement or judgment on account of permanent injury. In these situations the award will be partly on account of the plaintiff's expected future damages, such as medical expenses and lost wages. But it is also possible that the plaintiff will have insurance against some of these future expenses. To determine how much to reimburse the plaintiff's first-party insurers at the time of settlement, strictly speaking there should be a calculation not only of the portion of the award that duplicates past payments from collateral sources but also the portion that duplicates future payment from such sources. Otherwise the plaintiff will be overcompensated. But the complications entailed in attempting to make and implement such calculations are even more daunting than those I have already canvassed, because among other things they would involve "reimbursing" certain insurers for payments that they have not yet made. Except in the most substantial of cases, therefore, this whole issue tends to be ignored.

The lesson of all this, in my view, is that in the real world of tort law in practice, neither the majority nor the minority approach to the interaction of tort with collateral sources is wholly satisfactory. The majority approach preserves the possibility of optimal deterrence. But it does this by depriving some plaintiffs with large claims of any possibility of securing full compensation for their losses, by permitting some plaintiffs with smaller claims to be overcompensated, or by complicating the process of settlement to a far greater degree than otherwise seems desirable. The minority approach avoids some of these disadvantages, but only by sacrificing at least some potential deterrence. Where deterrence is not a concern, we would therefore expect the minority approach to be more attractive—as it was in the 9/11 context and often is in mass tort settings.

The Special Case of Life Insurance

Life insurance receives different, exceptional treatment in all of the situations I have just described. Like other sources of first-party insurance, under the majority collateral source rule, evidence of life insurance benefits paid to a decedent's survivors are not admissible in a wrongful death action brought by his or her heirs. As a consequence, like other insurance benefits, life insurance benefits are not deducted from any tort recovery a victim's survivors secure as a result of the victim's death. Wholly unlike the other sources of insurance, however, life insurers have no subrogation-based or other right to reimbursement out of the victim's tort recovery, either by contract provision, by statute governing statutory sources of recovery such as social security survivors' benefits, or by common law rule. Further, even in the minority of jurisdictions that have reversed the traditional collateral source rule and deduct other insurance benefits from a tort recovery, life insurance benefits are not deducted from a tort recovery. The result is that, in all jurisdictions, life insurance benefits are paid to and retained by a victim's beneficiary, on top of any tort recovery the beneficiary obtains on account of the victim's death. In these situations there is in a sense automatic and mandatory duplicate recovery.

I have partly formal and partly practical explanations for this unique treatment of life insurance. Whether I am right or wrong, at least I have an explanation, which is more than one can find anywhere else in the case law or scholarly commentary. Indeed, there is almost no reference at all to the tort treatment of life insurance in judicial opinions or in commentary, let alone any extended analysis of this treatment.

Both the principal purpose and main effect of life insurance typically is to replace a family's income on the death of an income-earning spouse or parent. Indeed, the growth of life insurance in the middle of the nineteenth century can be traced to life insurance salesmen's efforts to persuade men that they had a moral obligation to provide their families with a means of support in the event of their death.[8] Under this conception, life insurance provides income replacement that is analogous to disability insurance, which replaces lost income resulting from injury rather than death. And given this analogy, it is difficult to see why life insurance would not always have been treated the same way as disability insurance in the event of a tort recovery by the deceased's beneficiaries. Just as the plaintiff's disability insurer would have a right to reimbursement out of the plaintiff's tort recovery, why not subrogate life insurers to the tort rights of the deceased and his beneficiaries, by giving the life insurer a right of reimbursement out of any wrongful death recovery obtained by these parties?

The issue seems rarely to have arisen, but a formal explanation for insurers' not being granted subrogation rights by operation of law is as follows. The courts have long held that there is "equitable" subrogation, or subrogation by operation of law, only for indemnity insurance. Indemnity insurance is coverage that replaces a discrete, specific monetary loss. Fire insurance and health insurance are both forms of indemnity; they replace particular amounts of monetary loss. Life insurance, in contrast, does not provide indemnity for a discrete monetary loss but a lump sum regardless of the amount of loss resulting from the death of the party whose life is insured. Because life insurance did not provide a specific indemnity in this sense, the courts that addressed the issue held that life insurance was an investment or a way of assuaging grief, and therefore was not indemnity insurance.[9] Whether or not this way of thinking about the nature of life insurance was accurate, it is the reason that the few courts addressing the issue found that life insurance was not eligible to receive a judicially created right of subrogation.

Nonetheless, life insurers could have attempted to circumvent this obstacle by providing for a right to subrogation and reimbursement in their policies, and then testing the validity of such contract provisions by seeking to enforce them. Whether the investment and assuagement-of-grief rationales for life insurance would have stood in the way of an effort such as this is unclear, but the life insurers certainly could have tried, and they never did. So we must identify a practical explanation for the life insurers' failure to make this attempt.

My explanation for this failure is that the political and equitable optics of attempting to enforce a subrogation right would not have been in the life insurers' favor. Historically, tort recoveries for wrongful death were limited. There were sometimes relatively low monetary limits on the amount that could be awarded for wrongful death, and awards were ostensibly for economic loss only—wrongful death statutes were interpreted to preclude awarding survivors noneconomic damages to compensate them for their grief over the death of a loved one. There can be little doubt that juries sometimes awarded noneconomic losses anyway in the guise of compensating for economic loss, and that typically the courts looked the other way when this occurred. But the law on the books very often prohibited recovery for mental anguish or pain and suffering experienced by the victim's survivors as a result of his death. Over time, the states that had imposed monetary ceilings on the amount of awards raised these ceilings, and eventually removed them altogether. And eventually the prohibitions against awarding noneconomic damages for mental anguish and grief, which were often honored only in the breach, also were repealed. In the meantime, however, any life insurer seeking to enforce a contractual right of subrogation would have been demanding reimbursement out of a tort recovery paid to a deceased's survivors that would often have been considered unduly low and undercompensatory to begin with. Taking that approach would have reflected poorly on such a life insurer.

But even after the restrictions on wrongful death recoveries were removed and award levels became substantial, life insurers never created a contractual right to reimbursement in their policies, and never tested its validity in court. The explanation for this seeming default, I think, is that the life insurers probably still did not want, and even today do not want, the negative publicity that seeking reimbursement out of widows' and orphans' tort recoveries would generate. Somehow a health insurer seeking reimbursement for medical bills that it has already paid on behalf of an injured party does not conjure up the same image as a life insurer whose actions could be characterized as taking back the nest egg that a deceased parent or spouse had created for his or her family. So life insurers simply live with the no-reimbursement rule and do not attempt to set it aside by contract. The cost of life insurance coverage is marginally higher as a consequence, but the reason for that slightly higher cost is never mentioned.

In addition, it can be argued, most breadwinners do not purchase enough life insurance to protect their dependents against the income they will lose in the event of the breadwinner's death.[10] The absence of a reimbursement obligation in life insurance, when linked with the fact that most tort actions, including those for wrongful death, result in compromise settlements that are themselves undercompensatory, has the effect of counterbalancing the underpurchasing of life insurance. Tort settlements in wrongful death actions thus "top up" the typically inadequate life insurance benefits that have been purchased by or provided to surviving families.

The trouble with this explanation for the way things now stand, accurate though I think it may be, is that in large measure the rationale behind it would also be applicable to the collateral sources that are treated differently from life insurance. Arguably other forms of insurance also are underpurchased. Health insurance covers too high a percentage of low-cost treatment and not a high enough percentage of high-cost treatment; most people do not have enough insurance against being disabled for more than six months, which at any given age is about as likely to occur as dying. And almost all tort claims are compromised through settlements that pay plaintiffs less than their losses, especially considering the fact that plaintiffs' counsel are paid about one-third of every recovery.

Yet all the other forms of first-party insurance are subject to reimbursement out of tort recoveries, despite the fact that a no-reimbursement approach would have the effect of topping up the amount of compensation available to (nondeceased) tort victims who have losses that are not fully compensated by their tort recoveries. To be consistent, either we ought to be concerned across the board about avoiding overcompensation and apply the standard reimbursement rules to life insurance, or we ought to be concerned about undercompensation across the board and deny all first-party insurers a right of reimbursement. What is not consistent, on this view, is treating life insurance differently from all other forms of insurance.

Interestingly, as I noted at the beginning of this chapter, the one setting in which life insurance has not been treated differently from the other sources is under the 9/11 VCF. The VCF deducted all collateral sources, including life insurance benefits, from the amounts it would otherwise have paid to claimants. The VCF's approach is therefore worth examining, for it underscores both the unique treatment that life insurance receives within tort and the assumptions that lie at the foundation of the current approaches to coordination between tort and other sources of compensation for injury, illness, and death.

The 9/11 Fund

Congress's enactment of the VCF provoked considerable public controversy about both the measure of compensation the VCF employed and whether the victims of 9/11 should have been provided any special benefits at all. This controversy not only identified issues associated with the provision of compensation to the victims of terrorism but also was emblematic of the fundamental problems that beset tort actions involving thousands of claimants and hundreds of millions or billions of dollars. Increasingly, it is impossible for the resolution of tort actions of this size and scope to serve the traditional goals of tort law effectively. Instead they become occasions for the creation of ad hoc solutions that recognize the interests not only of plaintiffs, defendants, and their attorneys but also of employees and creditors of defendants, others with a stake in the local economies that are dependent on defendants' operations, and potential purchasers of the defendant or defendants.

In situations like these, tort—or in this case, the VCF itself—comes to serve as merely one of a series of ingredients of the system that provides compensation to tort victims. And one of the principal ingredients in addition to tort is first-party insurance. The compensation and liability issues arising out of 9/11 thus will continue to resonate within tort theory, even after the VCF itself is just a distant memory.

The VCF Framework

The principal impetus for the enactment of the VCF was the situation in which U.S. airlines found themselves immediately after 9/11.[11] It was clear that it would take a considerable period for air travel to return to its pre-9/11 levels, both because of the public's heightened fear of flying and because of the economic shock that resulted from the terrorist attacks. The airlines believed that a continuing threat that they would be held liable in tort for the failure to prevent their planes from being hijacked on 9/11 would create an additional, intolerable cloud on their viability as going concerns, and that many of them might fail as a result of the threat of this liability.

In the days that followed, the airlines persuaded the Congress that in order to avoid the economic dislocation that was in prospect, among other things they needed protection from tort liability. The airline stabilization legislation that was enacted less than two weeks after September 11 therefore immunized the airlines against tort liability for the consequences of 9/11, but only to the extent of any liability incurred in excess of the amount of their liability insurance. The airlines would remain potentially liable in tort, but no airline itself would ever have to make a monetary payout as a consequence of any judgment that it was negligent in connection with 9/11.

This extraordinary arrangement has gone largely unremarked on, mainly because of the attention that was given to the other features of the VCF. The de facto immunity from liability that the airlines secured obviously reflected the significance that the Congress and the interested parties attached to the airlines' liability insurance. Tort liability falling within the terms and limits of coverage would result in the spreading of losses beyond the individual airlines themselves, and to the extent that the airlines' insurers were reinsured, ultimately to the global financial markets. Here tort liability was subsumed by insurance; indeed, the tort liability of the airlines in the end was nothing but insurance.

The plaintiffs' bar successfully argued, however, that it would be unfair simply to immunize the airlines from any liability that was not insured. The 9/11 victims and their families, these attorneys contended, had to be provided with an alternative source of compensation for their losses. The legislation that was enacted therefore contained provisions designed to provide an alternative source of compensation. The VCF was established to provide automatic compensation to those who chose not to sue the airlines or other potential defendants, with the exception of suits against the terrorists and those who were allied with them, which would still be permitted.

Victims and their families who waived their right to sue in tort would apply to a Special Master for compensation. Under the 9/11 legislation the Special Master would determine the extent of the economic and noneconomic losses these claimants suffered, and award compensation "based on the harm to the claimant, the facts of the claim, and the individual circumstances of the claimant."[12] Under regulations promulgated by the Special Master, economic loss was calculated case by case, and noneconomic loss—pain and suffering by the victim, grief experienced by the survivors, and so on—was rebuttably presumed to be $250,000 for the victim and an additional $100,000 for each surviving spouse and dependent.

There was uncertainty about how many victims and their families would elect to receive VCF compensation and how many would sue in tort. Ultimately, however, the attraction of receiving automatic compensation, and the anticipated difficulties of recovering in tort from the airlines, prevailed. Over 97 percent of the families of deceased victims waived their tort rights by electing to receive compensation from the VCF. The VCF paid $7 billion to the victims and their families; the average award to the family of a deceased victim was over $2 million.[13]

These were in most respects what might be called "shadow" tort awards.[14] The compensation paid by the VCF was modeled on the types of compensation available in tort, though awards for noneconomic loss were undoubtedly lower on average than what would have been paid to successful tort claimants. In contrast to tort, of course, VCF compensation was automatic; claimants did not need to prove that they would have been successful in a tort suit.

In an important respect, however, the approach taken by the VCF departed radically from the tort model. The legislation required the Special Master to reduce the awards he would otherwise have made by the amount of collateral source compensation the claimant had received or would receive as a result of the terrorist-related aircraft crashes of September 11. The Special Master interpreted this requirement (in the view of most observers, correctly) to require offsetting payments not only by health and disability insurance but also by life insurance, pensions, and death benefit programs, though not the amount of self-contributions to pension plans or life insurance premiums paid by the deceased.[15] Thus, life insurance benefits payable to a VCF beneficiary, less the amount of any premiums the deceased had paid for the insurance, were deducted from the award. Pensions, less the amount the deceased had contributed, also were deducted. As a concession to political reality, though not necessarily consistently, charitable contributions paid to beneficiaries were exempted from the required offset, as were future collateral source benefits that were contingent on the occurrence of future events, such as (under social security survivorship benefits) the beneficiary not remarrying.

Loss, Need, and the Principles of Compensation

Tort seeks to compensate victims for the loss they have suffered. Need, or lack of it, is not relevant. If I negligently injure a billionaire, then she is entitled to be compensated for her loss, regardless of whether she actually needs the money. Similarly, the fact that even after I have received compensation for an injury, I still do not have the wherewithal to lead a satisfactory life, has no bearing on my tort rights.

Tort law's treatment of collateral sources such as health and disability insurance is largely consistent with this principle of compensating for loss, regardless of need. Under the traditional rule the plaintiff recovers regardless of payments made to him by these sources, but tends to be obligated to repay them out of his tort award. And under the modification that has been adopted in some states, payments from these sources are deducted from the tort award. Either way, loss but no more than loss is compensated. And, as we saw above, in view of the inadequate amounts of life insurance available to most people, and the fact that plaintiffs in wrongful death cases must pay one-third of any recovery to their lawyers, the treatment of life insurance in tort cases is not necessarily anomalous or inconsistent with the principle of compensating for loss rather than need.

The families of the 9/11 victims, however, regarded the VCF not only as a mechanism for compensating loss but also, at least in part, for addressing their needs. Many believed that the VCF was obligated to make awards that would enable them to lead satisfactory post-9/11 lives. It is no surprise, then, that the deduction of life insurance, pensions, and death benefits from awards made by the VCF proved to be the most controversial feature of the entire scheme. Rescue personnel such as firefighters tended to have earned average wages but were entitled to receive substantial death benefits from their employers. Deduction of these death benefits from VCF awards left the families of some of these victims with comparatively small recoveries. Moreover, there was a sense in which deducting life insurance benefits from an award failed to reward the prudence of those who had purchased life insurance. The families of those who had chosen to purchase life insurance, or to work in jobs that provided generous death benefits, were left no better off than those who had chosen not to do so. Having life insurance or death benefits turned out, under the circumstances, not to have advantaged them at all.

The validity of these criticisms depends very heavily on how the function of the VCF is conceived. One view is that, as a substitute for tort, the VCF should have been designed to provide nearly as full compensation for economic and noneconomic losses as tort, subject perhaps to a discount for the probability that tort suits would have been successful. To the extent that the VCF awards were offset by life insurance, death, and pension benefits, they failed as a rough substitute for tort. They failed, that is, to replace loss in the same way that tort would have replaced loss.

A different view is that the function of the VCF was not necessarily to compensate for all loss, but merely to provide a safety net, ensuring that the basic economic needs of the 9/11 victims' families would be met. This is a more modest view in one sense. But in another sense this view is more radical, for it allows need as well as loss to function as a compensation criterion. And once need comes into the picture, the criticisms of the approach the VCF took are more difficult to assess. On one hand, the deduction of life insurance and death benefits from the awards made to the families of comparatively wealthy victims was at least some concession to the notion that need rather than loss was a relevant consideration in determining the appropriate level of compensation to award. On the other hand, deducting these benefits from awards made to the families of lower-income victims such as firefighters was not need-sensitive. Deductions risked leaving this category of claimants with comparatively small awards that, even when combined with their life insurance and similar benefits, did not adequately satisfy their future financial needs.

This occurred because the amount of life insurance available to the family of a victim was a rough proxy for the wealth of a family, but only a very rough one. In the case of rescue personnel, the amount of their death benefits was not a proxy for their wealth, but for the riskiness of their occupations. The only way to be sure that award levels were need-sensitive would have been to means-test recoveries, and that was not accomplished merely by deducting life insurance and death benefits from the awards the VCF made.

Yet another angle from which to explore the role that may be played by need in measuring compensation is by reference to the way the VCF, or for that matter any coordination mechanism, allocates compensation responsibility. Deducting collateral source payments from a VCF or tort award would allocate primary compensation responsibility to the sources of these payments; allowing duplicate recovery followed by reimbursement of the source would allocate primary responsibility to the VCF or tort. For example, when health insurance benefits are deducted from a tort award, health insurance bears primary responsibility for medical expenses, and tort is merely a secondary source, responsible only for making up any compensation shortfall that remains after health insurance is exhausted. Similarly, deducting life insurance benefits from VCF awards allocated primary compensation responsibility to life insurance, leaving the VCF in a position of only secondary responsibility. In contrast, when insurance benefits are recoverable in tort and then reimbursed to the insurer, tort bears primary compensation responsibility, and insurance merely makes up any shortfall.

The question then becomes whether tort and programs like the VCF should have primary compensation responsibility or such responsibility should be shouldered by health, disability, and life insurance. On one hand, deterrence and corrective justice ordinarily argue for making liability sources primary, so that liable parties internalize the full cost of their activities and bear responsibility to victims. On the other hand, to the extent that ensuring compensation is the dominant concern, first-party insurance sources should be primary, because they are far more cost-effective means of compensation than tort, which has comparatively high administrative costs.

Using the most cost-effective method of distributing money, however, also will mean that there is more money available for victims, and therefore a greater probability that their needs can be satisfied. It is no surprise that the VCF, which did not have deterrence or corrective justice as a goal because neither the terrorists nor the airlines were being held financially responsible, would make first-party insurance, including life insurance, primary. That approach made federal funds available, but only to the extent that preexisting sources of compensation were inadequate.

Although there was an effectively unlimited supply of money to finance the VCF, that is hardly true in tort cases involving mass injury caused by private defendants. In situations where deterrence and corrective justice require it, we may nevertheless wish tort to continue to bear primary compensation responsibility, notwithstanding its inefficiency as a means of compensation. Continuing to make tort primary to first-party insurance, however, as the traditional, majority collateral source rule does, risks spending scarce tort dollars on losses for which first-party insurance could bear primary compensation responsibility. The minority approach reserves tort dollars to provide compensation only when first-party insurance is not inadequate.

The clash of values at the heart of this choice, I think, was ultimately the source of the debate about the VCF's treatment of collateral sources. The long-run significance of that debate for the tort system more generally, therefore, may well be that it highlights the question of how we should spend scarce tort dollars in a world where other sources of insurance are also readily available. And it is difficult to conceive of the issue in this way without thinking at least in part of the role that satisfying need ought to play in the choice.

The Future of Tort in a World of Insurance

The whole cluster of issues associated with the relation between tort and first-party insurance assumes its greatest importance in the mass tort cases that have come to be such a visible feature of the tort system over the last several decades. In a sense tort has divided into two worlds. The first is the normal world of sporadic injury. The second is the world of mass catastrophic loss. The tort system's prime values of deterrence and corrective justice often prove to have a much less important role to play in this second world than they play in the first. There comes a point at which the potential of tort liability to deter runs up against practical limits. No additional deterrence is created by threatening an actor with liability for more than its net worth. And in cases involving long-tail liability, both deterrence and corrective justice are already attenuated when the lion's share of the impact of massive liability is felt by shareholders who may not even have had a stake in the defendant at the time the actions that ultimately gave rise to injury were taken.

The occurrence of mass catastrophic loss is therefore more likely than sporadic loss to be the occasion for considering the best method of compensating those who have suffered loss, rather than emphasizing the redress and deterrence functions of liability. Almost inevitably the funds available to provide compensation to victims will tend to be finite in these situations, even if their absolute magnitude is comparatively large. And because trying hundreds or thousands of cases to a verdict is a practical impossibility, compromise settlements are the norm. Counsel and courts fashioning settlements cannot ignore the fact that the plaintiffs and the defendant are not the only interested parties. Employees, commercial creditors, sellers to and customers of the defendant, and taxpayers in the locations where the defendant does business, among others, have a stake in the defendant's future as a going concern. If what the plaintiffs demand is too onerous or a voluntary compromise is not feasible for other reasons, the defendant can seek to limit its liability through corporate reorganization. Through this device the defendant can obtain a judicially imposed form of settlement. And contributions to an overall settlement from liability insurers are much more likely to be forthcoming if payment of less than their maximum potential coverage responsibility is acceptable.

It also is in this context that placing a uniform monetary ceiling on the recovery of damages for pain and suffering, which in my view is otherwise of questionable merit, finds its most plausible (if still questionable) justification. Such ceilings disproportionately burden the most seriously injured victims and those with long-term or permanent loss, leaving those with less severe injuries with a right to full recovery for their pain and suffering. A sliding scale of some sort, as others have proposed, would be a much more equitable method of containing damages for pain and suffering, if that were thought to be desirable.[16] But to the extent that payment of actual out-of-pocket economic loss rather than compensation for intangible, noneconomic loss is a first priority, placing an otherwise unacceptably low and somewhat arbitrary ceiling on pain and suffering awards, as the VCF also did, may help to make scarce tort dollars more available for this higher compensation priority.

The 9/11 compensation experience is thus an emblem for the problems that we may face in the future. Some mass accidents or related disasters may be so catastrophic that the ordinary method of providing compensation in tort for the losses they cause may be unworkable. Tort in a world of catastrophic loss simply may not be able to function in the same way it does in a world of normal accidents. In these situations we may need to view tort more consciously as but one feature of the compensation universe, and to fashion tort liability with the availability of other sources of compensation in mind. The more first-party insurance we have, the more we may want to limit what we try to do with tort.

In a world where tort is but one of many sources of compensation for injury, illness, and death, there is an unavoidable tension between the accident prevention and corrective justice aims of tort law on the one hand and its loss spreading and compensation functions on the other. Imposing tort liability for losses that already have been or will be compensated by other insurance sources distributes scarce compensation resources to those likely to be in less need than those without access to their own sources of insurance.

The tension between the goals of tort law that is at its core has been reconciled by the tort system in different ways, but until the VCF was adopted, life insurance had always been exempted from the treatment accorded other sources of insurance. When the VCF treated life insurance like any other source of claimants' insurance, it not only opened up the possibility that life insurance could be treated this way in tort as well. It also brought forward the core question that is raised by the whole problem of how to treat other sources of compensation when a tort recovery has also been or will be obtained. This question cannot be camouflaged or sidestepped forever. When tort is recognized as just one element in a larger constellation of devices we employ to compensate for injury, illness, and death, tort's proper role within that constellation must be confronted.

As we saw earlier, both of the two conventional approaches each have serious flaws. What we need is a third way of dealing with the problem. A number of scholars, myself included, have proposed authorizing first-party insurance policyholders to sell their tort causes of action to their insurers in return for more insurance. Under these approaches, which may be called "full subrogation" or "unlimited insurance subrogation," a tort victim would continue to have formal tort rights, but her first-party insurance contract would provide that her total tort recovery—not merely the benefits already paid or payable by the insurer—would be returned to her insurer as subrogation reimbursement. The plaintiff would then be a plaintiff in name only, since the real party in interest would be her first-party insurer.

This general approach would preserve the deterrence that is a central feature of the traditional collateral source rule linked with subrogation, but would enable potential tort claimants to transform their right to recover pain and suffering damages into less expensive, or more broadly protective, first-party insurance. The details of this approach need to be worked out in more detail, and its proponents are doing so.[17] And this approach surely would run into considerable political opposition. But at least it points in a different and potentially promising direction, by attempting to preserve the benefits of tort, leaving the task of coordination to the institutions with a stake in its functioning, and making more effective use of the vast array of nontort sources of compensation that operate in parallel with tort.

—8—

Recurring Themes,
Sobering Constraints

In many ways the interactions between tort liability and insurance I have identified and analyzed in the preceding chapters speak for themselves. Like so much in law, these relationships have been, and continue to be, context dependent; they resist easy generalization. The interactions between auto liability and insurance, for example, have been very different from the interactions between products liability and insurance. Nonetheless, three features of the interaction between tort and insurance recurred frequently enough in my analysis to be worthy of further examination. In this chapter I want to extract these three themes from the material I canvassed in the preceding pages, briefly explore at a more general level the way these themes figure in contemporary interactions between tort and insurance, and ruminate about the lessons that might be learned from the history of the interaction between these fields.

The first recurring theme is that liability goes where the money is. Tort law continually seeks an available source of recovery, creating or expanding the liability of individuals and businesses that are likely to be covered by or have access to liability insurance. And liability insurance has usually responded, by creating new forms of insurance to meet the new liabilities when such insurance was not already available. The second theme involves the role insurance has played as an intermediary between injurer and victim, and the impact of this intermediating role on both the conduct of tort litigation and the making of new tort law by the courts. Insurance is not merely a source of money to pay judgments and settlements; insurers are de facto parties in tort litigation. Their involvement affects this litigation. The third theme is the increasing duplication of the functions performed by the tort and insurance systems. Tort liability increasingly has performed a loss-spreading function that is also the core purpose of insurance. Correspondingly, though to a lesser degree, insurance has come increasingly to duplicate the deterrence function of tort, by attempting to create incentives on the part of policyholders to prevent their losses from occurring. From both directions, the two systems have moved toward each other and have tended to overlap. Over time, then, tort becomes insurance, and insurance becomes tort.

Seeking an Available Source of Recovery

This first general feature of the relation between tort and insurance runs consistently through the history of tort law for the last century. Over most of this period there was a steady expansion of liability in a manner that sought out insured or otherwise financially solvent actors as potential defendants. The development of products liability and the breakdown of the no-duty rules that once pervaded negligence law, for example, each reflects this trend.

As we saw in earlier chapters, in these developments a party that previously faced no liability became a potential defendant under a new doctrine. These new forms of liability, however, did not substitute one defendant for another. The parties who were liable under the prior doctrine remained liable. In products liability, for example, the immediate seller remained liable for negligence. But now the manufacturer also was liable. And these additional defendants were usually in a better position to insure against their liability than were the original, sole defendants. In other cases a no-liability or limited-liability rule was supplanted by a rule that permitted the imposition of liability for the first time. Under the prior rules governing premises liability, for example, there was almost never liability to a social guest injured on a host's property. Once homeowner's liability insurance became widespread after the post–World War II housing boom, however, this strong protection of property owners weakened. Here, a no-liability rule was displaced by a liability rule that sought out preexisting insurance.

A variation on this theme occurred in the field of auto liability, where the relevant rules governing liability and the parties who were potentially liable remained essentially the same during the entire period. Here insurance expanded bit by bit to ensure that liable parties were covered. A judgment against an uninsured and impecunious driver is, after all, only a piece of paper. The addition of omnibus and drive-other-cars coverage to standard

policies, as well as the eventual adoption of compulsory insurance requirements, are examples of this phenomenon. In both ways, the presence of a
now-insured or otherwise solvent defendant in these instances enhanced
the chance that a deserving plaintiff would succeed in actually recovering
compensation.

Plaintiffs' lawyers, because they take cases on a contingency basis and decide whom to sue and what legal theory to allege, have been the vehicles for
the operation of this process. Indeed, partly for this reason tort law has not
expanded in areas where potential defendants are unlikely to be insured.
Similarly, the allegations in suits brought against insured defendants are
sometimes shaped to fit the availability of insurance coverage. It does a
plaintiff, and therefore a plaintiffs' lawyer, little good to allege battery, for
example, if the defendant's only substantial asset is insurance that covers liability for negligence but not for intentional or expected harm, which is the
gist of battery.[1]

Although the impetus for these new legal doctrines and insurance developments was to identify or create a potentially insured or solvent source of
recovery, it seems clear that once legal doctrines establishing new liabilities
are adopted, the liabilities tend to take on a life of their own. The insurance
justification that is present at the creation often then fades into the background. Thereafter the logical and conceptual structure of the doctrines
sometimes leads to their expansive application without regard to the availability of insurance against the expanded liability.

The insurance market may then respond in either of two very different
ways. In most situations the market meets the demand for insurance
against the new liability by extending coverage to the new potential defendants, or to the newly relevant causes of loss. Certainly this has been true of
medical malpractice and conventional products liability, as we saw in Chapters 4 and 5. A liability-and-insurance spiral then ensues. Liability is imposed where insurance is already in place or is expected to become
available. As liability expands both on paper and in practice, potential defendants purchase increasing amounts of insurance to protect themselves
against their expanding liability. And at least in part because of the availability of ever greater amounts of liability insurance, the frequency of suit
and the amount of awards and settlements increases. Liability insurance
thus contributes to the creation of its own demand.[2]

This liability-and-insurance spiral, however, occasionally is not the prevailing pattern. Sometimes insurers cannot, or will not, provide insurance against a new liability. For example, as Chapter 5 showed, in the 1980s the rise of retroactive, strict, and joint and several liability for pollution cleanup under CERCLA, the federal "Superfund" hazardous waste cleanup program, led to the virtual disappearance of pollution liability insurance rather than to its expansion. Expansive judicial interpretations of insurance policies that had seemed to insurers to provide only limited pollution liability insurance to their policyholders eventually caused the insurance industry to insert an "absolute" pollution exclusion into subsequently issued policies.

These two different insurance market reactions to new forms of liability suggest that ordinarily, the availability of insurance can set changes in the law of civil liability in motion that may eventually lead to the spread of even more insurance. Paradoxically, however, under some circumstances an expansion of liability not only may fail to elicit an expansion of coverage but also may even lead to a reduction in the scope of available insurance.

The lesson to be drawn from these experiences is that where civil liability goes, liability insurance will often, but not always, follow. Insurers' warnings that expanding liability may create problems of adverse selection, moral hazard, correlated loss, and juridical risk, may sometimes be exaggerated. The insurance market has proved remarkably capable of covering risks that insurers had previously been concerned would pose these problems, albeit sometimes without the levels of profit that insurers considered appropriate. But insurers are not always crying wolf. Some liabilities cannot be insured with enough confidence to make supplying private insurance against them worth doing.

Insurance as Intermediation

Insurance is not merely a device that provides indemnity to a tort defendant or compensation to a victim after a loss has occurred. In addition, in a variety of ways, insurance commonly serves as an intermediary between the plaintiff and the defendant in a tort suit. In part the intermediation function involves communication. Representatives of insurers are often conduits for the transmission of information from the insurer to the policyholder, and from the policyholder to the insurer. More important, however, because insurers have substantive rights and play well-defined roles in tort litigation, their presence also affects the actual outcomes of disputes and the direction in which tort law has a tendency to evolve.

Affecting Outcomes, Influencing Legal Change

The first way that liability insurers' presence affects litigation outcomes is this. The probability that the law will change is affected by the role played by liability insurers in tort cases. Appellate courts, especially, often confront the tension between deciding the dispute before them on the basis of the rules that existed when the conduct that is the subject of a tort suit occurred and making new rules of law. The nearly universal convention that any new rule that a court creates applies to the dispute at hand—retroactively, so to speak—contributes to this tension, because the parties cannot always reasonably have anticipated a rule change. Yet most uninsured individual defendants—physicians, drivers, homeowners, and tenants, for example—would be in no position to predict and adjust their behavior in advance in anticipation of potential legal change. The inability of such parties to anticipate the making of new law undoubtedly would act as something of a brake on the pace of legal change, because at the margin courts are reluctant to impose retroactive liability on certain uninsured defendants.

In contrast, when defendants such as these are covered by liability insurance, the impact of any unanticipated legal change is mitigated, because it is spread among the insurer's policyholders. The fact that auto, homeowner's, medical malpractice, and other forms of personal liability insurance have become so widespread undoubtedly is recognized by the courts and must in some cases relax or eliminate judicial concern that making new law will adversely impact individual litigants. And of course the courts also know that enterprises such as liability insurers actually are in a better position than individuals to anticipate legal change. In such a setting a court's reluctance to announce a new rule for the future, because of its impact on the parties to the immediate dispute, will decline. For these reasons, legal change is likely to be facilitated when defendants, especially individual defendants, are insured.

Second, the pace of legal change also may be affected by liability insurance because, other things being equal, plaintiffs, and plaintiffs' attorneys, are less likely to pursue claims against defendants with limited assets. New law is not made when claims are not brought at all; there can be legal change only when cases are tried and appealed. Therefore, the greater willingness of plaintiffs to pursue claims against insured defendants, and the greater ability of liability insurers, as distinguished from ordinary individuals, to litigate and appeal cases, create more numerous opportunities for legal change.

At least up to a point, the more opportunities there are for legal change to occur, the more frequently such change will actually occur. A critical mass of appellate cases presenting different factual situations and posing different legal issues is necessary before the potential for legal change reaches its maximum. The introduction and then the spread of liability insurance in the twentieth century would have accelerated the creation of a critical mass of such cases. And since tort law change in the courts has tended to be almost uniformly one-directional for the last century, the presence of liability insurers in tort cases has contributed to the expansion of tort liability.

Ironically, although in every case that resulted in tort law change, liability insurers opposed the expansion of liability, each time liability expanded insurers tended to benefit. The more such efforts at opposing legal change liability insurers unsuccessfully pursued, the greater the demand for their product eventually became. The greater the scope of liability with which defendants were threatened, the more liability insurance they bought. Over the long run, then, liability insurers won by losing. Insurers lost appeals that expanded liability, and expanded liability helped to create a $200-billion-a-year tort system in which liability insurance became exponentially more important than it once had been.

Third, the settlement patterns and procedures of insurers are different from those of uninsured defendants, whether they are individuals or businesses. As we saw in Chapter 3 and as other scholars have shown in more detail, liability insurers employ a bureaucracy that promotes routinized settlement.[3] Because liability insurance personnel have case loads to process, they settle cases by reference to rules of thumb that defendants themselves are less likely to employ. Similarly, liability insurers are the quintessential repeat-players in the system. They have reputations to establish and uphold, and they have portfolios of claims pending against them that automatically diversify the risks they face. Most defendants, in contrast, are infrequent or one-time players. Liability insurers are therefore likely in cases that are not routine to be less risk-averse than even sizable uninsured defendants. Liability insurers can afford not to settle cases that uninsured defendants with assets to protect would be more likely to settle.

Finally, and most obviously, the fact that a defendant is believed to be insured makes it more probable that a jury will impose liability on it. This is especially true of individual defendants in auto and malpractice cases. Although mention of liability insurance is a ground for a mistrial, jurors usually know, or think they know, when the defendant is insured. A jury might be reluctant to impose a substantial financial burden on an individual defendant in order to ensure compensation for a sympathetic plaintiff with a case that is not necessarily meritorious. The same jury, however, is likely to feel less compunction about imposing such a penalty on the defendant's liability insurer. Even if the law had remained static, then, the growth of liability insurance would have fueled increases in the percentage of successful tort suits and in the magnitude of recoveries in those suits.

Changing Relationships

As we saw in Chapter 1, from the beginning, liability insurers have provided not only indemnity to their policyholders but also a defense against suit, free of charge. Not only an attorney, but an attorney hired by the insurer, thus stands between the defendant and everything that happens in the lawsuit. Moreover, because in whole or at least in part it is the insurer's money that is directly in jeopardy in such instances, the defendant's relationship to the lawsuit, and to the plaintiff, is attenuated. In the polar but not unusual case in which there is no real prospect that a judgment for the plaintiff will exceed the amount of the defendant's insurance, or in which the defendant has no assets other than his insurance, for practical purposes the defendant is merely a testifying witness, if that.

In addition, because of the defendant's liability insurance, the plaintiff's relationship to the defendant is not at all direct. The plaintiff deals with a lawsuit through his or her attorney; and that attorney deals not with the defendant, but with the defendant's liability insurer or the attorney hired by the insurer to represent the defendant. And if—as is so common that it is routine—the plaintiff has already received payment for some of her losses from her own first-party insurers, then the plaintiff's relationship to the lawsuit itself is also attenuated. This is because the plaintiff, through contractual or equitable subrogation as I described it in Chapter 7, may be obliged to reimburse her insurers for their prior payments to her, out of her tort recovery or settlement. To this extent the plaintiff is a conduit for payment by the defendant, or its liability insurers, to the plaintiff's health and disability insurers.

Finally, defendants' litigation behavior may be affected when they are insured. When a liability insurer's money is at stake, it owns the lawsuit. Under most liability insurance policies the defendant's insurer has a right to control the defense and settlement of claims. The policy provides that, in return for coverage, the policyholder has a duty to cooperate in the insurer's defense of claims against it. Exactly how this all plays out varies, but clearly the provision of defense by the liability insurer affects what happens. On the one hand, cases against defendants whose only substantial asset is liability insurance are likely to be defended more vigorously than they would have been if the defendant were uninsured. After all, the insurer has real rather than the merely theoretical financial exposure of a judgment-proof, uninsured defendant. On the other hand, defendants who do have assets but also are insured are likely to be less devoted to their defense than they would be if their own money were directly at stake. In these situations, the probability that plaintiffs' tort suits will be successful may well be marginally increased because of the decreased stake that defendants have in the case. By experience-rating future premiums, insurers attempt to combat this subtle form of *ex post* moral hazard, but experience-rating of policyholders with infrequent claims is crude, and those with frequent claims are likely to have sizable deductibles or self-insured retentions that have this effect even apart from experience-rating.

In short, what is legally and logically a direct dispute between a plaintiff and a defendant actually takes place through a series of intermediaries, one of which is a liability insurer. Insurance thus separates the plaintiff and the defendant from each other, and in an important way from the lawsuit itself. Insurance attenuates the parties' relationship to each other, and to what is at stake in their dispute. Corrective justice, economic and political accountability, and the morality of civil liability all must be understood as taking place in this intermediated context.

The Duplication of Functions

The last major way tort law and insurance have influenced each other for more than a century has been through each system's adoption of purposes and policies imported from the other. Of all the instances of such cross-fertilization, the most important exchange has involved the loss-spreading and deterrence functions. By becoming increasingly concerned with loss spreading, tort has not only come to depend on the availability of liability insurance to potential defendants; tort also has actually become more like insurance. Similarly, insurance has developed the capacity to differentiate the premiums charged insureds on the basis of their potential for suffering loss, thus promoting loss prevention. In this respect, insurance has become more like tort.

As we saw in Chapter 2, beginning as early as the adoption of workers' compensation just after the turn of the twentieth century, the imposition of civil liability began to be justified on the basis of a loss-spreading rationale that is of course central to insurance as well. In workers' compensation this was not *tort* liability, strictly speaking, but it was *liability* just the same. Employers held liable for on-the-job injuries suffered by their employees would build the cost of compensation into the price of their products or services, it was said, and as a consequence the loss would be spread among the members of the purchasing public. This notion then came under broader consideration, not only in workers' compensation but also in connection with various forms of tort liability.

By the middle of the century there was a well-developed theory of what had come to be called enterprise liability, one of whose main features was the notion that the enterprises responsible for product-related and other injuries were in a better position than victims to pass the cost of these injuries along to the consuming public. Debates about the proper scope of tort liability have therefore long hinged at least in part on the question whether, and under what circumstances, potential injurers or potential victims are in a superior position to spread the risk of loss, by purchasing insurance or through other means. Loss-spreading capacity has thus become one of the components of the mainstream analysis of the proper scope of tort liability.

Conversely, a version of tort law's deterrence function has slowly been incorporated into insurance. Insurers attempt to charge premiums that are proportional to the degree of risk posed by the policyholder, for two reasons. First, this practice combats adverse selection—the tendency of those who are at above-average risk of suffering a loss to disproportionately seek insurance. Second, premium rating also helps to combat moral hazard—the decreased incentive of those who are covered by insurance to exercise care to avoid suffering losses. This is because future premiums will tend to reflect prior loss experience, at least to the extent that this experience is considered predictive of future risk. Insurers also often employ deductibles and coinsurance provisions in order to combat moral hazard. Premium rating, deductibles, and copayments are nothing less than an effort to promote what amounts to deterrence, by providing insureds with an incentive to optimize their losses, notwithstanding that they are insured against the risk of suffering loss.

Not only do insurers employ devices such as these in order to reduce moral hazard *ex ante*—that is, before loss has occurred. We have seen that sometimes the principal threat to the insurer is *ex post* moral hazard. Having health insurance, for example, rarely increases the probability that the policyholder will become sick or be injured. Such insurance, however, may well generate incentives to consume more health care than is optimal once the policyholder has become sick or injured. Managed health care is an attempt to deal with these incentives as they arise in health insurance, by carefully controlling the delivery of insured care. Stated bluntly, modern managed care represents an effort to deter the "overconsumption" of health care.

In short, tort has adopted loss spreading as one of its goals, and insurance has incorporated loss prevention into its structure. In theory this cross-fertilization could have been a uniformly good thing. Neither tort nor insurance is a pure or perfect system; under the proper circumstances the overlapping of functions might more effectively achieve the goals of each system than would the strict separation of the tort and insurance functions. Some of this desirable duplication of functions is exactly what has occurred. But along with some desirable duplication have come other effects on structural features of the system. It turns out that, for the reasons I note in the following pages, in a number of different settings neither system has performed the functions of the other very well.

Spreading Loss by Imposing Liability: Tort as Insurance

Tort often is not a cost-effective loss-spreading device. Because tort is largely fault-based and makes its necessary findings of fact in a highly individualized manner, tort is a very expensive form of loss insurance. As I have indicated at several points in previous chapters, tort on average pays less than half of its total expenditures to victims. In some fields, such as medical malpractice and products liability, it pays only one-third of its expenditures to victims. The rest goes to pay lawyers, liability insurers, and court costs. In sharp contrast, first-party insurance such as health and disability insurance pays a much higher percentage of its expenditures to victims—often over 80 percent—because most claims do not require litigation and their administrative costs are so much lower than tort.

Tort is also far less effective than insurance at controlling *ex post* moral hazard, because unlike health and disability insurance policyholders, tort plaintiffs are not subject to contractual devices and limitations such as managed care standards, copayment requirements, and deductibles that can be used to combat this threat. On the contrary, we saw in earlier chapters that the more medical care a tort plaintiff receives, and the longer she is out of work, the more damages a jury is likely to award her, and with no additional cost to her. As health insurance moves increasingly toward being universal, this multiplier effect is likely to influence tort costs even more than it does at present.

Tort often is not a terribly effective insurance mechanism for other reasons as well. One reason is that in certain settings tort risks promoting a version of adverse selection. In areas such as products liability and medical malpractice there is a contractual relationship, direct or indirect, between buyers and sellers. One component of the price of the seller's product or service will therefore take into account the cost of potential tort liability to the buyer or those affected by the product after the buyer acquires it. However, because it is extremely difficult, if not impossible, to charge different buyers different prices depending on their risk of loss, all buyers will tend to pay the same "tort insurance" premium as part of the product or service price. High-risk buyers may then tend to buy more of the product or service than low-risk buyers, because they will be getting more insurance for the same price. For certain products or services for which demand is highly inelastic, rates of purchase will not vary much, but there will still be cross-subsidies from low-risk to high-risk buyers.

Tort may create cross-subsidies of this sort not only from low-risk to high-risk potential victims but also from comparatively poor to comparatively wealthy potential victims. High-income purchasers of products and services pay the same "tort insurance" premium as low-income purchasers as part of their purchase price. But high-income purchasers recover more lost income in tort for the same tort "premium" when they are injured, because they have more income to lose. In effect, low-income product purchasers and health-care consumers subsidize high-income purchasers and consumers.

The final flaw in the effort to use tort as a loss-spreading device is this. Insurance does not function well in the face of correlated loss. The law of averages only works in favor of insurance when each risk the insurer accepts is independent of all the other risks it accepts. Otherwise the loss-spreading function cannot operate—either the insurer makes an enormous profit because no losses occur, or it is unable to pay claims because most or all policyholders have suffered a loss. Certain forms of tort liability, however, can be severely subject to correlated loss. A manufacturer of any product that is purchased or used by large numbers of people risks incurring liability to a substantial portion of these people or others affected by the product if the product turns out to be defectively designed or to carry an inadequate warning. The manufacturer in this situation is likely not to be a very good insurer, since it may incur catastrophic liability and become insolvent.[4] Of course, the manufacturer may be able to purchase liability insurance that protects against this risk to some extent, but then the insurer faces a similar problem and must find a way to diversify its risk. Mass tort liability, then, often is not a favorable setting for achieving loss-spreading goals. Yet, as we saw in Chapter 7, because deterrence considerations are often attenuated in mass tort cases, these cases have increasingly been dominated by compensation considerations that resonate more with loss spreading than with deterrence.

Preventing Loss While Insuring It: Insurance as Tort

Just as tort often is not a very effective insurance mechanism, so in certain settings insurance tends not to be very effective at loss prevention. The loss-spreading feature of insurance, after all, is fundamentally at odds with loss prevention. Only to the extent that the loss spreading entailed in an insurance scheme is limited can insurance promote loss prevention. In addition, the insurance categories created by premium rating can create safety incentives only if the policyholder can influence future premiums by preventing losses. When insurance categories are based on immutable features of the policyholder's make-up or activities, however, as they often are, there is no possibility that premium rating can promote safety. Rating based on past loss experience has the most potential to create safety incentives, since the policyholder's future premiums will vary directly with its current loss experience. But full experience-rating is statistically valid only for policyholders with a substantial base of losses. For other policyholders, experience-rating has only limited usefulness. The use of deductibles and the placement of limits on the amount of coverage that can be purchased also may produce safety effects, and I will have more to say about the greater use of these devices below.

It is true nonetheless that even when premium rating cannot directly impact safety levels, it may still may affect activity levels and, as a result, loss prevention, by influencing the allocation of resources toward safer activities. Activities that pose higher risks of loss will naturally be accompanied by higher insurance costs. Other things being equal, comparatively dangerous products will cost more than their safer substitutes because the former pose a greater risk of liability; similarly, surgery to correct a coronary blockage will cost more than noninvasive medical treatment for the same condition. Therefore, resources will tend to gravitate to activities that employ safer substitutes. Higher levels of safer activities, and lower levels of riskier activities, may be the result.

But just as some variables used in premium rating are immutable, some activities also are immutable. I can own fewer cars in order to reduce my auto insurance costs, even if my insurance premiums are based on the (unalterable) ages of those in my family who have drivers' licenses. But I cannot engage in less of the "activity" of living and thereby reduce my life or health insurance premiums. And if my workers' compensation or products liability insurance premiums are a function of my gross revenues, it would make no sense for me to sell fewer services or manufacture fewer products in order to minimize my insurance costs.

The most attractive and simple way for insurance to play a greater role in loss prevention would be to use more sizable deductibles. This is a recognized method of combating moral hazard and thereby creating incentives for the policyholder to optimize losses. The puzzle is why this device is not employed more frequently.

THE DYNAMICS OF CORPORATE INSURANCE PURCHASING.   There are a number of explanations for this puzzle. First, major corporate policyholders already tend to use large deductibles, or self-insured retentions, in their coverage programs. It is common, for example, for large U.S. corporations to retain self-insured responsibility for at least the first $1 million or more of liability that they incur under their CGL insurance policies.[5] For many of these businesses, this level of liability is reasonably predictable and steady from year to year. Purchasing first-dollar liability insurance would simply involve paying an insurer the cost of processing and paying highly expected losses, plus a loading charge. Beyond these highly predictable levels of liability, U.S. businesses tend to buy liability insurance. For small and medium-sized businesses, smaller deductibles make perfect sense. They cannot easily self-insure against very sizable liabilities.

It remains an interesting question, however, why the largest U.S. corporations purchase liability insurance the way they do, in the hundreds of millions of dollars per year subject only to retentions of a few million dollars. Why would some of the country's largest corporations, with tens or even hundreds of billions of dollars in annual revenues and tens of billions of dollars of net worth, purchase liability insurance in this way, in amounts that provide a mere $500 million or less of coverage each year? Surely the shareholders of such corporations are independently capable of bearing the risk of this amount of liability by diversifying their own portfolios. These corporations do not need to do the diversifying for their shareholders. It is true that a small or medium-sized business may be benefited by the purchase of liability insurance through its reassurance of its employees, suppliers, and customers that its resources will not be eroded by tort liability. Liability insurance for small and medium-sized businesses is in this sense a bonding mechanism.[6] But liability insurance covering a small percentage of a very large corporation's net worth does almost no such bonding.

One explanation might be that large corporations who buy liability insurance also buy risk-management services from the insurer that help the corporation reduce its losses, and thereby reduce the cost of insurance. Unfortunately, the factual premises on which this explanation rests are largely incorrect. Large liability insurers may have a base of knowledge that gives them a comparative advantage in risk management over small and medium-sized businesses. But liability insurers actually provide few risk-management services to sizable policyholders, and the policyholders know their businesses better than the insurers. General Electric knows more about how to make turbines and Boeing knows more about how to design airplane engines than their liability insurers, and both know at least as much as their insurers know about how to maintain safety on the factory floor. Each company has its own risk-management department, and there probably isn't much that their insurers could tell either company about how to reduce their losses beyond what they are already doing.

Two other explanations don't reflect terribly well on the system, but I think that they are more persuasive. Both involve corporate concerns about the reaction of the securities markets to uninsured liabilities. First, although major corporations are perfectly capable of self-insuring against the risk of incurring several hundred million dollars of tort liability, in any year when an uninsured liability is actually incurred, the corporation suffers a disruption that is reflected on its balance sheet. Suddenly a liability charge must be taken. Because the securities market may overreact to this shock, purchasing liability insurance is a method of smoothing the balance sheet from year to year. Further, since a corporation's management is likely to be heavily invested in the shares of the corporation and therefore less diversified than ordinary shareholders, management's self-interest is even more strongly served by avoiding shocks to the corporation's balance sheet.[7] Instead of periodically incurring a large liability that substantially erodes self-insurance reserves, the annual payment of an insurance premium results in less balance-sheet change from one year to the next. For very large businesses, then, purchasing insurance against what amounts to noncatastrophic liability is an inoculation against short-term financial instability rather than a meaningful transfer of risk. Once a large insured corporation incurs a liability, then of course it may be worth fighting with its insurers over who pays its liabilities, but obtaining this insurance may not always be the core purpose of the transaction in the first instance.

A second reason that very large corporations purchase insurance is related to the first. If a corporation did not purchase liability insurance and then incurred a substantial liability, the members of its board of directors would be likely to face a shareholders' suit alleging that the directors had breached their duty of care to the corporation by failing to buy liability insurance. The outcome of the suit would depend on whether a jury was persuaded that the decision not to buy insurance was within the bounds of good business judgment. Economists may immediately understand why it was prudent not to buy liability insurance protecting a small percentage of a large corporation's net worth, but the lay members of a jury, exercising 20/20 hindsight, may not have this understanding. Purchasing liability insurance avoids this risk.

The liability imposed on a corporation's directors in such a shareholder's suit would ordinarily be covered by the directors' D & O insurance in the absence of an applicable exclusion. And the amount of liability imposed on the individual directors—liability against which the corporation would be legally prohibited from indemnifying them—would be roughly equal to the loss the corporation suffered as a result of being uninsured. Indirectly, then, the D & O insurer could thereby become the corporation's CGL insurer. As a consequence, few if any D & O insurers would write coverage for a corporation that had not purchased CGL insurance, because to do so a D & O insurer would have to engage in what amounted to double underwriting—first for the direct D & O risk, and then for the indirect, unpurchased CGL risk. In short, partly because they could not easily buy D & O insurance without also buying CGL insurance, even large corporations purchase the latter.

Thus, it is not at all obvious that it would be in major corporations' interest to purchase CGL insurance if it were not for their concern about balance sheet smoothing and about access to D & O insurance. Apart from this concern, if such corporations were going to buy insurance at all, it probably would make a lot more sense for them to purchase liability insurance that incepted when liability in excess of several-hundred-million-dollars was incurred—in effect, insurance subject to a several-hundred-million-dollar deductible—rather than buying insurance as they do now, so that their coverage terminates, rather than begins, at this liability level. Interestingly, the decreasing reliability of CGL insurance that I analyzed in Chapter 5 has been moving them in that direction, but only very slowly.

ENCOURAGING LARGER DEDUCTIBLES AND HIGHER LIMITS OF COVERAGE.   A broader question flowing from this analysis is whether it would be preferable for all policyholders, large and small, purchasing all kinds of insurance, to purchase less insurance against small losses and more insurance against large ones. Certainly insurance theory suggests that scarce dollars should be spent on protection against large rather than small losses. Exactly how much insurance against small rather than large losses ordinary individuals purchase is not entirely clear. Nonetheless, I have the strong impression from reading the insurance trade press for 30 years, as well as from conversations with insurance professionals, that the typical individual insurance consumer tends to purchase coverage subject to comparatively small deductibles. The result is that there is more coverage against small losses, and less against large losses, than would be available if much more sizable deductibles were the norm.

One reason policyholders follow this practice, which is seemingly so contrary to their interest, is that they appear to want to get something tangible for their premium dollars. Policyholders who must pay a substantial portion of a small or moderate loss out of their own pockets sometimes feel that their insurance coverage has been inadequate. And in health insurance many policyholders whose coverage is employment based do not directly pay a premium bill at all, and therefore consider themselves to have been denied an entitlement when they must pay a deductible or copayment for a health-care bill. In this situation policyholders may think of themselves as having guaranteed health care rather than health insurance. Copayment obligations are then regarded as gaps in that guarantee, rather than as a sensible way to manage care and to increase the amount of coverage provided for large losses.

As a result of these consumer attitudes toward insurance, brokers, agents, employers, and other intermediaries may find that a sizable portion of their individual customers or employees are more likely to be satisfied with their service if insurance pays a high percentage of their small losses. There are far more customers with small and moderate losses for these intermediaries to keep satisfied than there are customers who suffer very large losses that exhaust the limits of their coverage because they did not purchase enough of it. For this reason, insurance agents and other intermediaries may not encourage the use of larger deductibles and the purchase of correspondingly higher amounts of coverage than they otherwise might.

A second reason that policyholders probably have too much coverage against small losses and not enough against large losses is that deductibles or coinsurance of any kind in consumer auto liability or homeowners' liability insurance—and certainly substantial deductibles or coinsurance—could complicate application of the insurer's duties to defend and settle claims against the policyholder. With no deductibles or coinsurance the insurer's duties are established. The liability insurer must defend all claims that would fall within coverage if they were successful, and must accept reasonable offers to settle claims made by the party suing the policyholder. In contrast, if these forms of liability insurance were subject to deductibles or coinsurance, new policy provisions reflecting new, more complicated, and probably bifurcated duties would have to be prepared and approved. For example, insurers might not be permitted to settle suits against their policyholders without the policyholders' agreeing to pay the applicable deductible as part of the settlement. Rules regarding the circumstances under which the policyholder could be asked, or required, to pay a deductible into a settlement would have to be developed. And then litigation over the scope of these rules would probably ensue. Insurers find it preferable to leave well enough alone and to sell liability insurance to individuals without such deductibles.

A final reason for the absence of sizable deductibles in most forms of insurance is that insurers' premium revenues may be higher when they sell coverage subject to small rather than large deductibles. While it is true that the same premium could buy more coverage if it were subject to a larger deductibles, policyholders are motivated to spend as little as possible on insurance. Encouraging the use of larger deductibles probably would not create an occasion for most policyholders to spend the same premium on more insurance coverage. Instead many would buy no more or only a little more coverage, for a lower premium. Since the interest of insurance company managers tends not to be simply to maximize profitability but also to operate ever larger enterprises, managers' incentives cut against pressing for larger deductibles by their policyholders. As a consequence, there may be less institutional pressure than would be desirable for using larger deductibles or coinsurance, because that risks decreasing insurers' revenues.

But the practice of employing no deductibles or very low ones is not in policyholders' interest. The primary function of insurance is to spread the risk of losses that policyholders cannot effectively bear themselves. Comparatively small losses can more easily be managed individually; it is large losses that are most in need of insuring. Using small deductibles and no coinsurance spends scarce premium dollars on insurance against small losses, sacrificing the opportunity to encourage the purchase of more insurance against large losses. This practice also undermines the capacity of insurance to promote loss prevention, because ordinary policyholders have so little at stake in the risk of high-probability, low-severity losses. Larger deductibles and coinsurance would more effectively help to combat both *ex ante* and *ex post* moral hazard. If insurance were restructured to include large copayments by policyholders, it could simultaneously and more effectively spread the most severe losses and help to prevent losses from occurring.

The question is how to get there. The least intrusive approach would be a regulatory requirement promulgated by state insurance commissioners that the purchasers of consumer insurance be given an explicit choice among deductibles and coinsurance that vary more than those that are currently offered. A slightly more intrusive approach would be a regulatory default rule that required a substantial deductible or coinsurance provision unless the insurance purchaser expressly opted for a smaller copayment. It would also make sense to develop optional auto liability and homeowners' liability insurance policies that would be subject to declining deductible levels and coinsurance as the amount of liability incurred increased. Under such policies, the insurer's duty to defend and privilege of settling would continue as they now stand; the policyholder would have to abide by the settlement decisions of the insurer. These decisions would result in a coinsurance obligation on the part of the policyholder that functioned much like a retrospective premium calculated at the end of the policy period. This would leave policyholders a bit vulnerable to surcharges at the end of the policy period. But in return for this vulnerability, policyholders would be afforded larger amounts of coverage. In each of these ways, policyholders would be encouraged to buy more insurance against devastatingly large losses, and less insurance against smaller, more individually manageable losses.

Sobering Constraints

The decades-long process of attempting to employ tort liability to promote loss spreading, and to use insurance to promote loss prevention, has been far from completely successful. Indeed, I hope that I have showed that part of what influences the character of contemporary tort law and insurance is precisely that each system is sometimes asked to do more than it can do effectively. Tort cannot be a thoroughly satisfactory loss-spreading device, and insurance cannot be a wholly effective loss prevention device. Yet often over the last century, tort law, or insurers' own practices, or both, have evolved to demand precisely that. When we try to obtain more loss spreading from tort and more loss prevention from insurance than either system can comfortably generate, then the social and economic costs that we must pay often are substantial. Throttling back on the amount of the cross-functions these systems perform would seem to be the natural solution to this problem, but the two systems are now so intertwined that this simple approach is not feasible. Over a century of mutual influence and development has fused the two systems together in many ways that cannot be undone.

Just as important, whether reform is desirable is always a "compared to what" question. Cutting back on tort liability and shifting some of tort's loss-spreading functions back into insurance may be a sensible thing to do when considered independently. But such a move also may reduce the deterrent effect of the threat of liability. The question then is whether other devices we use to promote deterrence—market forces and governmental safety regulation, for example—can and will pick up the slack. Alternatively, as I suggested at the conclusion of Chapter 7, life, health, and disability insurers might be given full rights of subrogation on behalf of their policyholders, as I and others have proposed elsewhere. Then individuals would not necessarily have to bring tort suits. Rather, they would receive more generous insurance benefits in return for transferring all their tort rights to their insurers. Such an approach could streamline tort litigation at the same time that it preserved the deterrent effect of the threat of liability.[8]

Just as using tort to promote loss spreading as much as we do now may not be sensible, using insurance to promote safety also is often a game that is not worth the candle, especially if doing so unduly hinders the capacity of insurance to achieve loss spreading. The more accurately liability insurance premiums differentiate among policyholders on the basis of their risk of incurring liability, the more consistent such insurance will be with loss prevention, but the less loss spreading this insurance will entail. Conversely, the less premium differentiation liability insurance employs, the less consistent it will be with loss prevention, but the more loss spreading it will promote. The point holds not only for liability insurance, but for insurance against first-party losses as well. Insurance is always locating itself somewhere on the continuum of effects running from pure loss spreading at one extreme to maximizing its capacity to prevent losses at the other extreme. The practical question is whether the mix of loss spreading and loss prevention promoted by any particular insurance arrangement is optimal, and whether legal regulation that might change this mix is appropriate or, on the contrary, will do more harm than good. In most instances we could promote loss prevention and optimal loss spreading more effectively by incorporating larger deductibles in all forms of insurance, rather than by attempting to create loss prevention incentives through ever more refined premium differentiation.

The lesson that I think should be drawn from this analysis, and indeed in many respects from this book as a whole, is that we should be using the tort and insurance systems mainly for what they do best, and certainly only for what they can do with some measure of adequacy. The twentieth-century recognition that tort is a mixed system that pursues a series of incompletely compatible purposes must be leavened by a twenty-first-century recognition that there are some purposes now pursued by tort that only insurance can achieve effectively; that there are some functions of tort that insurance can perform in at best a supplementary manner; and that there are some goals that neither tort nor insurance as we now know them can effectively achieve. Looking to other means of achieving ideals that each of these systems has proved it is not capable of giving us to the full extent we desire would be a far more sensible way to proceed. In important respects in both of these fields, then, it may truly be said that less is more.

Notes

Introduction

1. There is much work, both scholarly and popular, on American litigiousness generally. See, e.g., Thomas F. Burke, *Lawyers, Lawsuits, and Legal Rights: The Battle over Litigation in American Society* (Berkeley, Calif., 2002); Robert A. Kagan, *Adversarial Legalism: The American Way of Law* (Cambridge, Mass., 2001); Philip K. Howard, *The Death of Common Sense: How Law Is Suffocating America* (New York, 1994). There is, similarly, much general work on litigiousness and the functioning of tort. See, e.g., Peter A. Bell and Jeffrey O'Connell, *Accidental Justice: The Dilemmas of Tort Law* (New Haven, Conn., 1997). General works that place the role played by insurance in tort in context, in various ways, include Tom Baker and Jonathan Simon (eds.), *Embracing Risk: The Changing Culture of Insurance and Responsibility* (Chicago, 2002); Mark Rahdert, *Covering Accident Costs: Insurance, Liability, and Tort Reform* (Philadelphia, 1995); Kenneth S. Abraham, *Distributing Risk: Insurance, Legal Theory, and Public Policy* (New Haven, Conn., 1986); and Kent D. Syverud, "On the Demand for Liability Insurance," 72 *Texas Law Review* 1629 (1994).

2. See, e.g., John Fabian Witt, *The Accidental Republic* (Cambridge, Mass., 2004); Jacob S. Hacker, *The Divided Welfare State* (New York, 2002); David A. Moss, *When All Else Fails* (Cambridge, Mass., 1996). On both the partiality of the system and the historical interaction of the private and public approaches, see Jennifer Klein, *For All These Rights* (Princeton, N.J., 2003).

3. I have based this calculation, with adjustments of my own that I will describe below, on Towers-Perrin Tillinghast, *U.S. Tort Costs and Cross Border Perspectives: 2006 Update* 15 (2006), www.towersperrin.com/tillinghast. This report estimates total direct torts costs of over $260 million, but the estimate includes more than merely personal injury costs. In addition, the methodology used by Towers-Perrin Tillinghast (TPT) to compute total tort costs has been the subject of controversy. See, e.g., Americans for Insurance Reform,

"Tillinghast's 'Tort Cost' Figures Vastly Overstate the Cost of the American Legal System," January 6, 2004, www.insurance-reform.org. But the TPT data is the most recent and most comprehensive available, and it includes estimates stretching back to 1950, and therefore makes longitudinal, order-of-magnitude comparisons possible. I will use TPT data throughout the book, though where other data is available I will use it as well. In my view some of the criticisms of the TPT data are not justified, but some are. For example, I think that the cost of defending particular tort claims, which TPT includes in its estimates, is appropriately considered part of the direct cost of the tort system. I have therefore included this cost in my adjusted estimates. Similarly, notwithstanding TPT's critics, I think that the cost of resolving an auto fender-bender or other such claim without any lawsuit is appropriately considered a direct cost of the tort system, because the payment is the result of a legal obligation with its source in tort law. However, TPT does not explain how it has arrived at its estimates for the amounts of self-insured and uninsured tort liability. Lacking any alternative reliable estimate, I have included in my own estimate the TPT figure, which is roughly one-third of the total, though it should probably be taken with a grain of salt. On the other hand, TPT's estimates also include 22 percent for insurance company administrative expenses not associated with particular tort claims. I do not think that salaries or the cost of advertising, for example, are "direct" costs; I have therefore deducted these expenses from the TPT data in making the estimate in the text, and I will continue to make similar deductions when referring to TPT data throughout the book.

4. See Lynn M. LoPucki, "The Essential Structure of Judgment Proofing, 51 *Stanford Law Review* 147 (1998); "The Death of Liability," 106 *Yale Law Journal* 1 (1996). Individuals also have certain shelters, though they are more limited. See Stephen G. Gilles, "The Judgment-Proof Society," 63 *Washington & Lee Law Review* 603 (2006).

5. See, e.g., William O. Douglas, "Vicarious Liability and Administration of Risk," 38 *Yale Law Journal* 584 and 720 (pts. 1 and 2) (1929); Fleming James, Jr., "Contribution among Joint Tortfeasors: A Pragmatic Criticism," 54 *Harvard Law Review* 1156 (1941).

6. See Guido Calabresi, *The Costs of Accidents* (New Haven, Conn., 1970).

7. See George L. Priest, "The Current Insurance Crisis and Modern Tort Law," 96 *Yale Law Journal* 1521 (1987); Richard A. Epstein, "Products Liability as an Insurance Market," 14 *Journal of Legal Studies* 645 (1985).

8. See Jon Hanson and Kyle D. Logue, "The First-Party Insurance Externality: An Economic Justification for Enterprise Liability," 76 *Cornell Law Review* 129 (1990); Gregory Keating, "The Theory of Enterprise Liability and Common Law Strict Liability," 54 *Vanderbilt Law Review* 1285 (2001).

9. See W. Page Keeton et al., *Prosser and Keeton on Torts* 589 (St. Paul, Minn., 5th ed. 1984).

10. 150 P.2d 436 (Cal. 1944).

11. The literature on tort reform, both general and specific, is voluminous. A sample of recent general work, both pro and con, includes the following: Paul Ruschmann, *Tort Reform* (Philadelphia, 2006); Eric Helland and Alexander Tabarrok, *Judge and Jury: American Tort Law on Trial* (Oakland, Calif., 2006); William Haltom and Michael McCann, *Distorting the Law: Politics, Media, and the Litigation Crisis* (Chicago, 2004); Robert A. Levy, *Shakedown: How Corporations, Government, and Trial Lawyers Abuse the Judicial Process* (Washington, D.C., 2004); Michael McKasy and Debra Stephens, *Tort Law Update: Rising above Tort Reform* (Seattle, 2004); Philip K. Howard, *The Collapse of the Common Good: How America's Lawsuit Culture Undermines Our Freedom* (New York, 2002); Thomas H. Koenig and Michael L. Rustad, *In Defense of Tort Law* (New York, 2001); Stephen Daniels and Joanne Martin, "The Strange Success of Tort Reform," 53 *Emory Law Journal* 1225 (2004); Philip K. Howard, "Is Civil Litigation a Threat to Freedom?" 28 *Harvard Journal of Law & Public Policy* 97 (2004); Linda S. Mullenix, "The Future of Tort Reform: Possible Lessons from the World Trade Center Victim Compensation Fund," 53 *Emory Law Journal* 1315 (2004); Deborah L. Rhode, "Frivolous Litigation and Civil Justice Reform: Miscasting the Problem, Recasting the Solution," 54 *Duke Law Journal* 447 (2004); Gary R. Smith, introduction, "The Future of Tort Reform: Reforming the Remedy, Re-balancing the Scales," 53 *Emory Law Journal* 1219 (2004); Michael B. Dann, "Jurors and the Future of 'Tort Reform,'" 78 *Chicago-Kent Law Review* 1127 (2003); Deborah J. La Fetra, "Freedom, Responsibility, and Risk: Fundamental Principles Supporting Tort Reform," 36 *Indiana Law Review* 645 (2003).

12. For an extensive survey and analysis of these positions, see John C. P. Goldberg, "Twentieth-Century Tort Theory," 91 *Georgetown Law Journal* 513 (2003).

13. The data on the issue is analyzed in Don DeWees, David Duff, and Michael J. Trebilcock, *Exploring the Domain of Accident Law: Taking the Facts Seriously* (New York, 1996); Gary Schwartz, "Reality in the Economic Analysis of Tort Law: Does Tort Law Really Deter?" 42 *UCLA Law Review* 377 (1994).

14. For analysis of the role played by inadvertence in negligent behavior, see Mark F. Grady, "Res Ipsa Loquitur and Compliance Error," 142 *University of Pennsylvania Law Review* 887 (1994).

15. Tillinghast Towers-Perrin, *U.S. Tort Costs: 2003 Update* 17 (2004), www.towersperin.com. For a survey of the various sources paying compensation, see Deborah R. Hensler et al., *Compensation for Accidental Injuries in the United States* (Santa Monica, Calif., 1991).

16. James S. Kakalik and Nicholas M. Pace, *Costs and Compensation Paid in Tort Litigation* 72 (Santa Monica, Calif., 1986).

17. Committee for Economic Development, *Who Should Be Liable?* 53 (New York, 1989) (estimates of 35–45 percent); Stephen D. Sugarman, *Doing Away with Personal Injury Law: New Compensation Mechanisms for Victims, Consumers, and Business* 23–24 (New York, 1989) (citing estimates of 37–40 percent).

18. Kenneth S. Abraham, "Twenty-First-Century Insurance and Loss Distribution in Tort Law," in M. Stuart Madden (ed.), *Exploring Tort Law* 86–91 (New York, 2005).

1. The Dawn of a New Era

1. See, e.g., The Thorns Case, Y.B. Mich. 6 Ed. 4, f. 7, pl. 18 (1466).

2. 35 N.Y. 210 (1866).

3. See, e.g., Mayor of New York v. Lord, 18 Wend. 126 (N.Y. 1837).

4. For the fullest expression of this subsidy thesis, see Morton J. Horwitz, *The Transformation of American Law, 1780–1860* (Cambridge, Mass., 1977).

5. Lawrence M. Friedman, *A History of American Law* 351 (New York, 3d ed. 2005).

6. Peter Karsten, *Heart versus Head: Judge-Made Law in the Nineteenth Century* 101–106 (Chapel Hill, N.C., 1997).

7. Horwitz, *The Transformation of American Law,* 202.

8. Speaking of the barratry defense early in the nineteenth century, the Massachusetts Supreme Judicial Court noted that it was the duty of a ship's owner to entrust it to a captain "of competent skill, prudence, and discretion." The insurer was not responsible for losses arising from the captain's "negligence, ignorance, or willful misconduct" because "the principle of an implied warranty on the part of the assured, that every thing shall be done to prevent a loss, pervades the whole subject of marine insurance." Cleveland v. Union Insurance Company, 8 Mass. 308, 321–322 (1808); see also Grim v. Phoenix Insurance Company, 13 Johns 451 (N.Y. 1816) (fire damage caused by negligence not covered under marine insurance).

9. For example, Phillips's 1823 *Treatise on the Law of Insurance* noted that "a person cannot protect himself by insurance against the loss occasioned by his own fraudulent acts and misconduct." An agreement indemnifying against such loss would be "obviously opposed to the general interest of a community." And there was "the same objection, in a smaller degree, against sustaining a contract to indemnify a man against the consequences of his own negligence." Insurance against loss caused by the policyholder's negligence would put the insurer "wholly in the power of another, and it could

operate only to the injury of the parties, and to the community of which they were members." See Willard Phillips, *Treatise on the Law of Insurance* 158 (New York, 1823); Horwitz, *The Transformation of American Law,* 202 (quoting Phillips).

10.   The change seems to have already begun to occur when Kent published the first edition of his *Commentaries* in 1826. By that time there was a division of authority regarding the barratry defense: "[I]t is a vexed question, rendered more perplexing by well-balanced decisions, and in direct opposition to each other, whether a loss by fire proceeding from negligence, be covered by a policy insuring against fire." 3 James Kent, *Commentaries on American Law* 253–254 (New York, 1826).

11.   On the few occasions when the validity of devices that looked like liability insurance were called into question prior to the Civil War, concern was voiced about the incentives that would be created if such insurance was permitted. For example, something resembling liability insurance was occasionally hidden in the interstices of first-party policies themselves. First-party marine insurance against the loss of ships and cargo at sea sometimes covered liability for the "running down" of one ship by another. But this form of coverage was also subject to the barratry defense of the policyholder's negligence, except under unusual circumstances. An English court early in the nineteenth century had indicated that "it would be an illegal insurance to insure against what might be the consequences of the wrongful acts of the assured," but created an exception where the policyholders also commonly functioned as insurers and were therefore "as much interested to extend the principle of loss as to restrain it." Delanoy v. Robson, 5 Taunt. 605 (1814). That is, the court thought (whether or not correctly) that the moral hazard that would be created by liability insurance where the insurer was in other situations the potential victim would be no greater than in ordinary marine insurance. So the running-down insurance that was sometimes included in marine insurance policies was valid under these circumstances, though not necessarily under others. See also Mary Coate McNeely, "Illegality as a Factor in Liability Insurance," 41 *Columbia Law Review* 26, 27 (1941).

12.   Brown v. Kendall, 60 Mass. 292 (1850).

13.   Horwitz, *The Transformation of American Law,* 202.

14.   In 1873, for example, the U.S. Supreme Court agonized about the validity of agreements relieving common carriers of their duties. The question, said the Court, was whether such agreements may introduce evils against which it was "the direct policy of the law to guard," and whether "a modification [of the common law high duty of care] which gives license and immunity to negligence and carelessness on the part of a public carrier or his servants, is

not so evidently repugnant to that policy as to be altogether null and void; or, at least, null and void under certain circumstances." New York Central R. Co. v. Lockwood, 84 U.S. 357, 360 (1873). The Court went on to hold that the particular agreement at issue in that case was invalid. Underscoring the point, the Court quoted a New York decision expressing concern about the effects of that state's rule permitting abrogation of a common carrier's duty of high care to its passengers: "'The fruits of this rule,' says Judge Davis, 'are already being gathered in increasing accidents, through the decreasing care and vigilance on the part of these corporations; and they will continue to be reaped until a just sense of public policy shall lead to legislative restriction upon the power to make this kind of contract.'" Id. at 368, quoting Stinson v. New York Central Railroad Co., 32 N.Y. 337 (1865).

15. 304 U.S. 64 (1938).

16. 117 U.S. 312 (1886).

17. The insurer's brief certainly tried to make it sound that way, opening with the following statement: "For many years past a conflict has been going on between common carriers on the one side and the public who employ them on the other, the carrier seeking by various devices of phraseology in his bills of lading to secure exemption, not only from the rigorous rules of the common law, but also from all responsibility to the owners of property entrusted to him. As the practice of insurance has increased and become more general the insurance companies have necessarily been drawn into this conflict, and one of the latest of the carriers' devices in seeking to evade responsibility is by attempting to obtain the benefit of any insurance effected by the owner upon his property." Brief for Appellant at 1, Phoenix (October 16, 1882).

18. 117 U.S. at 325.

19. 117 U.S. at 324.

20. John Fabian Witt, *The Accidental Republic: Crippled Workingmen, Destitute Widows, and the Remaking of American Law* 12–17 (Cambridge, Mass., 2004).

21. The rule originated in Farwell v. Boston & Worcester R.R. Corp., 45 Mass. 49 (1842).

22. See, e.g., Gilman v. Eastern R. Co, 95 Mass. 433 (1866) (duty to provide competent fellow employees); Northern Pacific R. Co. v. Herbert, 116 U.S. 642 (1886) (different department doctrine); Dayharsh v. Hannibal & St. J. R. Co., 15 S.W. 554 (Mo. 1891) (vice-principal doctrine). For discussion, see G. Edward White, *Tort Law in America* 51–55 (New York, expanded ed. 2003).

23. For discussion of these developments, see Friedman, *A History of American Law*, 422–424.

24. 1 James Harrington Boyd, *A Treatise on the Law of Compensation for Injuries to Workmen* 8–9 (Indianapolis, 1913).

25. Harry Perry Robinson, *The Employers' Liability Assurance Corporation Ltd. 1880–1930* (London, 1930).

26. Charles E. Hodges, *The First American Liability Insurance Company* 10 (New York, 1957).

27. See Raymond N. Caverly, "The Background of the Casualty and Bonding Business in the United States," 6 *Insurance Counsel Journal* 62, 63 (1939).

28. Act of May 14, 1887, ch. 270, 1887 Mass. Acts 899 (current version at Mass. Gen. Laws Ann. Ch. 153 (West 2005).

29. Boston & A.R. Co. v. Mercantile Trust & Deposit Co. of Baltimore, 34 A. 778, 786–787 (Md. 1896).

30. Trenton Pass. R. Co. v. Guarantors Liability Indemnity Co., 37 A.609, 611 (N.J. 1897).

31. Boston & A.R. Co. v. Mercantile Trust & Deposit Co. of Baltimore, 34 A. 778, 786–787 (Md. 1896).

32. Breeden v. Frankfort Marine, Accident & Plate Glass Ins. Co., 119 S.W. 576 (Mo. 1909). To my knowledge Gary Schwartz was the first modern scholar to take note of the dissent in Breeden. See Gary Schwartz, "The Ethics and the Economics of Tort Liability Insurance," 75 *Cornell Law Review 313* (1990).

33. 119 S.W. at 581. True to its principles, the dissent listed a parade of horribles that would follow the majority's decision: "If this so-called species of insurance is valid, then by the same course of reasoning a physician or surgeon may insure against his acts of malpractice, or other negligent acts in the sick room, and act with perfect impunity. And, based upon the same authorities relied upon by counsel for respondent in this case, the Supreme Court of Pennsylvania, in a recent case, has just held that the owner of an automobile may insure against all damages he may be compelled to pay to any third person in consequence of his negligence in operating the same . . . Already we see mere children, almost daily, driving automobiles, with their attending dangers, along our streets at a high rate of speed, from 20 to 30 miles an hour. Would any sensible man suppose for a moment that parents would tolerate that recklessness for a moment if they were not indemnified against all damages which might flow from such conduct? Certainly not." Id. at 584–585.

34. Horwitz, *The Transformation of American Law,* 226–237.

35. Boston & A.R. Co. v. Mercantile Trust & Deposit Co. of Baltimore, 37 A. 778, 786 (Md. 1896); see also Trenton Pass. R. Co. v. Guarantors Liability Indemnity Co., 37 A. 609, 611 (N.J. 1897) ("The insured is held to the performance of his duty of vigilance both by his liability notwithstanding the indemnity, and by the fact that the vigilant carrier would obtain better terms in making the contracts of insurance.").

36. Ann M. Kelchburg, *A History of the Continental Insurance Company* 103 (New York, 1979).

37. Travelers Insurance Company, *Travelers: 100 Years* 54–55 (Hartford, 1964).

38. Edwin W. De Leon, *Manual of Liability Insurance* 3, 17 (New York, 1909).

39. Id. at 18, 35.

40. Premiums for Manufacturers' Employers' Liability insurance, for example, were based on total employee compensation paid, whereas premiums for Landlord's Public Liability insurance were based on the total area and frontage of the premises, and the number and kind of elevators onsite, if any. A refined set of premium classes and subclasses was also developed. By 1908 there were 20 major classifications based on the type of business covered (e.g., Bakers, Chemical and Paint Manufacturers, Coal Mines, and Meat Packing) and often dozens of subclasses within each class. The Leather and Shoe class, for example, distinguished Leather Embossing from Counter, Heel, and Sole Cutters. Id. at 43–52.

41. Id. at 18.

42. See, e.g., Randolph E. Bergstrom, *Courting Danger: Injury and Law in New York City, 1870–1910* 21 (Ithaca, N.Y., 1992) (27 percent in 1910); Lawrence M. Friedman and Thomas D. Russell, "More Civil Wrongs: Personal Injury Litigation, 1901–1910," 34 *American Journal of Legal History* 295, 303 (1990) (19 percent in Alameda County, California, state court from 1901 to 1910).

43. Robert A. Silverman, *Law and Urban Growth: Civil Litigation in the Boston Trial Courts, 1880–1900* 105–113 (Princeton, N.J., 1981).

44. Bergstrom, *Courting Danger*, 20.

45. Lawrence M. Friedman, "Civil Wrongs: Personal Injury Law in the Late 19th Century," 1987 *American Bar Foundation Law Journal* 351, 359.

46. Friedman and Russell, "More Civil Wrongs," 295.

47. Frank W. Munger, "Social Change and Tort Litigation: Industrialization, Accidents, and Trial Courts in Southern West Virginia, 1872 to 1940," 36 *Buffalo Law Review* 75, 82 (1987).

48. U.S. Department of Commerce, *Statistical Abstract of the United States, 1910,* table 23, p. 51 (Washington, D.C., 1911).

49. Bergstrom, *Courting Danger*, 33.

50. Friedman and Russell, "More Civil Wrongs," 295.

51. Friedman and Russell, "More Civil Wrongs," 303.

52. Silverman, *Law and Urban Growth*, 106.

53. Bergstrom, *Courting Danger*, 21.

54. Silverman, *Law and Urban Growth*, 105.

55. Bergstrom, *Courting Danger*, 21.

56. Friedman, "Civil Wrongs," 361.

57. See Fenton v. Fidelity & Cas. Co. of New York, 56 P. 1096 (Or. 1899).

58. See William R. Vance, *Handbook on the Law of Insurance* 607–608 (St. Paul, Minn., 1904).

59. Id. at 55.

2. The Original Tort Reform

1. Randolph E. Bergstrom, *Courting Danger: Injury and Law in New York City, 1870–1910* 21 (Ithaca, N.Y., 1992).

2. For example, from 1880 to 1890, 41 work injury suits (12 percent of all personal injury suits) were filed in state court in Alameda County, California. From 1901 to 1910, 63 such suits (19 percent of all personal injury suits) were filed. Lawrence M. Friedman and Thomas D. Russell, "More Civil Wrongs: Personal Injury Litigation, 1901–1910," 34 *American Journal of Legal History* 295, 303 (1990). A higher percentage of such suits (55 percent) was filed in federal court during the latter period, perhaps because of the involvement of the Union Pacific and Southern Pacific railroads; they were frequent defendants in the suits, and their presence supported federal court jurisdiction based diversity of citizenship.

3. See *Report to the Legislature of the State of New York by the Commission Appointed under Chapter 518 of the Laws of 1909 to Inquire into the Question of Employers' Liability and Other Matters* 5 (Albany, N.Y., First Report 1910).

4. See Price V. Fishback and Shawn Everett Kantor, *A Prelude to the Welfare State: The Origins of Workers' Compensation* 35–37 (Chicago, 2000).

5. Id. at 41. Two studies reported larger percentages of compensation, but these were biased upward because of an artificial assumption that some of the victims in these studies had no medical expenses. See id. at note d.

6. Crystal Eastman, *Work-Accidents and the Law* 120–121 (New York, 1910).

7. Fishback and Kantor, *A Prelude to the Welfare State*, 209–211.

8. Fishback and Kantor, *A Prelude to the Welfare State*, 49, found limited evidence that higher wages were paid in certain dangerous employments during this period.

9. United States Department of Commerce, *Statistical Abstract of the United States* table 58, p. 123 (Washington, D.C., 1905).

10. Fishback and Kantor, *A Prelude to the Welfare State*, 72.

11. John Fabian Witt, *The Accidental Republic: Injured Workingmen, Destitute Widows, and the Remaking of American Law* 71–102 (Cambridge, Mass., 2004).

12. Id. at 92–101.

13. Kenneth S. Abraham, "Liability Insurance and Accident Prevention: The Evolution of an Idea," 64 *Maryland Law Review* 573 (2005).

14. See David A. Moss, *Socializing Security: Progressive-Era Economics and the Origins of American Social Policy* 9 (Cambridge, Mass., 1996).

15. Eastman, *Work-Accidents and the Law,* 105–114.

16. Travelers Insurance Company, *The Travelers: 100 Years* 55–56 (Hartford, 1964).

17. U.S. Department of Commerce, *Statistical Abstract of the United States* table 298, p. 582 (Washington, D.C., 1910).

18. A. M. Best Company, *Best's Aggregates and Averages Property/Casualty United States & Canada* 413 (Oldwick, N.J., 2005).

19. *Wainwright Commission Report,* 31.

20. Witt, *The Accidental Republic,* 116.

21. "Wage-Earners' Life Insurance," in Osmond K. Frankel (ed.), *The Curse of Bigness* 5 (New York, 1934).

22. Id. at 10.

23. U.S. Department of Commerce, *Statistical Abstract of the United States* table 316, p. 554 (Washington, D.C., 1914).

24. See Morton Keller, *The Life Insurance Enterprise, 1885–1910* 245–264 (Cambridge, Mass., 1963); Shepard B. Clough, *A Century of American Life Insurance* 215–232 (New York, 1946); Mark J. Roe, "Foundations of Corporate Finance: The 1906 Pacification of the Insurance Industry," 93 *Columbia Law Review* 639, 656–674 (1993).

25. Lawrence M. Friedman, *A History of American Law* 357 (New York, 3d ed. 2005).

26. Witt, *The Accidental Republic,* 119–122.

27. See Fishback and Kantor, *A Prelude to the Welfare State,* 12–147; Harry Weiss, "Employers' Liability and Workmen's Compensation," in John R. Commons (ed.), *History of Labor in the United States, 1896–1932,* 575–577 (New York, 1966); Eliza K. Pavalki, "State Timing of Policy Adoption: Workmen's Compensation in the United States, 1909–1929," 95 *American Journal of Sociology* 592 (1989); Price V. Fishback and Shawn Everett Kantor, "The Adoption of Workers' Compensation in the United States, 1900–1930," *Journal of Law and Economics* 305 (1988); Richard A. Epstein, "The Historical Origins and Economic Structure of Workers' Compensation Law," 16 *Georgia Law Review* 775 (1982).

28. Eastman, *Work-Accidents and the Law,* 220.

29. *Wainwright Commission Report,* 7.

30. Id. at 67.

31. John Fabian Witt, "Speedy Fred Taylor and the Ironies of Enterprise Liability," 103 *Columbia Law Review* 1, 39–40 (2003).

32. Years of enactment can be found in Fishback and Kantor, "The Adoption of Workers' Compensation in the United States, 1900–1930," 319–320.

33. Francis B. Tiffany, *Death by Wrongful Act* 178 (St. Paul, Minn., 1893); Rex

Malone, "American Fatal Accident Statutes: The Legislative Birth Pains," 1965 *Duke Law Journal* 673, 695–706.

34. The data in this paragraph is drawn from Fishback and Kantor, *A Prelude to the Welfare State*, 23, 59–61, 90.

35. Id. at 1, 65–66.

36. See, e.g., James R. Chelius, "Liability for Industrial Accidents: A Comparison of Negligence and Strict Liability Systems," 5 *Journal of Legal Studies* 293, 305 (1976).

37. See, e.g., Michael J. Moore and W. Kip Viscusi, *Compensation Mechanisms for Job Risks: Wages, Workers' Compensation, and Product Liability* 121–135 (Princeton, N.J., 1990).

38. Price V. Fishback, "Liability Rules and Accident Prevention in the Workplace: Empirical Evidence from the Early Twentieth Century," 16 *Journal of Legal Studies* 305, 322 (1987).

39. Fishback and Kantor, *A Prelude to the Welfare State*, 80.

40. Id. at 152; U.S. Department of Commerce, *Statistical Abstract of the United States* 314 (Washington, D.C., 1929).

41. Arthur Larson and Lex K. Larson, *Larson's Workmen's Compensation Law* §150.01 (New York, 3d ed. 2000).

42. Walter F. Dodd, *Administration of Workmen's Compensation* 521 (New York, 1936).

43. Id. at 519.

44. Witt, *The Accidental Republic*, 120.

45. See G. F. Michelbacher and Thomas M. Nial, *Workmen's Compensation Insurance* 299–314 (New York, 1925).

46. Dodd, *Administration of Workmen's Compensation*, 710.

47. See, e.g., "Workmen's Compensation—Discussion," 12 *American Economic Review* 153, 160 (supp. March 1922).

48. See, e.g., "Compensation Insurance Law Found Faulty in Practice," *New York Times*, December 7, 1930, 147; "Investigators Urge Sweeping Reforms in Compensation Act," *New York Times*, December 23, 1932, 1.

49. See, e.g., Herman Somers & Anne Somers, "Workmen's Compensation: Unfulfilled Promise," 7 *Industrial and Labor Relations Review* 32, 41 (October 1953).

50. *Report of the National Commission on State Workmen's Compensation Laws* (Washington, D.C., 1972).

51. This data is reported in "California Comp. Reforms Would Trim Billions in Costs," *Business Insurance*, September 15, 2003, 3; "The Workers' Compensation Crisis in California," 1 *California Economic Policy* 6 (2005); "For the Record," *Business Insurance*, June 3, 2002, 23; and California State Auditor,

Report No. 2003–108.1, California's Workers' Compensation Program 28 (Sacramento, 2003).

52. "Workers' Compensation: The Industry's Quiet Crisis?" Insurance Information Institute website, www.iii.org.

53. David Neumark, "The Workers' Compensation Crisis in California," 1 *California Economic Policy* 10 (2005).

54. Cal. Lab. Code §4658(d) (West Supp. 2006).

55. Thomas A. Eaton, "Revisiting the Intersection of Workers' Compensation and Product Liability: An Assessment of a Proposed Federal Solution to an Old Problem," 64 *Tennessee Law Review* 881, 883 (1997), citing Lawrence W. Soular, Alliance of American Insurers, and American Insurance Association, *A Study of Large Product Liability Claims* 1 (Chicago, 1986). For discussion of the issues associated with these arrangements, see Andrew Klein, "Apportionment of Liability in Workplace Injury Claims," 26 *Berkeley Journal of Empirical & Labor Law* 65 (2005); Paul Weiler, "Workers' Compensation and Product Liability: The Interaction of a Tort and a Non-Tort Regime," 50 *Ohio State Law Journal* 825 (1989).

56. See, e.g., American Law Institute, 2 *Enterprise Responsibility for Personal Injury* 187–198 (Philadelphia, 1991).

3. Drivers, Lawyers, and Insurers

1. For discussion of the way recurring sets of similar claims often end up being treated similarly, see Samuel Isaacharoff & John Fabian Witt, "The Inevitability of Aggregate Settlement," 57 *Vanderbilt Law Review* 1571 (2004).

2. Jonathan Simon, "Driving Governmentality: Automobile Accidents, Insurance, and the Challenge to the Social Order in the Inter-War Years, 1919–1941," 4 *Connecticut Insurance Law Journal* 521 (1998).

3. U.S. Department of Commerce, *Statistical Abstract of the United States* table 600, p. 677 (Washington, D.C., 1923).

4. Id. at table 318, p. 316 (1931).

5. Edison L. Bowers, *Compulsory Automobile Insurance* 23 (New York, 1929).

6. The lesser duty of care to passengers actually was first adopted by common law decision in Massaletti v. Fitzroy, 118 N.E. 168 (Mass. 1917). When courts in other states rejected the Massaletti approach, a number of state legislatures adopted the rule by statute. See Andrew Kull, "The Common Law Basis of Automobile Guest Statutes," 43 *University of Chicago Law Review* 798, 812 (1976).

7. Prosser stated firmly, for example, that "the statutes are generally acknowledged to have been the result of persistent and effective lobbying on the part of liability insurance companies." W. Page Keeton et al., *Prosser and Keeton on the Law of Torts* §34, at 215 (St. Paul, Minn., 5th ed. 1984). But the sources

he cited contain similarly undocumented assertions. Very modest confirmation of the role played by the insurers can be found in "Insurance News," *Wall Street Journal,* July 18, 1927, 11, and "Asks Curb on 'Racket,'" *New York Times,* June 1, 1930, 1.

8. *Report by the Committee to Study Compensation for Auto Accidents to the Columbia University Council for Research in the Social Sciences* 121–122 (Philadelphia, 1932).

9. The full name of the Plan is *Report by the Committee to Study Compensation for Auto Accidents to the Columbia University Council for Research in the Social Sciences* (Philadelphia, 1932).

10. Id. at 55–56.

11. Id. at 160–161.

12. See, e.g., Young B. Smith, "Compensation for Automobile Accidents: A Symposium—The Problem and Its Solution," 32 *Columbia Law Review* 784, 792 (1932).

13. See, e.g., August G. Lilly, "Compensation for Automobile Accidents: A Symposium—Criticism of the Proposed Solution," 32 *Columbia Law Review* 803, 805 (1932); P. Tecumseh Sherman, "Grounds for Opposing the Automobile Accident Compensation Plan," 3 *Law & Contemporary Problems* 599, 600–601 (1936).

14. Frank Grad, "Recent Developments in Automobile Accident Compensation," 50 *Columbia Law Review* 300, 307 (1950).

15. Jerry S. Rosenbloom, *Automobile Liability Claims* 4 (Homewood, Ill., 1968)

16. My account of the evolution of the auto policy in the following paragraphs draws heavily from John Eugene Pierce, *Development of Comprehensive Insurance for the Household* 153–197 (Homewood, Ill., 1958).

17. See, e.g., Robinson v. Fidelity & Casualty Company of New York, 57 S.E. 2d 93 (Va. 1950); Peterson v. Maloney, 232 N.W. 790 (Minn. 1930); Dickinson v. Maryland Casualty Company, 125 A. 866 (Conn. 1924).

18. See, e.g., Mullen v. Hartford Accident & Indemnity Company, 191 N.E. 394 (Mass. 1934) (liability for injury caused by oil leaking from insured vehicle is covered); Quality Dairy Company v. Fort Dearborn Casualty Underwriters, 16 S.W. 2d 613 (Mo. Ct. App. 1929) (liability for harm resulting from detachment of wagon from insured vehicle is covered); Owens v. Ocean Accident Guarantee Corporation, 109 S.W. 2d 928 (Ark. 1937) (liability for dropping patient prior to loading her into an insured ambulance is covered).

19. 1 Alan I. Widiss, *Uninsured and Underinsured Motorist Insurance* 10–11 (Cincinnati, 2d ed. 1985). Widiss explains that the antecedent of UM coverage was unsatisfied judgment insurance, which had been sold by a few companies since 1925, but which required that the insured actually reduce a claim to a judgment that later proved to be uncollectible.

20. H. Jerome Zoffer, *The History of Automobile Insurance Rating* 3 (Pittsburgh, 1959).

21. Id. at 10–14.

22. Selwyn Enzer, *Some Impacts of No-Fault Automobile Insurance: A Technology Assessment* 88 (Menlo Park, Calif., 1974).

23. Insurance Information Institute, *Insurance Facts* 13 (New York, 1976).

24. Susan B. Carter et al. (eds.), 4 *Historical Statistics of the United States* table DF 340, p. 830 (New York, 2006).

25. Id. at table DF 214, p. 811.

26. Melvin M. Belli (ed.), *Trial and Tort Trends* ix–x (San Francisco, 1955).

27. For discussion of Belli's career and his role in NACCA, see John Fabian Witt, *Patriots and Cosmopolitans: Hidden Histories of American Law* (Cambridge, Mass., 2007).

28. Belli, *Trial and Tort Trends, 277.*

29. See, e.g., Melvin M. Belli, *The More Adequate Award* (San Francisco, 1952).

30. 1 *Defense Law Journal* v., 3, 273–359 (1957).

31. Tillinghast-Towers Perin, *U.S. Tort Costs: 2003 Update* appendix 1A (2004), www.towersperrin.com.

32. See U.S. Department of of Commerce, *Statistical Abstract of the United States* table 78, p. 62 (Washington, D.C., 1970), table 151, p. 100 (Washington, D.C., 1981), table 136, p. 93 (Washington, D.C., 1990).

33. See id. at table 149, p. 99 (Washington, D.C., 1981).

34. U.S. Department of Health and Human Services, Centers for Medicare and Medicaid Services, *National Health Expenditures by Type of Service and Source of Funds, CY 1960–2004,* www.cms.hhs.gov/NationalHealthExpendData/02_NationalHealthAccountsHistorical.asp#TopOfPage.

35. Id.

36. See H. Laurence Ross, *Settled Out of Court* 108 (Chicago, 1970); Edward C. German, "Techniques of Evaluation," in Roger A. Needham (ed.), *Evaluation of a Personal Injury Case* 21 (New York, 1971).

37. Ross, *Settled Out of Court,* 19.

38. Alfred F. Conard et al., *Automobile Accident Costs and Payments* 3 (Ann Arbor, 1964).

39. Defense Research Institute, *The Revolt against Whiplash* (Syracuse, N.Y., 1960). These articles had such titles as "Whiplash: An Unacceptable Medical Term" and "How to Forestall the Use of the Term 'Whiplash' in the Hearing of Jurors."

40. See Tom Baker, "Liability Insurance as Tort Regulation: Six Ways That Liability Insurance Shapes Tort Law in Action," 12 *Connecticut Insurance Law Journal* 1 (2005).

41. Conard et al., *Automobile Accident Costs and Payments,* 149.

42. Id. at 151.
43. Id. at 179.
44. See, e.g., Clarence Morris and James C. N. Paul, "The Financial Impact of Automobile Accidents," 110 *University of Pennsylvania Law Review* 913 (1962).
45. Deborah R. Hensler et al., *Compensation for Accidental Injuries in the United States* 107–108 (Santa Monica, Calif., 1991).
46. The academic debates that proceeded virtually simultaneously with the development of practical proposals for reform are reflected in Walter J. Blum and Harry Kalven, Jr., *Public Law Perspectives on a Private Law Problem* (Boston, 1965); Guido Calabresi, "Fault, Accidents, and the Wonderful World of Blum and Kalven," 75 *Yale Law Journal* 216, 225–232 (1965); Guido Calabresi, "The Decision for Accidents: An Approach to Nonfault Allocation of Costs," 78 *Harvard Law Review* 713, 720–734 (1965); Walter J. Blum and Harry Kalven, Jr., "The Empty Cabinet of Dr. Calabresi: Auto Accidents and General Deterrence," 34 *University of Chicago Law Review* 239 (1967); and Guido Calabresi, "Does the Fault System Optimally Control Primary Accident Costs?" 33 *Law & Contemporary Problems* 429, 443–445 (1968).
47. Robert E. Keeton and Jeffrey O'Connell, *Basic Protection for the Traffic Victim* (Boston, 1965).
48. See Walter J. Blum and Harry Kalven, Jr., "Ceilings, Costs, and Compulsion in Auto Compensation Legislation," 1973 *Utah Law Review* 341.
49. "The Drama with a Cast of 100 Million," 4 *Trial* 26 (February/March 1968).
50. Daniel Patrick Moynihan, foreword to Jeffrey O'Connell, *Ending Insult to Injury: No Fault Insurance for Products and Services* x–xi (Urbana, Ill., 1975).
51. For discussion see G. Edward White, "The Unexpected Persistence of Negligence," in his Tort Law in America 244–290 (New York, expanded ed. 2003).
52. An analysis of the studies concluded that "no-fault states appear to have lower accident rates and a lower rate of driver negligence generally than found in tort states . . . there exists little reason to believe that no-fault insurance affects incentives to drive safely for the vast majority of drivers." David S. Loughran, *The Effect of No-Fault Automobile Insurance on Driver Behavior and Automobile Accidents in the United States* 37 (Santa Monica, Calif., 2001).
53. 116th Cong., 1st Sess., Hearing before the Committee on Commerce, Science, and Transportation, U.S. Senate 24–25 (June 9, 1999). Nevertheless, with great persistence and ingenuity, Jeffrey O'Connell continues to propose variations on the elective no-fault theme. See, e.g., Jeffrey O'Connell and John Linehan, "Neo No-Fault Early Offers: A Workable Compromise between First and Third-Party Insurance," 41 *Gonzaga Law Review* 103 (2005/2006).

54. See Calfarm Ins. Co. v. Deukmejian, 48 Cal. 3d 805, 771 P.2d 1247 (1989).

55. For a catalogue of these reforms, see Joseph Sanders and Craig Joyce, "'Off to the Races': The 1980s Torts Crisis and the Law Reform Process," 27 *Houston Law Review* 207, 217–223 (1990).

56. Insurance Research Council, *Trends in Auto Injury Claims* 4 (Wheaton, Ill., 2d ed. 1995).

57. Insurance Information Institute, *Insurance Fact Book 2006* 49 (New York, 2006).

58. Id. at 43.

59. A state-by-state breakdown of these requirements can be found at the Insurance Information Institute website, www.iii.org/media/hottopics/insurance/compulsory/.

60. Stephen Carroll and Allan Abrahamse, "The Frequency of Excess Auto Personal Injury Claims," 3 *American Law and Economics Review* 228 (2001) (finding that as much a 42 percent of soft tissue injury losses are in excess of the amount that would be predicted in the absence of fraud or expense padding).

4. The Physicians' Dilemma

1. For discussion of the studies, see Tom Baker, *The Medical Malpractice Myth* 118–137 (Chicago, 2005); Michelle M. Mello and David M. Studdert, "The Medical Malpractice System: Structure and Performance," in William M. Sage and Rogan Kersh (eds.), *Medical Malpractice and the U.S. Health Care System* 17–21 (New York, 2006); David A. Hyman and Charles Silver, "The Poor State of Health Care Quality in the U.S.: Is Malpractice Liability Part of the Problem or Part of the Solution," 90 *Cornell Law Review* 893, 937–942 (2005); Tom Baker, "Reconsidering the Harvard Medical Malpractice Study Conclusions," 33 *Journal of Law, Medicine, and Ethics* 501 (2005); David M. Studdert, Michelle M. Mello, and Troyen A. Brennan, "Medical Malpractice," 350 *New England Journal of Medicine* 283 (2004); Patricia M. Danzon, "Liability for Medical Malpractice," in Anthony J. Cuyler and Joseph P. Newhouse (eds.), 1B *Handbook of Health Economics* 1339, 1368 (New York, 2000).

2. Worthington Hooker, *Physician and Patient* 277 (New York, 1849).

3. Reference to this form of defense insurance can be found, for example, in State ex rel. Physicians' Defense Co. v. Laylin, 76 N.E. 567 (Oh. 1905), and App. Ct. v. Physicians Defense Co., 126 Ill. App. 509 (1906).

4. "A Happy Device," *Washington Post,* July 29, 1904, 6; Sutherland v. Fidelity and Cas. Co. of New York, 175 P. 187 (Wash. 1918); App. Ct. v. Fidelity and Cas. Co. of New York, 209 Ill. App. 284 (1917).

5. Note, "Problems of Negligent Malpractice," 26 *Virginia Law Review* 919 (1940).

6. Note, "The California Malpractice Controversy," 9 *Stanford Law Review* 731 (1957).

7. Note, "Medical Malpractice and Medical Testimony," 77 *Harvard Law Review* 333 (1963).

8. Huffman v. Lindquist, 234 P.2d 34, 45–46 (Cal. 1951) (Carter, J., dissenting).

9. "Medical Malpractice and Medical Testimony," 337.

10. The doctrine was applied to this set of facts in the 1920s. See Moore v. Ivey, 264 S.W. 283 (Ct. App. Tex. 1924).

11. Ybarra v. Spangard, 154 P.2d 687 (Cal. 1944).

12. The seminal case addressing the issue is President of Georgetown College v. Hughes, 130 F.2d 810 (D.C. Cir. 1942). By the early 1970s Prosser could say that the "immunity of charities is clearly in full retreat." William Prosser, *Handbook of the Law of Torts* 996 (St. Paul, Minn., 4th ed. 1971). For a chronicle of subsequent developments, see Note, "The Quality of Mercy: 'Charitable Torts' and Their Continuing Immunity," 100 *Harvard Law Review* 1382 (1987).

13. Kenneth S. Abraham and Paul C. Weiler, "Enterprise Liability and the Evolution of the American Health Care System," 108 *Harvard Law Review* 381, 386–392 (1994).

14. "Problems of Negligent Malpractice," 919.

15. See Paul Starr, *The Social Transformation of American Medicine* 284, 299–300 (New York, 1982); Ronald L. Numbers, *Almost Persuaded: American Physicians and Compulsory Health Insurance, 1912–1920* (Baltimore, 1978).

16. Sylvia A. Law, *Blue Cross: What Went Wrong?* 12 (New Haven, Conn., 1976).

17. U.S. Department of Commerce, *Statistical Abstract of the United States* tables 78 and 80, pp. 62–63 (Washington, D.C., 1970); U.S. Department of Commerce, *Statistical Abstract of the United States* table 136, p. 93 (Washington, D.C., 1990).

18. Patricia M. Danzon, *Medical Malpractice: Theory, Evidence, and Public Policy* 60 (Cambridge, Mass., 1985).

19. U.S. General Accounting Office, *Medical Malpractice: Six Case Studies Show Claims and Insurance Costs Rise Despite Reforms* table 2.4, p. 17 (Washington, D.C., 1986).

20. Id. at table 2.6, p. 18.

21. The 1960 figure is derived from Mark Kendall and John Haldi, "The Medical Malpractice Insurance Market," in U.S. Department of Health, Education, & Welfare, *Report of the Secretary's Commission on Medical Malpractice Appendix* 509 (Washington, D.C., 1973). For the 1980 figure, see Insurance Infor-

mation Institute, *1984/1985 Property/Casualty Fact Book* 29 (New York, 1985).

22. U.S. Department of Commerce, *Statistical Abstract of the United States* table 151, p. 104 (Washington, D.C., 1980); *Statistical Abstract of the United States* table 134, p. 92 (Washington, D.C., 1990).

23. Tom Baker, "Medical Malpractice and the Insurance Underwriting Cycle," 54 *DePaul Law Review* 393 (2005).

24. Id. at 399, fig. 1.

25. Richard Boyle, "Medical Malpractice Screening Panels: A Judicial Evaluation of their Practical Effect," 42 *University of Pittsburgh Law Review* 939, 941 (1981).

26. See, e.g., Best v. Taylor Machine Works, 689 N.E. 2d 1057 (Ill. 1997); Sofie v. Fibreboard Corporation, 771 P. 2d 711 (Wash. 1989).

27. Patricia M. Danzon, *New Evidence on the Frequency and Severity of Medical Malpractice Claims* 26–27 (Santa Monica, Calif., 1986).

28. On screening panels, see Albert Yoon, "Mandatory Arbitration and Civil Litigation: An Empirical Study of Medical Malpractice in the West," 6 *American Law & Economics Review* 95, 99 (2004).

29. Kyle D. Logue, "Toward a Tax-Based Explanation of the Liability Insurance Crisis," 82 *Virginia Law Review* 895 (1996).

30. Anne Gron and Andrew Winton, "Risk Overhang and Market Behavior," 74 *Journal of Business* 591 (2001); Baker, "Medical Malpractice and the Insurance Underwriting Cycle," 409.

31. Studies of the impact of the reforms are summarized and evaluated in U.S. Congress, Office of Technology Assessment, *Impact of Legal Reforms on Medical Malpractice Costs* (Washington, D.C., 1993), and U.S. Congress, Congressional Budget Office, *The Effect of Tort Reforms: Evidence from the States* (Washington, D.C., 2004). Among the prominent studies are W. Kip Viscusi and Patricia H. Born, "Damages Caps, Insurability, and the Performance of Medical Malpractice Insurance," 72 *Journal of Risk & Insurance* 23, 32 (2005), finding a 16–17 percent impact on losses as compared to other states; W. Kip Viscusi and Patricia H. Born, "Medical Malpractice Insurance in the Wake of Liability Reform," 24 *Journal of Legal Studies* 463, 482–485 (1995). These findings are consistent with Danzon's earlier findings that a cap on liability reduced awards by 19 percent. Danzon, *Medical Malpractice,* 78.

32. Catherine M. Sharkey, "Unintended Consequences of Medical Malpractice Damages Caps," 80 *New York University Law Review* 391 (2005).

33. American Law Institute, 2 *Enterprise Responsibility for Personal Injury* 113–126 (Philadelphia, 1991). For an elaboration, see Kenneth S. Abraham and Paul C. Weiler, "Enterprise Medical Liability and the Evolution of the American Health-Care System," 108 *Harvard Law Review* 381 (1994). An

update on enterprise medical liability thinking is provided in Randall R. Bovbjerg and Robert Berenson, "Enterprise Liability in the Twenty-First Century," in Sage and Kersh, *Medical Malpractice and the U.S. Health Care System*, 191.

34. Paul Weiler et al., *A Measure of Malpractice* 43, 69–71 (Cambridge, Mass., 1993).

35. Id. at 73–74.

36. See Tom Baker, "Reconsidering the Harvard Medical Malpractice Study Conclusions," 33 *Journal of Law, Medicine, & Ethics* 501 (2005).

37. Id. at 144–152.

38. Bernard Black et al., "Stability, Not Crisis: Medical Malpractice Claim Outcomes in Texas, 1988–2002," 2 *Journal of Empircal Studies* 207 (2005).

39. Baker, *The Medical Malpractice Myth*, 53–54.

40. U.S. General Accounting Office, *Medical Malpractice Insurance: Multiple Factors Have Contributed to Increased Premium Rates* 15 (Washington, D.C., 2003).

41. Kenneth E. Thorpe, "Medical Malpractice 'Crisis': Recent Trends and the Impact of State Tort Reforms," *Health Affairs Web Exclusives 2004*, W-20, W-23.

42. "Lawyers vs. Patients," *Wall Street Journal,* May 1, 2002, A18.

43. "Insurers' Missteps Helped Provoke Malpractice 'Crisis,'" *Wall Street Journal,* June 4, 2002, A1, A8.

44. "The Third Generation: Start-up Medical Malpractice Companies," *National Underwriter: Property & Casualty,* July 25, 2005, 19 (describing study identifying 90 new companies writing medical malpractice insurance since 2002).

45. Bernard Black et al., "Stability, Not Crisis," 207; U.S. General Accounting Office, *Medical Malpractice Insurance,* 19.

46. Id. at 10.

47. HEALTH Act of 2005, S. 354, 109th Cong., secs. 4–5.

48. See Baker, *The Medical Malpractice Myth,* 174–178; William M. Sage, "Malpractice Reform as a Health Policy Problem," in Sage and Kersh, *Medical Malpractice and the U.S. Health Care System,* 30.

5. Products Liability, Environmental Liability

1. 152 Eng. Rep. 402 (Ex. 1842).

2. 110 N.E. 1050 (N.Y. 1916).

3. See James A. Henderson, Jr., "*MacPherson v. Buick Motor Co.,* Simplifying the Facts While Reshaping the Law," in Robert L. Rabin and Stephen D. Sugarman (eds.), *Tort Stories* 41 (New York, 2003).

4. See, e.g., Mazetti v. Armour and Co., 135 P. 633 (Wash. 1913).

5. George L. Priest, "The Invention of Enterprise Liability: A Critical History of the Intellectual Foundations of Modern Tort Law," 19 *Journal of Legal Studies* 461 (1985). Representative articles include William O. Douglas, "Vicarious Liability and Administration of Risk (pts. 1 and 2)," 38 *Yale Law Journal* 354, 720 (1929); Lester W. Feezer, "Capacity to Bear Loss as a Factor in the Decision of Certain Types of Tort Cases," 78 *University of Pennsylvania Law Revew* 805 (1930); Charles O. Gregory, "Trespass to Negligence to Absolute Liability," 37 *Virginia Law Review* 359 (1951); Leon Green, "The Individual's Protection under Negligence Law: Risk Sharing," 47 *Northwestern Law Review* 751 (1953).

6. 150 P.2d 436 (Cal. 1944).

7. See, e.g., Fleming James, Jr., "Products Liability," 34 *Texas Law Review* 44 (1955).

8. William L. Prosser, "The Fall of the Citadel," 50 *Minnesota Law Review* 791 (1966).

9. 377 P.2d 897 (Cal. 1963).

10. Fleming James, Jr., "Accident Liability Reconsidered: The Impact of Liability Insurance," 57 *Yale Law Journal* 545, 569 (1948).

11. See Guido Calabresi, "Some Thoughts on Risk Distribution and the Law of Torts," 70 *Yale Law Journal* 499 (1961); "Fault, Accidents, and the Wonderful World of Blum and Kalven," 75 *Yale Law Journal* 216 (1965); "The Decision for Accidents: An Approach to Nonfault Allocation of Costs," 78 *Harvard Law Review* 713, 720–734 (1965); "Does the Fault System Optimally Control Primary Accident Costs?" 33 *Law and Contemporary Problems* 429 (1968).

12. See Richard A. Posner, A Theory of Negligence, *Journal of Legal Studies* 29 (1972); Walter J. Blum and Harry Kalven, Jr., *Public Law Perspectives on a Private Law Problem* (Boston, 1965); Walter J. Blum and Harry Kalven, Jr., "The Empty Cabinet of Dr. Calabresi: Auto Accidents and General Deterrence," 34 *University of Chicago Law Review* 239 (1967).

13. See, e.g., Borel v. Fibreboard Paper Products Corp., 493 F.2d 1076 (5th Cir. 1973) (asbestos); In re A.H. Robins Co. Inc. "Dalkon Shield" IUD Products, 406 F. Supp. 540 (MDL 1975) (the Dalkon Shield).

14. The seminal market share liability case is Sindell v. Abbott Laboratories, 607 P.2d 924 (Cal. 1960).

15. American Law Institute, *Restatement (Third) of the Law of Products Liability* §2 (St. Paul, Minn., 1998).

16. See James A. Henderson, Jr., and Theodore Eisenberg, "Inside the Quiet Revolution in Products Liability," 39 *UCLA Law Review* 731 (1992); Gary Schwartz, "The Beginning and the Possible End of the Rise of Modern American Tort Law," 26 *Georgia Law Review* 601 (1992); James A. Hender-

son, Jr., and Theodore Eisenberg, "The Quiet Revolution in Products Liability: An Empirical Study of Legal Change," 37 *UCLA Law Review* 479 (1990).

17. See James A. Henderson, Jr., "Echoes of Enterprise Liability in Product Design and Marketing Litigation," 87 *Cornell Law Review* 958 (2002).

18. Dawson v. Chrysler Corp., 630 F.2d 950, 962–963 (3d Cir. 1980) (Adams, J.).

19. See, e.g., MacDonald v. Ortho Pharmaceutical Corp., 475 N.E. 2d 65 (Mass. 1985) (holding that a jury could find that a warning on a contraceptive was inadequate because it referred to the risk of death from a blood clot in the brain without using the word "stroke").

20. See, e.g., Reyes v. Wyeth Laboratories, Inc., 498 F.2d 1264 (5th Cir. 1974).

21. See, e.g., Boomer v. Atlantic Cement Co., 257 N.E. 2d 870 (N.Y. 1970).

22. U.S. v. Hooker Chemicals and Plastics Corp., 850 F. Supp. 993, 1020 (W.D. N.Y. 1994).

23. The key provisions, for present purposes, are §§106 and 107, 42 U.S.C. §§9606 and 9607.

24. Id.

25. Roger C. Henderson, "Insurance Protection for Products Liability and Completed Operations—What Every Lawyer Should Know," 50 *Nebraska Law Review* 415, 416 (1971).

26. Id.

27. See Michael D. Green, "The Paradox of Statutes of Limitations in Toxic Substances Litigation," 76 *California Law Review* 965 (1988).

28. See, e.g., Beryllium Corp. v. American Mutual Liability Ins. Co., 223 F.2d 71 (3d Cir. 1955).

29. The nature of these different risks is carefully teased out in Tom Baker, "Insuring Liability Risks," 29 *Geneva Papers* 128 (2004).

30. Id. at 131–139.

31. 102nd Cong., First Sess., Hearings before the Subcommittee on the Consumer of the Committee on Commerce, Science, and Transportation, U.S. Senate 63–64 (September 12 and 19, 1991) (testimony of Deborah R. Hensler).

32. See, e.g., W. Kip Viscusi, *Reforming Products Liability* 14–31 (Cambridge, Mass., 1991); Marc Galanter, "Real World Torts: An Antidote to Anecdote," 55 *Maryland Law Review* 1093 (1996).

33. See, e.g., Jackson Township Municipal Utilities Authority v. Hartford Accident and Indemnity Company, 451 A.2d 990 (N.J. Super. 1982).

34. See, e.g., Morton International, Inc. v. General Acc. Ins. Co., 629 A.2d 831 (N.J. 1993). The pollution exclusion saga is explored at some length in American States Ins. Co. v. Koloms, 687 N.E.2d 72 (Ill. 1997), and Kenneth S. Abraham, *Environmental Liability Insurance Law* 145–163 (Englewood Cliffs, N.J., 1991).

35. See Kenneth S. Abraham, "The Maze of Mega-Coverage Litigation," 97 *Columbia Law Review* 2102 (1997).

36. See, e.g., Keene Corp. v. Ins. Co. of N. America, 667 F.2d 1034 (D.C. Cir. 1981).

37. Stephan J. Carroll et al., *Asbestos Litigation* 105–106 (Santa Monica, Calif., 2005.

38. 509 U.S.764 (1993).

39. The literature on the crisis is extensive. See, e.g., Kenneth S. Abraham, "Making Sense of the Liability Insurance Crisis," 48 *Ohio State Law Journal* 399 (1987); George L. Priest, "The Current Insurance Crisis and Modern Tort Law," 96 *Yale Law Journal* 1521 (1987); Symposium, "Perspectives on the Insurance Crisis," 5 *Yale Journal on Regulation* 367 (1988); Kyle D. Logue, "Toward a Tax-Based Explanation of the Liability Insurance Crisis," 82 *Virginia Law Review* 895 (1996). A prescient piece that was published just before the crisis is Richard A. Epstein, "Products Liability as an Insurance Market," 14 *Journal of Legal Studies* 645 (1985).

40. David G. Owen, "Special Defenses in Modern Products Liability Law," 70 *Missouri Law Review* 1, 45 (2005).

41. Towers-Perrin Tillinghast, *U.S. Tort Costs: 2004 Update* appendix 4 (2005), www.towersperrin.com.

42. Richard E. Stewart and Barbara D. Stewart, "The Loss of the Certainty Effect," 4 *Risk Management and Insurance Review no. 2* 29 (2001).

43. Little has been published about the relationship between insurers and policyholders in particular mass tort cases. Much of what I relate in the following paragraphs is based on my own 20 years of experience as consulting counsel in insurance coverage litigation associated with mass tort and similar cases, mostly (though not exclusively) on behalf of policyholders. Passing reference to the role played by insurers in mass tort can be found in Stephen J. Carroll, *Asbestos Litigation* xxvi (Santa Monica, Calif., 2005; Michael D. Green, *Bendectin and Birth Defects: The Challenges of Mass Toxic Substances Litigation* 207 (Philadelphia, 1996); Peter H. Schuck, *Agent Orange on Trial: Mass Toxic Disasters in the Courts* 155 (Cambridge, Mass., 1987); and Richard B. Sobol, *Bending the Law: The Story of the Dalkon Shield Bankruptcy* 116–117 (Chicago, 1991).

44. The rules governing the effect of a finding of tort liability on the coverage question vary from state to state and depend in part on whether the liability insurer is actually defending the case or merely contributing to the insured's costs of defense. If the primary insurer or insurers are merely contributing to the insured's costs rather than actually furnishing defense counsel, as is typically the case in major mass tort actions, the insured is more likely to be bound (in its claim for coverage) by a jury decision that harm was expected

or intended. And even when the primary insurer or insurers are defending and therefore are estopped to assert a finding of liability for intentionally causing harm as a defense in the policyholder's claim for coverage, this estoppel does not necessarily bind the excess insurers, who have no duty to defend.

6. Which Came First, the Liability or the Insurance?

1. The story of this evolution and its historical context is told very insightfully in Robert L. Rabin, "The Historical Development of the Fault Principle: A Reinterpretation," 15 *Georgia Law Review* 925 (1981).

2. *Restatement of the Law Torts: Liability for Physical Harm* §7, Proposed Final Draft no. 1 (Philadelphia, April 6, 2005). This statement of the law has its critics, who argue that it is important as a matter of principle and sometimes for practical purposes to recognize that the existence of a duty is logically prior to liability for negligence. For a debate about this and related questions, see Symposium, "The John W. Wade Conference on the Third Restatement of Torts, September 15–16, 2000," 54 *Vanderbilt Law Review* 639–1465 (2001). The most prominent attack on the *Restatement* formulation can be found in John C. P. Goldberg and Benjamin C. Zipursky, "The *Restatement (Third)* and the Place of Duty in Negligence Law," id. at 657.

3. W. Page Keeton et al., *Prosser and Keeton on Torts* 589 (St. Paul, Minn., 5th ed. 1984).

4. Williard J. Obrist, *The New Comprehensive General Liability Insurance Policy* (Milwaukee, 1966).

5. The account in this paragraph and the several paragraphs that follow draws on John Eugene Pierce, *The Development of Comprehensive Insurance for the Household* 106–121, 296–298 (Homewood, Ill., 1958).

6. Hugh Harbison, "Legal Environment for All Lines Insurance," in Dan M. McGill (ed.), *All Lines Insurance* 25 (Philadelphia, 1960).

7. U.S. Department of Commerce, *Statistical Abstract of the United States* table 571, p. 455 (Washington, D.C., 1960).

8. See Stephen C. Yeazell, "Re-financing Civil Litigation," 51 *DePaul Law Review* 183, 188 (2001).

9. For discussion of these reasons in no-duty and similar cases, see James A. Henderson, Jr., "Expanding the Negligence Concept: Retreat from the Rule of Law," 51 *Indiana Law Journal* 476 (1976).

10. See, e.g., cases cited in Keeton et al., *Prosser and Keeton on Torts,* 396–399.

11. See Robert L. Rabin, "*Rowland v. Christian:* Hallmark of an Expansionary Era," in Robert L. Rabin and Stephen D. Sugarman (eds.), *Torts Stories* 89 (New York, 2003). In fact, Christian was only an apartment tenant, but she

had purchased tenant's insurance protecting her property that was accompanied by personal liability insurance analogous to what was provided by homeowner's policies.

12. Rowland v. Christian, 443 P.2d 561 (Cal. 1968).

13. See Dan B. Dobbs, *The Law of Torts* §237, at 615–620 (St. Paul, Minn., 2000).

14. 107 N.W.2d 859 (Minn. 1961).

15. Cases that abolished interspousal immunity include Klein v. Klein, 376 P.2d. 70 (Cal. 1962) and Brown v. Gosser, 262 S.W.2d 480 (Ky. 1953). Cases that abolished parent-child immunity include Gibson v. Gibson, 479 P.2d 648 (Cal. 1971), Gelbman v. Gelbman, 245 N.E.2d 192 (N.Y. 1969), and Groller v. White, 122 N.W.2d 193 (Wis. 1963). Statutes that abolished parent-child immunity in auto cases only include 1975 North Carolina Laws c. 685 §1 (codified at N.C. Gen. Stat. Ann. §1–539.21 (1981)) and 1967 Conn. Pub. Acts 596 §1 (codified at Conn. Gen. Stat. Ann. §52–572c (1981)).

16. See e.g., Meyer v. State Farm Mutual Automobile Insurance Company, 689 P.2d 585 (Colo. 1984); Jennings v. Government Employees Insurance Company, 488 A.2d 166 (Md. 1985); Mutual of Enumclaw Insurance Company v. Wiscomb, 643 P.2d 441 (Wash. 1982).

17. The seminal cases on point are Wendt v. Servite Fathers, 76 N.E. 2d 342 (Ill. App. 1947), and President and Directors of Georgetown College v. Hughes, 130 F.2d 810 (D.C. Cir. 1942).

18. For discussion of the impact of insurance premiums on volunteer organizations, see Charles Robert Tremper, "Compensation for Harm from Charitable Activity," 76 *Cornell Law Review* 401 (1991); Jeffrey D. Kahn, "Organizations' Liability for Torts of Volunteers," 133 *University of Pennsylvania Law Review* 1433 (1985).

19. See, e.g., Arkansas Volunteer Immunity Act, 1987 Ark. Acts 390 §2 (codified at Ark. Code Ann. §§16–6–101–105 (1987)); 1987 Iowa Acts Ch. 212 §19 (codified at Iowa Code Ann. §613.19 (1987)); 1987 Mont. Laws Ch. 437 §1 (codified at Mont. Code Ann. §27–1–732 (1987)).

20. 42 U.S.C. §14503.

21. The classic opinion poking fun at the arbitrariness of the impact rule is Bosley v. Andrews, 142 A.2d 263 (Pa. 1958) (Musmanno, J., dissenting).

22. See, e.g., Philadelphia Contributorship Ins. Co. v. Shapiro, 798 A.2d 781 (Pa. 2002). A number of states have held, however, that mental anguish or emotional distress does fall within the terms of policies covering liability for "bodily injury, sickness, or disease." See, e.g., Lavanant v. General Accident Ins. Co. of America, 595 N.E. 2d 819 (N.Y. 1992).

23. See American Law Institute, *Restatement (Second) of the Law of Torts*, §313(2) (St. Paul, Minn., 1965).

24. See, e.g., Thing v. La Chusa, 771 P. 2d 814 (Cal. 1989).

25. See, e.g., Molien v. Kaiser Foundation Hospitals, 616 P.2d 813 (Cal. 1980) (spouse of patient negligently informed that she had sexually transmitted disease can sue physician for emotional distress).

26. The relevant provisions in contemporary standard-form homeowner's and auto liability insurance policies may be found in Kenneth S. Abraham, *Insurance Law & Regulation* 190, 646 (New York, 4th ed. 2005).

27. Accounts of the overall evolution of liability in this field include Barry J. Koopmann, "A Rule of Which Procrustes Would Be Proud: An Analysis of the Physical Injury Requirement in Negligent Infliction of Emotional Distress Claims under Iowa Law," 51 *Drake Law Review* 361 (2003); Christina Hull Eikhoff, "Out with the Old: Georgia Struggles with Its Dated Approach to the Tort of Negligent Infliction of Emotional Distress," 34 *Georgia Law Review* 349 (1999); Leslie Benton Sandor and Carol Berry, "Recovery for Negligent Infliction of Emotional Distress Attendant to Economic Loss: A Reassessment," 37 *Arizona Law Review* 1247 (1995); and Martha Chamallas with Linda Kerber, "Women, Mothers, and the Law of Fright: A History," 88 *Michigan Law Review* 814 (1990).

28. See Ernest J. Weinrib, "The Case for a Duty to Rescue," 90 *Yale Law Journal* 247 (1980).

29. Robert L. Rabin, "Enabling Torts," 49 *De Paul Law Review* 435 (1999).

30. Kline v. 1500 Massachusetts Avenue Apartment Corp., 439 F. 2d 477 (D.C. Cir. 1970).

31. Tarasoff v. Regents of the University of California, 551 P.2d 334 (Cal. 1976).

7. Collateral Sources, Mega-Liability

1. Kenneth R. Feinberg, 1 *Final Report of the Special Master for the September 11th Victim Compensation Fund of 2001* 1 (Washington, D.C., 2004).

2. Stephen J. Carroll, *Asbestos Litigation* xxvi. (Santa Monica, Calif., 2005).

3. See Kenneth S. Abraham, "Twenty-First Century Insurance and Loss Distribution in Tort Law," in M. Stuart Madden (ed.), *Exploring Tort Law* 91 (New York, 2005).

4. See Kenneth S. Abraham and Lance Liebman, "Private Insurance, Social Insurance, and Tort Reform: Toward a New Vision of Compensation for Illness and Injury," 93 *Columbia Law Review* 75, 94–98 (1993).

5. See Duncan v. Integon General Ins. Co., 482 S.E. 2d 325 (Ga. 1997); Johnny C. Parker, "The Made Whole Doctrine: Unraveling the Enigma Wrapped in the Mystery of Insurance Subrogation," 70 *Missouri Law Review* 723 (2005); Elaine M. Rinaldi, "Apportionment of Recovery between Insured and Insurer in a Subrogation Case," 34 *Tort & Insurance Practice Journal* 803 (1994).

6. See Associated Hospital Service of Philadelphia v. Pustilnik, 396 A.2d 1332 (Pa. Super. 1979).

7. Tom Baker, "Blood Money, New Money, and the Moral Economy of Tort Law in Action," 35 *Law & Society Review* 272 (2001).

8. See Viviana A. Rotman Zeliser, *Morals & Markets: The Development of Life Insurance in the United States* 94–101 (New York, 1979); Tom Baker, "On the Genealogy of Moral Hazard," 75 *Texas Law Review* 237 (1996).

9. Well into the twentieth century, in fact, it was an open question whether even health insurance that guaranteed care and directly reimbursed physicians provided an indemnity, and therefore whether it carried with it an equitable right of subrogation even in the absence of a contract provision affording the insurer subrogation rights. See, e.g., Michigan Medical Service v. Sharpe, 64 N.W. 2d 713 (1954).

10. See Kyle D. Logue, "The Current Life Insurance Crisis: How the Law Should Respond," 32 *Cumberland Law Review* 1 (2001).

11. For extended analysis of a whole range of issues associated with the enactment and implementation of the VCF, see Symposium, "After Disaster: The September 11 Compensation Fund and the Future of Civil Justice," 53 *De Paul Law Review* 205 (2003).

12. Pub. L. No. 107–42, 115 Stat. 230 [codified at 49 U.S.C. §40101], §405 (b)(1).

13. Feinberg, 1 *Final Report of the Special Master,* 52–55, 100.

14. 104 C.F.R. §104.44.

15. Id., §104.47(a).

16. See, e.g., James F. Blumstein, Randall R. Bovbjerg, and Frank A. Sloan, "Beyond Tort Reform: Developing Better Tools for Assessing Damages for Personal Injury," 8 *Yale Journal on Regulation* 171 (1991); Randall R. Bovbjerg, Frank A. Sloan, and James F. Blumstein, "Valuing Life and Limb in Tort: Scheduling 'Pain and Suffering,'" 83 *Northwestern University Law Review* 908 (1989).

17. See Kenneth S. Abraham, "Twenty-First-Century Insurance and Loss Distribution in Tort Law," in Madden, *Exploring Tort Law* 106–110; Charles Fried and David Rosenberg, *Making Tort Law* 91–92 (Cambridge, Mass., 2003); Robert Cooter and Steven D. Sugarman, "A Regulated Market in Unmatured Tort Claims: Tort Reform by Contract," in Walter Olson (ed.), *New Directions in Liability Law* 174 (New York, 1988); Jeffrey O'Connell and Janet Beck, "Overcoming Legal Barriers to the Transfer of Third-Party Tort Claims as a Means of Financing First-Party No-Fault Insurance," 58 *Washington University Law Quarterly* 55 (1979).

8. Recurring Themes, Sobering Constraints

1. Tom Baker, "Liability Insurance as Tort Regulation: Six Ways That Liability Insurance Shapes Tort Law in Action," 12 *Connecticut Insurance Law Journal* 1, 4–9 (2005); Ellen Smith Pryor, "The Stories We Tell: Intentional Harm and the Quest for Insurance Funding," 75 *Texas Law Review* 1721 (1997).

2. Kent D. Syverud, "On the Demand for Liability Insurance," 72 *Texas Law Review* 1629 (1994).

3. John Fabian Witt and Samuel Isaacaroff, "The Inevitability of Aggregate Settlement: An Institutional Account of American Tort Law," 57 *Vanderbilt Law Review* 1571 (2004).

4. See Richard A. Epstein, "Products Liability as an Insurance Market," 14 *Journal of Legal Studies* 645 (1985).

5. On the use of deductibles, and the complications they pose, see Kent D. Syverud, "The Duty to Settle," 76 *Virginia Law Review* 1113, 1185–1193 (1990).

6. For this and other explanations for the purchase of liability insurance that seem applicable to small and medium-sized businesses, see David Meyers and Clifford W. Smith, "On the Corporate Demand for Insurance," 55 *Journal of Business* 281 (1982).

7. Tom Baker and Sean Griffith, "The Missing Monitor in Corporate Governance: The Directors' and Officers' Liability Insurer," 95 *Georgetown Law Journal* 1795 (2007).

8. See Kenneth S. Abraham, "Twenty-First-Century Insurance and Loss Distribution in Tort Law," in M. Stuart Madden (ed.), *Exploring Tort Law* 106–110 (New York, 2005); Charles Fried and David Rosenberg, *Making Tort Law* 91–92 (Cambridge, Mass., 2003); Robert Cooter and Steven D. Sugarman, "A Regulated Market in Unmatured Tort Claims: Tort Reform by Contract," in Walter Olson (ed.), *New Directions in Liability Law* 174 (New York, 1988); Jeffrey O'Connell and Janet Beck, "Overcoming Legal Barriers to the Transfer of Third-Party Tort Claims as a Means of Financing First-Party No-Fault Insurance," 58 *Washington University Law Quarterly* 55 (1979).

Index

269